*For Hillis Miller*
*with respect and admiration*

# The Voice of the Heart

## the working of
## Mervyn Peake's imagination

LIVERPOOL ENGLISH TEXTS AND STUDIES, 48

# The Voice
# of the Heart

### the working of
### Mervyn Peake's imagination

G. Peter Winnington

LIVERPOOL
UNIVERSITY PRESS

First published 2006 by
Liverpool University Press
4 Cambridge Street
Liverpool L69 7ZU

*British Library Cataloguing-in-Publication data*
A British Library CIP record is available


ISBN 1 84631 022 9 cased (ISBN-13 978 1 84631 022 5)
ISBN 1 84631 030 X limp (ISBN-13 978 1 84631 030 0)

Typeset in Garamond by
BBR Solutions Ltd, Chesterfield
Printed and bound in the UK by
Bell & Bain Ltd, Glasgow

# Contents

# Acknowledgments

My publishers join me in thanking Sebastian Peake, representing the Mervyn Peake Estate, for generous permission to make numerous quotations from Peake's works and to reproduce his paintings, drawings and illustrations. Chris Beetles kindly provided several images which Alison Eldred scanned. Acknowledgement is made to the library of University College London for quotations and images from Peake's manuscripts.

I am most grateful to several friends who reacted to this book while it was slowly taking shape. Lawrence Bristow-Smith read my original notes and encouraged me to dig deeper. Hugh Brogan and Colin Manlove were helpfully critical of the opening of the first draft. Pierre François commented on the second with the frankness of friendship and the perspicacity of scholarship, and Stuart Olesker made incisive observations on the next-to-last draft. Kenneth Graham offered useful last-minute suggestions. For all their generosity of time and attention, the final product – and its faults – remain very much my own.

# Illustrations

# Abbreviated references and editions quoted

Verse quotations are from the first published editions, since they alone were prepared and corrected by Peake. (Some later editions contain misprints or silently revert to an earlier version or draft.) Quotations from the Titus books are from recent impressions of the corrected text first printed in the King Penguin edition. The place of publication is London unless otherwise specified.

AW    'The Artist's World', a radio talk in the series entitled 'As I see it', broadcast by the BBC 1947. First fully transcribed in MPR 8 (Spring 1979), 3–5.

BI    'Book Illustration', a radio talk in the series entitled 'As I see it', broadcast by the BBC 1947. First fully transcribed in MPR 9 (Autumn 1979), 14–23.

BiD    'Boy in Darkness' in *Sometime, Never: Three Tales of Imagination* by William Golding, John Wyndham and Mervyn Peake. Eyre & Spottiswoode, 1956, pp. 155–224.

BN    *A Book of Nonsense*. Peter Owen, 1972.

Cave    *Anima Mundi, or The Cave*. Mervyn Peake Society, 1996. Not paginated. Peake's notes on the play, reproduced in facsimile as a kind of frontispiece to the edition, were transcribed only in PS 5 (October 1997), iii: 28–29.

CLP    *The Craft of the Lead Pencil*. Wingate, 1946.

Convoy    'The Glass Blowers' in *Convoy*, No. 4 (July 1946), 23–27. Reprinted in MPR 18 (Spring 1984), 3–7 and MPMA 70–72.

CSDA    *Captain Slaughterboard Drops Anchor*. Country Life, 1939. To situate quotations I have numbered the pages, starting from the hand-drawn title leaf; the story begins on page 2. This works with all subsequent reprints except the 1967 Macmillan/Academy edition in which the text was revised and typeset.

D        Introduction to *Drawings by Mervyn Peake*. Grey Walls Press,
         dated 1949, published 1950.
G        *Gormenghast* (1950). Vintage, 1998.
Gb       *The Glassblowers*. Eyre & Spottiswoode, 1950.
HRNE     'How a Romantic Novel was Evolved' in *A New Romantic
         Anthology* edited by Stefan Schimanski and Henry Treece. Grey
         Walls Press, 1949, pp. 80–81.
LF       'London Fantasy' in *World Review* n.s. 6 (August 1949), 55–59.
LLU      *Letters from a Lost Uncle* (1948). The first two editions were
         unpaginated, so I have situated quotations by the pagination in
         Methuen's third edition of 2001. If you care to count the pages,
         this system also works for the second edition of 1976, but not for
         the first, for it contained a double-page spread that was omitted
         from later editions (and subsequently lost). To appreciate the
         drawings, I recommend the first or second edition, as the third
         reproduces clumsy alterations that Peake made late in life.
MP       *Mr Pye* (1953). Harmondsworth: Penguin, 1972. (The first
         edition is too rare for convenient reference.) I have checked my
         quotations against the first edition and corrected them where
         the Penguin is in error (misprinting 'islands' for 'islanders' and
         'underline' for 'underlie', for instance).
MPMA     *Mervyn Peake: The Man and His Art* edited by G. Peter
         Winnington. Peter Owen, 2006.
MPR      *Mervyn Peake Review*. Mervyn Peake Society, 1975–98.
MS       The manuscripts of the Titus books are deposited in the library
         of University College London, call number MS ADD 234. They
         are identified by box number (in arabic figures) and notebook
         (in roman). Further information in MPR 12 (Spring 1981),
         29–30.
NAAL     *The Norton Anthology of American Literature* edited by Nina
         Baym *et al.* 5th Edition. 2 Vols. New York & London: Norton,
         1998.
NAEL     *The Norton Anthology of English Literature* edited by M.H.
         Abrams *et al.* 7th Edition. 2 Vols. New York & London: Norton,
         2000.
NODE     *The New Oxford Dictionary of English*. Oxford: Oxford Univer-
         sity Press, 1998.
P&D      *Poems and Drawings*. Keepsake Press, 1965.
PP       *Peake's Progress*. Harmondsworth: Penguin, 1981. Neither the

hardback edition (Allen Lane, 1978) nor the Penguin reprint of 2000 is reliable. See Winnington, 'Editing Peake', 4–7 for information on the corrections made for the 1981 edition.

PS  *Peake Studies*. Orzens, Switzerland, 1988– (home page http://www.peakestudies.com).

RoB  *Reverie of Bone*. Bertram Rota, 1967.

RTO  'The Reader Takes Over', a BBC panel discussion of *Titus Groan*, recorded in 1947, transcribed and printed in MPR 10 (Spring 1980), 4–16.

RWR  *Rhymes without Reason*. Eyre & Spottiswoode, 1944. The second edition omits three poems and their corresponding illustrations.

S&S  *Shapes and Sounds*. Chatto & Windus, 1941.

SP  *Selected Poems*. Faber, 1972.

TA  *Titus Alone* (1959). Vintage, 1998.

10P  *10 Poems*. Mervyn Peake Society, 1993. Not paginated.

TG  *Titus Groan* (1946). Vintage, 1998.

WiD  'What is Drawing?' in *Athene* [Journal of New Society of Art Teachers] 8 (April 1957), iii: 21. Reprinted in MPR 15 (Autumn 1982), 3.

W&D  *Writings and Drawings*. Academy; New York: St Martin's, 1974.

# Works cited

N.B. As a full primary and secondary Peake bibliography can be found at http://www.peakestudies.com, and the editions used in this book are identified in the list of abbreviated references, the following bibliography lists only the other works cited in this book. Unless otherwise specified, the place of publication is London.

Amis, Kingsley, *New Maps of Hell: a survey of science fiction*. New York: Harcourt, Brace Jovanovich, 1960.

Batchelor, John, *Mervyn Peake: a biographical and critical exploration*. Duckworth, 1974.

Fowler, Roger, 'How to see through language'. *Poetics* 11 (1982), 213–35.

François, Pierre, '*Mr Pye*: an Ovidian Curse for a Dichotomized Evangelist', PS 6 (April 1999), ii: 39–47.

Gilmore, Maeve, *A World Away*. Gollancz, 1970.

Kermode, Frank, *The Genesis of Secrecy*. Harvard University Press, 1979.

Laski, Marghanita, *Ecstasy: a study of some secular and religious experiences* (1961). Repr. New York: Greenwood Press, 1968.

Manlove, C.N., *Modern Fantasy*. Cambridge: Cambridge University Press, 1975.

Miller, J. Hillis, *The Disappearance of God: five nineteenth-century writers* (1963). Cambridge, MA: Belknap Press of Harvard University Press, 1975.

Mills, Alice, *Stuckness in the Fiction of Mervyn Peake*. Amsterdam/New York, NY: Rodopi, dated 2005, published 2006.

Smith, P.G., *Mervyn Peake: a personal memoir*. Gollancz, 1984.

Speth, Lee. 'Cavalier treatment: a Connecticut Yankee in Gormenghast.' *Mythlore* 6 (Spring 1979), 2: 46–47.

Stanzel, Franz K., *A Theory of Narrative*. Trans. Charlotte Goedsche. Cambridge: Cambridge University Press, 1984.

Storr, Anthony, *Solitude*. (Originally published as *The School of Genius*, 1988.) HarperCollins, 1997.

Watney, John, *Mervyn Peake*. Michael Joseph, 1976.

Wescott, Mabel Ingalls, *Let Me Linger and Other Poems*. Boston, MA: Meador, 1937.

Winnington, G. Peter, 'Editing Peake', MPR 13 (Autumn 1981), 2–7. (Lists the corrections made to the King Penguin editions and to the Penguin *Peake's Progress* (1981).)

——, *Vast Alchemies: the life and work of Mervyn Peake*. Peter Owen, 2000.

——, 'Peake, Knole, and *Orlando*', PS 7 (October 2000), i: 24–29.

——, 'Parodies and Poetical Allusions', PS 7 (April 2002), iv: 25–29.

Yorke, Malcolm, *Mervyn Peake: my eyes mint gold. A life*. John Murray, 2000.

# Introduction

Now that he's dead 'is secrets die with him
Like some lost language, or a hieroglyph
Time-shallowed on a stone.
                                                    (*The Wit to Woo*, PP277)

'There is no exquisite beauty,' says Bacon, 'without
some strangeness in the proportions.'
    Edgar Allan Poe, *Broadway Journal*, 12 April 1845.

THIS IS THE FIRST critical monograph on Mervyn Peake's work as a whole – the first, that is, to take account of his poems, plays, short stories and graphic work (paintings, drawings and illustrations, both to his own works and those by others), as well as his novels about Titus Groan and Mr Pye. There have been biographies (by Watney, Winnington and York, in that order) and memoirs (by Gilmore and Smith), but very little criticism. Half of John Batchelor's pioneering study, *Mervyn Peake: a biographical and critical exploration* (1975), analysed Peake's prose and poetry in general terms, but did not relate them to his graphic work. Tanya Gardiner-Scott's *Mervyn Peake: the evolution of a dark romantic* (1989) concentrated on the three Titus books, especially the third, treating them as gothic, and ignored everything else. A study by Alice Mills (which appeared only after this book was finished) examines the notion of *Stuckness in the Fiction of Mervyn Peake*. Colin Manlove devoted a chapter of *Modern Fantasy* (1975) to the Titus books but, because they did not fit his conception of fantasy, he ended by condemning them as 'products of a real, even a great literary ability strangled in its own toils' (257).

Considering that *Titus Groan* was published 60 years ago, this amounts to a tiny body of criticism. Yet Peake's work has been popular, particularly

among university students. The three Titus books have been continuously
in print ever since they were paperbacked in the late 1960s, and they have
been translated into at least two dozen different languages. The first two
volumes regularly feature in lists of the best novels. *Mr Pye, Selected Poems*
and *A Book of Nonsense* have remained in print since the mid-70s, and
Peake's illustrations for *Treasure Island, The Rime of the Ancient Mariner,
Alice's Adventures in Wonderland* and *Through the Looking-Glass* have
been reissued time and again (the last two quite recently in simultaneous
luxury and popular editions). First editions of his books and his paintings
and drawings command large sums in the auction rooms. So while he has
found favour in the eyes of both educated readers and collectors, Peake
has been almost entirely neglected by critics.

One of the reasons for this is quite simple: Peake's work is anomalous.
Asked in a radio discussion of *Titus Groan* whether he had tried to fit his
book 'into any known literary form', he answered that for him there are

> two kinds of books, one of which is on the classic side, where there is the
> mould – the mould which one accepts, then pours one's words into. ...
> And then there's the other, which is not, I think, necessarily a formless
> thing [but which] creates its own form.        (MPR 10 (Spring 1980), 14)

By his own admission then, the Titus books are *sui generis*, with their own
form, created (like the works of the Bright Carvers) in 'a highly stylized
manner peculiar to themselves' (TG15).

Unfortunately for Peake, critics like pigeon-holes and they resent
a writer whose work they cannot easily classify. Typical is the reaction
of Kingsley Amis. In his survey of science fiction, *New Maps of Hell*, he
dismissed Peake as 'a bad fantasy writer of maverick status' (153). One
wonders where Peake's fault lies: is he 'a bad writer' or does he write
'bad fantasy'? (For that matter, does he in fact write fantasy?) As for his
'maverick status', who assigned him that, if not Mr Amis? Just so long as
no one has shown what Peake was actually doing, it is easier to say what
his work is *not* than what it *is*, and easier still to damn him for not fitting
into a convenient category. The observation by Maurice Collis (reviewing
*Gormenghast*) to the effect that

> the unusualness of *Titus Groan* put the critics on their mettle; they tried
> their best to fathom its mood and discover whether it was an extravaganza,
> a vision or what, but found it impossible to pin down Mervyn Peake,
>                                    (*World Review*, n.s. 22 (December 1950), 77–78)

remains as true today as it was 60 years ago. To borrow Peake's own words once again, his writing 'defies the very convention that gives it form' (D8).

Practically all the articles and dissertations about Peake's work (listed in Parts G, H and I of 'Peake in Print' on the *Peake Studies* website: www.peakestudies.com) have taken one of three approaches. They attempt to 'explain' the work by the life, or to prove some preconception about it (that it's political allegory, for instance), or else treat it as an example of a genre (like the gothic or the grotesque) in order to compare Peake with other writers. All too often, the secondary literature tells us more about the critics than about the works they study. As Peake observed,

> There are always those who wish to limit art to within the boundaries of their own faculties: to recognize only such work as reflects their own attitude to life and aesthetics. And this is natural, if unintelligent. A man is unable to see anything other than himself. A mule faced with an El Greco can only glare in a mulish way: can only receive what mules can receive. Similarly, a particular man can see only his own reflection.          (D9)

I too stared mulishly at Peake's work for many years. Only when I began to listen to it with what *The Genesis of Secrecy* so colourfully calls 'uncircumcised ears' (Kermode 16) did things begin to fall into place. This made me, in Peake's words, 'a slightly different man' and I came to 'see a slightly different picture … until the canvas or the drawing [bore] no relation to the work [I] stared at five years earlier' (D9). I hope that the resulting book reveals more about the working of Peake's mind than mine.

My aim has been to identify, without presupposition or judgment, the main themes, motifs and structural patterns of Peake's prose and verse, relating them where relevant to his drawings and illustrations. Thus I treat all his works as products of the same mind and therefore mutually illuminating. Rather than generalize from a single instance, I supply many examples, irrespective of quality. A plodding poem can reveal quite as much of Peake's technique as an exquisite drawing, and sometimes more, just as cracks and crannies offer more of a handhold for the climber than smooth marble.

That comparison leads me to another of my aims. As so much of Peake's writing involves metaphor, literalized metaphor and even metaphors of literalized metaphor, I have endeavoured to respect his imagery. That is, because the meaning changes when you change the image, I have done my best to keep my metaphors (dead and alive) aligned with Peake's.

In short, I have tried to respect the unique form of Peake's works by dealing with them in and on their own terms, grouping my findings in chapters whose titles reflect his preoccupations rather than pre-established concepts. Peake did not deal in abstract notions, and gave even a term like *perspective* an unexpected slant. Furthermore, he was fundamentally indifferent to politics; an event like the Korean war reputedly inspired in him no more than a pun: 'The only Korea I'm interested in is my own.' He used political terms as metaphors, and I have treated them as such.

The result differs substantially from anything yet written on Peake. No one has discussed even so basic a theme as love or identified the ubiquitous motif of the island in his work, to start with, nor has anyone related his shorter works to the Titus books. As for his plays, there is not a line of criticism to be found, apart from reviews of *The Wit to Woo* while it was being performed in 1957. So although I have read practically all the secondary literature and even (as editor of *The Mervyn Peake Review* and then of *Peake Studies*) published much of it, I make little reference to it. To have discussed and argued with it would have doubled the length of this book. Here and there I may make an observation or draw a conclusion similar to one critic's or another's but, since I am taking all Peake's work into account, the path by which I have arrived at it has been my own.

A word about irony. Whenever you feel like exclaiming, 'Oh the irony of it!' rest assured that I would be doing so too, on practically every page, were it not that the repetition would be tedious. It is a deliberate omission.

In Peake's short story, 'The Connoisseurs', two art critics break a beautiful vase to find out whether it's genuine – and it was. If after reading this book Peake's work remains intact for you – better, if you return to it with rekindled interest and fresh understanding – then I shall have achieved my aim. For this is by no means the whole Peake.

# Heart

Either everything is understood at once, by the heart,
or it is never understood at all.                    (MP167)


### To Live at all Is Miracle Enough

To live at all is miracle enough.
The doom of nations is another thing.
Here in my hammering blood-pulse is my proof.
[…]
Swung out of sunlight into cosmic shade,
Come what come may the imagination's heart
Is constellation high and can't be weighed.

Nor greed nor fear can tear our faith apart
When every heartbeat hammers out the proof
That life itself is miracle enough.
                                          (Gb3)


MERVYN PEAKE IS BEST known for his novels *Titus Groan, Gormen-ghast* and *Titus Alone*. They are often called the 'Gormenghast trilogy' but since they are about the eponymous hero rather than his castle home it is more accurate to call them 'the Titus books'. The appellation is, however, significant: it's the place rather than the plot that remains in the mind. Rarely has a literary castle caught the imagination of so many readers.

In the space of less than 25 years Peake also produced thousands of drawings and book illustrations, hundreds of paintings, more than two hundred poems, a dozen plays, another novel, a novella and a handful of short stories. What was the creative process that makes Gormenghast so memorable and facilitated so many works in so many media in so short a time? Although Peake was not given to theorizing, he wrote of what drawing meant for him in the Introduction to a book of his *Drawings*. In so doing he supplies some answers to my question. So this chapter is based on a close reading of that Introduction, illustrated with quotations from his poems and the experiences of his fictional characters.

AT THE CENTRE OF the poem printed as the epigraph to this chapter, 'To Live at all is Miracle Enough', Peake writes: 'the imagination's heart / Is constellation high and can't be weighed' (Gb3). In this I hear an echo of Shakespeare's definition of love in Sonnet 116: 'It is the star ... / Whose worth's unknown although his highth be taken' (NAEL 1: 1038). Whether I am right or wrong, Peake's statement confirms something that stands out in all his work: for him, the heart, traditionally the seat of love, is also the seat of the imagination, moved alike by beauty and by fear. (Although this sounds highly Wordsworthian, Peake was not necessarily influenced by Wordsworth.) In his work we find the heart and the imagination pulsing in parallel at moments of great emotion. This is because, 'When beauty rides into the hollow heart / It is as something that comes home again / As though for anchorage' (Gb39). In the golden oak forest, 'Fear' (G132; Peake's capital) spurs Titus to venture on and encounter the Thing, the feral girl from the mud huts who lives alone in the woods around Gormenghast. For Peake, love, the heart and the imagination are three components of a single process: love expresses our most important feeling; with its beats the heart signals our response to emotion, the vital visceral level of life; and the imagination dwelling in the heart is inspired by those emotions. Together they form the miracle of what it is to be alive – and creating.

The making of a work of art begins in the heart. In phrases like 'art should be artless, not heartless' (TA49), Peake uses the heart as a kind of shorthand for the combination of all three notions. So when he states that 'poetry is a ritual of the heart' (G176) he is talking of experiences accompanied by powerful emotions like love or fear that the imagination has drawn upon and expressed in words. Without heart, Peake tells us, the work of an artist is merely mechanical, characterized by

> the lethal stillness of good taste and moderation, that landlocked harbour where the craft of an artist can gaze at its own image in the water, year after year, its woodwork freshly painted, its canvas neat and trim, its cargo rotting.                                                    (D8)

Notice how the pun on 'craft', which neatly extends through 'painted', 'canvas' and 'cargo', builds on the image of beauty riding at anchor in the heart. The heart must be open to the world and let beauty enter. Nor can imagination substitute for the heart: 'a drawing may be brilliant in a dozen ways and yet be empty. It may be outlandish, bizarre, and it would seem original, but its heart may be missing' (D7–8). As a teacher of life drawing, Peake knew that he could not influence this basic process in his students, 'for in the end the miracle is all that counts, and miracles cannot be taught' (WiD). Without the heart, then, fed by love and fired by the imagination, miracles can no more be performed than we can live.

Peake seems to have been acutely aware of the beating of his heart, that 'rattling dice' in his chest. It throbs and hammers in his poetry, and in his fiction his characters are equally conscious of it, from Nannie Slagg's refrain of 'Oh my poor heart!' to the singing of the bird in Keda's bosom. Its pulsing accompanies all the major scenes in his novels and stories, whether it be the moments when Titus discovers colour and beauty or the set scenes shot through with fear, such as the duels that occur in each of the Titus books. Nor is it just the physical sensation of having a heart in one's body – leaping, dancing, throbbing or pounding, as the case may be – that is so important to Peake. He associates two other qualities with it: sound and (more unexpectedly) space. I'll examine them in that order.

Peake's characters frequently hear their hearts beating. Flay, seeking the apartment in which the Twins are incarcerated, listens intently in the hollow halls beneath the castle (also called the silent halls), but 'there was never any sound but the beating of his own heart' (G301). Some characters can even hear another's heart. When Steerpike has entered Fuchsia's attic, early in *Titus Groan*, he sees her approaching and feigns a faint; as she bends over him, 'in the protracted and deathly stillness he could hear a heart beating. It was not his own' (TG153). The blind Lamb, in 'Boy in Darkness', has the most acute hearing of all: in the 'hollow silence' of his underground home, he 'could hear the beating of four hearts' (BiD222). So where there is silence, the heart can be heard quite as keenly as it can be felt.

Sound plays a fundamental role in Peake's creative process. For him the beating of his heart is the voice of his imagination at work. While writing *Titus Groan*, he made sketches of the characters: 'The drawings were never exactly as I imagined the people,' he tells us, 'but were near enough for me to know when their voices lost touch with their heads' (HRNE 80). Sound was the touchstone; the drawings mere approximations. The triple synaesthesia of sight, sound and touch implied by checking with drawings how voices keep contact with their bodies confirms the seamless continuity for Peake of imagining by hearing the heart, and then drawing. It applies throughout his creative work. And it is the notion with which he opens his Introduction to *Drawings*: 'The voice of a pencil. Its lilt; its pitch; its suave and silver argument or the husky stuttering of its leaden dagger. The voice of ink, of chalk, of pigment or stone.' Each medium has a voice of its own that expresses what Peake hears in his heart, 'varying voices that, soundless, can be like tumult or as faint as a whisper in the next room' (D7).

The oxymoron of 'soundless voices' that are 'like tumult' points to the problem encountered by all artists who attempt to translate the experience of one perceptual mode in the terms of another. It is probably because Peake's natural gifts included *voice* as the first step of his creative process that he became a writer as well as a painter and draughtsman. Without it, he might have drawn and painted with equal skill, but he would probably not have written prose and poetry as he did. He certainly treasured this transmutation of one perceptual mode into another; he called it 'alchemy', the making of gold out of base metals.

Creating a work means transferring these voices (or 'accents') from the heart and the imagination onto the paper or canvas. Until the pencil begins to draw, 'The paper is breathless / Under the hand' (D7, epigraph). On first reading, we might think that the paper is 'breathless' with expectation, but Peake has another, more important thought in mind: the pencil (or pen, or brush) *breathes life* into the paper (or canvas). As he puts it in his Introduction, 'they make their way, these accents, through the arm and fingers to a canvas … [or] to the square yawn of a paper page as empty of life as the manless moon' (D7). A blank sheet of paper, like the moon in space, gapes speechless at the world, waiting for the artist to animate it. Under Peake's hand, drawing, writing and painting bring the work of art to life, enabling it to speak with the voice of his heart.

During the war Peake was commissioned to record glassblowers making cathode ray tubes in a Birmingham factory. He was surprised to find himself suddenly inspired by their balletic movements as they blew down their hollow rods and turned the gobbet of molten glass on the end into a vase-like shape. Their act of breathing shape into lifeless sand (like so much moon dust!) struck a chord in him. He not only made some of his best paintings, but also wrote about them in both prose and verse (see MPMA 70–73). Phrases like 'A rhythm of breath is wheedling

Dr Prunesquallor and his sister Irma with her
'corsage of hand-painted parrots'.

alchemy / From the warlock sand' (Gb19; 'warlock' is another favourite word) reveal that he sensed in their actions a correspondence with how he breathed life into his own creations.

In his Introduction, Peake defines the 'authority' of a great work of art in terms of *voice*. For him, a great drawing

> is doubly alive, firstly through its overtones and echoes which show it to be borne rapidly or languorously along one of the deep streams that wind back through time to a cave in Spain. The authority, as it were, of a chorus of voices.

A great work should also speak with 'the authority of the single, isolated voice' of the individual artist. He should have a

> voice that is not afraid to speak quietly if such is natural to it, when the fashion favours the bull-mouthed orators. Nor is afraid to shout across the lethal stillness of good taste and moderation.        (D8)

Here Peake expresses his basic stance as an artist: he refused to compromise with fashion or conventional good taste, choosing to express his own voice, at the cost of worldly success. Here too there is tragic irony: he was in his mid-30s when he wrote that this individual voice 'is the kind of authority that races against time for a few feverish seasons'. Ten years later disease robbed him of his steady hand and his ability to concentrate; ten more and he was dead.

In claiming that the voice of authority in a work is 'borne rapidly or languorously along one of the deep streams that wind back through time to a cave in Spain', Peake presents the sequence of his own process in reverse, travelling back from the work on paper or canvas, up the bloodstream in the arm to the cave, or heart, where it originates. As we have seen, the heart and the imagination can be heard most clearly in places where there is no other sound. In Peake's fiction such places are Fuchsia's attic, the hollow halls and the Lamb's underground mine, all of which are silent cave-like spaces. In silence, then, Peake listens to the voice of the imagination in his heart; transposed onto paper or canvas, it becomes the voice of the work of art.

This brings us to the notion of *space*. Peake associates the imagination with space, the vast, empty and silent interstellar space of the universe. The idea was already there in the first quotation I made, 'the imagination's heart / Is constellation high' (Gb3) and it is repeated in many forms throughout his work. We have 'the firmament' of Titus's imagination in

*Gormenghast* (85), and 'the imagination's astral touch' which makes 'the brain's gray spaces … / Flare into focus' (RoB15). What is more, because Peake's imagination resides in his heart, he houses the whole universe in there: 'Beneath my ribs are the spaces / Of the Pleiades', he told his wife (Yorke 95). So 'When beauty rides into the hollow heart' (Gb39), that hollowness equates to the infinite capacity of Peake's heart to accommodate his equally infinite imagination.

This can be illustrated by that moment in *Gormenghast* when Titus comes across a flight of beautifully painted stairs and climbs to a landing colonized by tiny grey mice. Up there

> a window let in the light and, sometimes, the sun itself, whose beams made of this silent, forgotten landing a cosmos, a firmament of moving motes, brilliantly illuminated, an astral and at the same time a solar province; for the sun would come through with its long rays and the rays would be dancing with stars.                                    (G49)

All these astronomical allusions added to the silence of the place make it inevitable that Titus should make his momentous discovery 'with his imagination dilated and his heart hammering aloud' (G50). We might also note how the conjunction of grey mice with coloured stairs parallels 'the imagination's astral touch' which makes 'the brain's gray spaces … / Flare' (RoB15). Similarities such as these reveal the patterns of Peake's imaginative process.

These patterns permeate his work. In a poem about bomb damage in wartime London, for instance, he describes houses whose 'wounds'

> taunt the hollow
> World of their emptiness that yawns and opens
> Into a firmament beneath their ribs
> That knows no planets, but a few dead stars.
>                                    (S&S6)

Here the yawning cavities opened up by the exploding bombs beneath the 'ribs' of the houses echo Peake's intimate sense of having the universe in his heart, but (understandably enough) their 'firmament' has gone dead.

The same conjunction of motifs occurs in an early poem about a wood in autumn. Because, as Peake puts it, 'A stillness … / Escapes my ear, but knocks my heart', the colours of the leaves inspire him:

Then leaps my heart to the bone gate,
And at the gate the baffled heart
Knocks impotent for space.

(RoB29)

Unlike his ears, his heart 'hears' the silence and demands more space than the 'gate' (his ribcage) can allow for his imagination to create the poem itself. This sense of constriction – and its resolution – lies at the heart (or should we say 'under the heart'?) of one of Peake's most memorable poems, 'Grottoed beneath Your Ribs Our Babe Lay Thriving' (Gb4–5).

Given his sense of the immense possibilities of the imagination within that cavern beneath his ribs, we might expect Peake to be particularly moved by pregnancy. And indeed, soon after the birth of his first child, he addressed to his wife a poem that follows the babe's evolution, in four numbered stanzas, from foetus to separate individual. The phrase 'Grottoed beneath your ribs' opens each stanza, changing to 'Grottoed no longer' in the fourth. The first evokes the moment of conception: in the 'sky' there passed a 'green meteor with a flickering / Trail that stayed always yet was always moving;' with 'qualms of love' this sperm 'set fire the nine-month burden'. So the foetus is seen as a 'fire-boy knocking at the osseous belfry / Where thuds the double-throated chord of loving'. The womb has become a 'belfry' where the sound of the beating heart, the vocal chord of love, echoes with a harmonious pun on the umbilical cord. (The image of the pelvic area as a belfry is used to comic effect in *Titus Groan*: Irma's hips sway when she talks 'as though, like a great bell, they were regulated and motivated by a desire to sound, [and] they all but chime. … Her sharp, unpleasant voice … contrasted to the knell her pelvis might have uttered' (TG460). Irma, of course, is childless.)

In the second stanza, having its own beating heart,

our babe no more
May hear the tolling of your sultry gong
Above him where the echoes throb and throng
Among the breathing rafters of sweet bone.

(Gb4)

Instead, 'He lies alone / With air and time about him and the drone / Of space for his immeasurable bed'. (There is a similar pairing of the droning sound of silence with the heart in *Titus Alone*: 'The silence droned like a bee in the heart of a flower' (152).) As the foetus develops it acquires its own 'immeasurable' space. When finally it 'knocks at the gate' and is born, the child can 'Stretch [its] small wrinkled limbs in shrill delight' – is there an echo of Blake's 'Lamb' here? – for it has gained a corresponding space in the outside world, where 'the brilliant daybreak / Flares heavenward in a swathe of diamond light'. The notion of light, which has been conspicuously absent so far, enters the poem with the meteor-sperm in the otherwise dark sky, develops with growing images of fire, and exits, 'heavenward', in this sparkling blaze. Thus Peake draws a parallel between the creative process as he experienced it and the growth and birth of a child.

This parallel between human gestation and the birth of a work of art is partially literalized in *Titus Groan* and repeated throughout Peake's work. There is a sense in which the first two books about Titus Groan recapitulate at great length the development of a work of art (whether visual or verbal) and the third dramatizes its existence in the outer world. Numerous metaphors and metatextual comments support this reading, as when Titus realizes that 'he could never turn back the pages' of his life (TA28), and I will develop it in later chapters. So when Batchelor claims that *Titus Groan* is filled with metaphors of birth (83), he is only half right. The metaphors are of creation, of which gestation and birth are but one expression.

This brings us to the next stage in Peake's creative process: putting the work onto paper or canvas. Beginning as a whisper in the heart, his inspiration travels down his arm and hand to express itself through his pen, pencil or brush. It demands space, 'a canvas like a field of untrodden snow' or 'the square yawn of a paper page' on which to organize 'a cold chaos of stone' and bring life to 'the manless moon' (D7). Just as the voice in the heart becomes the voice of the work, so the work requires a space as vast as the firmament where it was conceived. With space as with sound, there is a parallel between inner and outer worlds.

Bridging these two worlds there is but the nib of the pen, the lead of the sharpened pencil, the bristle of the brush, or the blade of the chisel. (I know of no extant piece of sculpture by Peake, but he did carve in his youth; Watney 51 reproduces a photograph of him, mallet in hand, at work on a piece of stone. The 'chaos of stone' just mentioned shows that he had sculpture in mind quite as much as painting or drawing.) Artists experience this crucial moment of bringing their creation across the threshold of their inner world and out into the 'real' world in many different ways. Peake compares it to stepping over the edge of a cliff: the 'rattling dice' that he hears in his chest 'Proclaim the edge of precipice /

At whose hid boulders, stands a soundless sea' (10P). The creative process requires that he commit himself in this act. Consequently the notion of the *edge* takes on tremendous importance in his work.

In each of Peake's novels, characters take existential decisions on the edge of a precipice: Keda steps out into space in hope and exultation; Mr Pye sits on a cliff edge to reflect on his problems and ultimately drives a horse and carriage over the brink in despair. Unlike Keda, he soars into the sky on miraculous wings. Fuchsia's moment is tragic, in keeping with her character. On the window-ledge above the flood she is merely playing with the idea of suicide when she is disturbed, turns, loses balance and falls, to drown in the water below.

For Peake, the edge is the threshold between life and death, the pivot or hinge on which life turns. In *Titus Groan* he endlessly repeats the word as he recounts the feud between Flay, the thin and bony servant, and Swelter, the fat and flatulent chef. Swelter sharpens a kitchen cleaver to 'an uncommonly keen edge' (146), to 'a screaming edge' (423), to 'an edge as set up a new sensation – that of killing, as it were, without knowing it' (424). Flay observes him honing 'the already razor-keen edge' on a grindstone, putting his ear to 'the shivering edge … as though to listen for a thin and singing note to take flight from the unspeakable sharpness of the steel' (210), and divines his intentions. So he fetches an old sword from the armoury, cleans off the rust and gives it 'a point and an edge in the Stone Lanes. Compared to the edge which Swelter had given to the cleaver the sword was blunt but it was murderous enough' (403). Thus equipped they are 'on the edge of violence' (408). Their duel ends with Swelter tripping on the sill of a doorway (another *edge*, you will note) and falling with an almighty splash into a 'lake' of rainwater. In a parody of the scene in Tennyson's *Idylls of the King* when Sir Bedivere returns Excalibur to the lake, 'the cleaver sailed from his grasp and, circling in the moonlight, fell with a fluke of flame in the far, golden silence of the lake' (438). Thereupon Flay skewers him with his sword. He and Lord Sepulchrave tip the vast cadaver over the edge of the roof and drag it off as a sacrifice to the owls in the Tower of Flints. Throughout this subplot, the edge is the fulcrum on which life and death pivot for Flay and Swelter. When it tips in favour of Flay, Swelter trips, topples – and is tipped.

Peake's act of creation, which might have been just 'a matter of making marks' on paper or canvas (D9), proves to be a highly existential moment. It expresses his identity. 'Who is one?' he asks. 'What is one's elemental name … one's core? … Is it made of iron, or of atmosphere?' (D10). Nor is this all; the resulting work is also faced with an edge or precipice, on which, unlike the artist, it must remain balanced:

> when the finest examples of any master's work are contemplated, the first thing one finds is that they have that most magisterial of qualities, 'equipoise'. They are compelling because they are not 'classic' and because they are not 'romantic'. They are both and they are neither. They are balanced upon a razor's edge between the passion and the intellect, between the compulsive and the architectonic. (D9)

So Peake leads an acrobatic existence: he has to 'go over the edge', commit himself and reveal who he is – his 'elemental name' – in order to achieve this ideal balance in his work. Like a glassblower, 'he is the lyric-juggler' (*Convoy* 25).

Committing oneself like this requires an appropriate medium. Does the inspiration

> breathe best through ink or paint or chalk? Are monsters made to feel at home, or seraphs, or Lord Mayors, or sunsets, or lamplit bedrooms, or race horses painted with coloured vaseline?
>
> This is the problem of the artist – to discover his language. It is a lifelong search, for when the idiom is found it has then to be developed and sharpened. (D10)

As the French say, *le style, c'est l'homme*. Define the style and you define the artist. Nor is this all. 'Worse than no style is a mannerism – a formula for producing effects.' Not committing oneself is 'suicide' (D10). Going over the edge may seem like death, but it creates an original work of art and gives the artist a new life.

With each work, Peake asks himself whether he is just applying a formula, or creating a masterpiece of equipoise that will transform the paper it is drawn or written on 'into a cosmos of such vibrancy' that it makes viewers or readers feel as though they inhabit 'a land of the dead' (D7). This is the miracle he desires. Lest he be accused of exaggerating, he continues:

> If I am asked whether all this is not just a little 'intense' – in other words, if it is suggested that it doesn't really matter, I say that it matters fundamentally. For one may as well be asked, 'Does life matter?' – 'Does man matter?' If man matters, then the highest flights of his mind and his imagination matter. His vision matters, his sense of wonder, his vitality matters.

It gives the lie to the nihilists and those who cry 'Woe!' in the streets. For art is the voice of man, naked, militant, and unashamed.

This melodramatic and romantic position underlies all Peake's work.

To produce such miraculous works, artists face the challenge of breaking the habits of everyday life, of listening with the inner quite as much as with the outer ear, and of looking at the objects around them with fresh eyes. 'A loaf of bread is not worth drawing, nor is anything else, unless it is seen, as it were, for the first time' (D10).

> Once there was a yellow chair against a blue wall. It was seen by a painter
> – not because it was a chair – but because a yellow shape sang out against
> the blue plaster. [It would of course *sing out* for Peake.] It was not some-
> thing to sit on, but a glory in the brain of Van Gogh.     (AW3)

Peake compares the effort of rising to this challenge to breaking a window: 'the creation of a work of art' requires 'the smashing of another window-pane' (D9). He sums this thought up with the notion that

> Each day we live is a glass room
> Until we break it with the thrusting
> Of the spirit and pass through
> The splintered walls to the green pastures
> Where the birds and buds are breaking
> Into fabulous song and hue
> By the still waters.

The Biblical echoes should not be lost upon us; they lead straight into the second half of the poem:

> Each day is a glass room unless
> We break it: but how rare's the day
> We have the power to raise the dead
> And walk on air to the green pastures!
> For the clouded glass, or clay,
> Is blind with usage, though the Lord
> Walk the still waters.
>
>                               (Gb17)

In other words, those miracles (comparable to giving birth, raising the dead and walking on water) that occur when artists produce exceptional work (and in their joy feel as though they are walking on air) are still performed. This is neatly exemplified by Mr Pye who, having grown

'The smashing of another window pane'.
In the cross-hatched background, the words
'First Poems by Mervyn Peake' can be made out, confirming
the link between this image and creativity.

wings, asks his god, 'What can I do with wings, for pity's sake?' There is no reply. 'The room was quite silent save for a moth at the window, which fluttered up and down the glass' (MP132). There is his answer, if Mr Pye could but recognize it: with wings he can extricate himself from his predicament, but to do it he needs to shatter the glass cage of everyday thinking. However, fly he does, in the end; a miracle.

Such things do not happen every day because habit obscures the artist's vision. The best he can do is to struggle on, although the result may often be desperately insignificant. Peake likens this to trying to reach a 'swan arrogant' that rides within his heart,

> Beneath the muscled branches of thick thought
> Holding my brain at bay. Each day
> I wrench the boughs apart until
> I can no longer hold them. From the well
> Of my confusion the dead waters rise
> In layers of silence widening my eyes
> With nothingness.
>
> (S&S21)

The 'swan arrogant' is ironic, for poets traditionally compare their own verse to that of others as a swallow to a swan. Peake admits the arrogance of reversing the comparison. And one wonders whether the problem, on this occasion, was that he was desperately *looking* rather than *listening*. At any rate, at such moments he feels tempted to seek inspiration in pain itself:

> Rather than a little pain, I would be thief
> To the organ-chords of grief
> That toll through me
> With a burial glory.
> […]
> Cold grief,
> I would be thief
> Of you,
> Until my bones breed hemlock through and through.
>
> (S&S18)

When the drive to be creative starts to feed upon itself, the act of committing the work to paper or canvas can be disturbed to the point of awakening thoughts of self-destruction, suicide.

Peake's metaphor for the last step in his creative process is the theatre.

First heard as a whisper in the heart, each fresh inspiration travels 'to a canvas like a field of untrodden snow, to a cold chaos of stone, to the square yawn of a paper page.' These, he continues, are 'the imponderable platforms: the breathless theatres' (D7) or hollow halls where his work comes to life. Just as the stage can be made to represent any space, from a claustrophobic cell to a shoreless sea, so Peake perceives his page or canvas as an infinitely adaptable space that mirrors or replicates the space that his imagination enjoys in his heart. The imagination is commonly compared to a theatre in the mind that is contemplated through introspection. With Peake, however, this comparison does not apply to the moment of imagining, but to the time of realization, whether writing, drawing or painting. For most of his creative career his 'stage' was paper, canvas or stone, which can be bought, carried away and enjoyed at home.

The significance of the theatre for Peake should not be underestimated. It combines the two fundamental features of his imaginative process – the voice associated with physical action – and it implies the existential question raised by every performance: will it come alive? What is more, because his 'paper stage is set afresh each day, stands bare for all to take, to strut, to mime upon, to creep or float across' (D7), it reflects the Sisyphean existence of the artist who has to break out of his glass room anew each day. It also introduces – and this is crucial – the sense that has been absent so far from Peake's creative process: sight. We have observed how Peake begins with the synaesthesia of sound as sensation in the heart; now is the moment when finally he *sees* his work. Readers coming away from *Titus Groan* and *Gormenghast* with intense visual images may find it hard to accept that he *heard* and *felt* his works long before he *saw* them.

Peake's writing reflects this sequence. In his poems the first statement generally vehicles an auditory perception, and the second a physical action or sensation; occasionally it's the reverse. In either case, sight – perception of shape, line, colour and perspective – comes in third place. To describe seeing a beautiful girl, only to have 'the magic' of 'her loveliness … crumble, and break' as soon as he hears her voice, he reorders his experience to open the poem with 'And then I heard her speak' (Gb34). The same sequence characterizes his prose, as I showed in *Vast Alchemies* (189) with reference to the first page of *Titus Groan*. I could equally well have quoted the opening words of *Gormenghast*: 'Suckled on shadows; weaned, as it were, on webs of ritual: for his ears, echoes, for his eyes, a labyrinth of stone' (7). It's the same with Mr Pye's Great Pal, whom he cannot 'hear and touch and see' (MP60). This is not to say that seeing was any less important for Peake; it just came after hearing and feeling in his creative sequence.

Like Dickens, who once claimed that 'every writer of fiction writes in effect for the stage', Peake had a lifelong affair with the theatre. His first uncompleted project was an opera; his first contract was to design the costumes and scenery for a play. When he turned his attention back to the stage in the 1950s, he made plays out of *Titus Groan* and *Mr Pye*, as Dickens did with some of his stories. In all, Peake embarked on something like 20 plays; and his last great unfinished work was an opera of Gormenghast. If we include projected works in his oeuvre, plays outnumber prose works two to one. Today he is known for his illustrations, his novels and stories, and his poetry. He would have wished to be equally known as a dramatist.

The young Dickens aspired to be an actor and later exhausted himself by giving dramatic readings from his novels. Peake saw himself rather as a director, and attended many of the rehearsals of his play, *The Wit to Woo*, at the Arts Theatre in London in 1957; he collapsed when it was not the success he had dreamed of. For him, writing novels was like directing plays – or rather, impros. He assigned the roles and left the situation to develop. 'What can be as exciting as setting a scene and peopling it?' he exclaimed to Maurice Collis. 'To be in *half* control of them, that is the thing. … One's characters must have free will' (letter dated 4 March 1947 printed in MPR 19 (Summer 1985), 15; Peake's emphasis). So he allowed his imagination to 'take its own course' and his characters to 'take their way' (from Peake's notes on *Titus Groan* quoted by Watney 128).

The theatre is a vehicle for much of Peake's work, rather as Cheeta used a ruined house to stage her revenge. 'The great crater of the Black House that had until recently yawned to the moon was now filled with something other than its mood. Its emptiness gone, it listened as though it had the power of hearing' (TA215). Be it paper, canvas or ruin, Peake breathes life into his stage, animating it with characters that he only half controls, and they act out his works before his eyes. To the evident ekphrasis of his descriptive writing, the theatre adds a quality of observed action. The intense vitality of what Peake witnessed made him want to write in the present tense, even to break into running commentary. Long sections of *Titus Groan* were originally written thus and only later transposed into the past.

As creator, director, and at the same time spectator of his own works, Peake asks, 'what should we hope for as the curtain rises and lays bare the

gratuitous stage where, unhindered, a man may cry his ghostly manifesto?'
And the answer is 'a miracle', one of those 'works that are not excellent
of their kind but are a new kind of excellence' (D7). For many people,
the Titus books possess just this quality. After reading *Gormenghast*, C.S.
Lewis told Peake that it has 'the hallmark of true myth. … What one may
call "the gormenghastly" has given me a new Universal' and he thanked
him 'for adding to a class of literature in which the attempts are few and
the successes very few indeed' (letter dated 10 February 1958 quoted by
Yorke 213).

H AVING FOLLOWED THE MAIN steps of Peake's creative process through
his Introduction to *Drawings*, I propose to illustrate this sequence
in the experience of his fictional characters.

High under the roof of Gormenghast Fuchsia has appropriated three
attic rooms as her own secret domain where she can daydream to her
heart's content. Even before she enters them, 'a thin beam' of morning
sunlight, 'filled with slowly moving motes like an attenuate firmament
of stars' (78), signals that this is the world of the imagination. This first
room is filled with a heterogeneous assortment of objects that recall her
childhood; they are the furnishings of her imagination.

In the second attic, 'silence was there with a loud rhythm. The halls,
towers, the rooms of Gormenghast were of another planet' (80). Fuchsia
responds by catching at 'a thick lock of her hair and dragg[ing] her own
head back as her heart beat loudly and, tingling from head to foot, little
diamonds appeared at the inner corners of her eyes' (80). This corresponds to the first step of Peake's sequence, with its characteristic features
of the sound of silence, the beating of the heart, physical sensations, and
a hint of 'diamond light' (Gb5).

This second room is Fuchsia's 'attic of make-believe, where she would
watch her mind's companions advancing or retreating across the dusty
floor'. It is like a stage, to which she gains access by going down a few
steps. 'The rafters above the steps' actually form a low proscenium arch,
for they 'were warped into a sagging curve so that it was not possible to
obtain more than a restricted view of the room beyond' (80). To reach
her third attic, Fuchsia has to descend these steps and cross the 'stage':

> As she stepped forward on the empty boards, it was for her like walking
> into space. Space, such as the condors have shrill inklings of, and the cock-
> eagle glimpses through his blood. …

> It was here that she would see the people of her imagination, the fierce
> figures of her making, as they strolled from corner to corner, brooded
> like monsters or flew through the air like seraphs with burning wings, or
> danced, or fought, or laughed, or cried.                              (80)

This replicates Peake's own theatrical space, his floor 'to strut, to mime
upon, to creep or float across' (D7), down to the repetition of the
'monsters' and 'seraphs' (D10) that people it.

Climbing to a balcony, Fuchsia turns and sees 'the great stage below
her as empty as an unremembered heart' (81). In addition to all that has
gone before, this confirms that to forget the heart is to forget the imagination, to be sterile, uncreative, and therefore dead. If an artist looks at
his page or canvas and forgets his heart, he cannot give life to it; he is
dissociated from his imagination. Fuchsia, of course, is intensely alive:
'With what characters she had filled this lost stage of emptiness!' (80). 'At
a call' she can 'set in motion the five main figures of her making' (81). Of
these figures, Peake describes but two:

> Munster, who would crawl along the rafters and drop chuckling into the
> middle of the floor in a cloud of dust and then bow to Fuchsia before
> turning and searching for his barrel of bright gold.                 (81)

Munster recalls Peake himself, whose eyes 'mint gold' (Gb11). (If the
name suggests 'monster', it's self-parody.) The second, equally typical
figure, is accompanied by a domesticated wild animal:

> The Rain Man, who moved always with his head lowered and his hands
> clasped behind him ... had but to lift his eyelid to quell the tiger that
> followed him on a chain.                                             (81)

One thinks of Captain Slaughterboard with his Yellow Creature, the Lost
Uncle with his turtle, and Muzzlehatch with his monkey (and even a
whole zoo). The figments of Fuchsia's imagination are those of her creator,
and like him she does not find it easy, at first, 'to understand them or to
tell them what to do' (81). In short, her attic theatre and the working of
her imagination correspond to Peake's own creative process.

The second passage comes in *Gormenghast* when Titus slips out of the
castle for the first time and glimpses the Thing in the oak wood. (He
is but seven years old; in the first draft of this episode, however, he was
fourteen, the same age as Fuchsia at the beginning of *Titus Groan*.) He
is about to discover a miraculous world that reflects his imagination. By

escaping like this (if only for a day) from the deadening ritual of the castle, he is breaking the glass cage of routine to reach those 'green pastures / Where the birds and buds are breaking / Into fabulous song and hue' (Gb17). The landscape Titus discovers is predictably Edenic and green, filled with birdsong and insects 'with the morning sunbeams dancing over them' (103). There is even a snake that 'slid down a rockface like a stream of water' (104). At the sight of it, the narrator (or Titus, it is not clear which) wonders, 'What was this shock of love?' (104).

Riding away from the castle and up Gormenghast mountain, Titus looks back to see his home rising above the mist-filled valley like an island on a white sea. In place of Peake's blank page, we have the mist, and Titus wonders 'Was there no pulse beneath the vapour? Not a heart beating? For surely the weakest heart would reverberate in such white silence and thud its double drum-note in far gullies' (102). At this moment it seems to him as if 'the heart of the world had ceased to beat' and he 'realized in full what it was to be alone. The solitude was of a kind he had never experienced before' (101). The conditions for staging the fruits of his imagination are fulfilled.

Feeling intensely alive, Titus glimpses Gormenghast forest in the distance and his curiosity 'burn[s]'. Wondering 'what brooded within those high and leafy walls' he sets off towards it, 'his truant conscience … stunned beneath the hammers of his excitement' (103). Reaching the edge of the forest, he dismisses his pony, finding himself 'truly alone' (104) for the first time. As he enters the wood we would expect Titus to go over a metaphorical precipice. He does not. Peake interrupts this account to tell us what is happening at the castle school.

In Bellgrove's classroom the air is 'breathless' with a silence that has 'a loudness of its own' because the pupils are playing 'a game of high and dangerous hazards' (106). A boy leaps out of the window, a hundred feet above the ground, swings on a tree branch like a trapeze artist, and flings himself back in through the window. So although Titus himself does not step over an edge to 'walk into space' (TG80) at this point, the sequence is none the less observed in the text: the other pupils do it for him. Moreover, the difficulty and danger of the boys' game contrasts with the Thing's effortless 'flight' among the trees in the following chapter.

On the fringe of the forest, Titus is about to enter a theatre, for he finds himself facing

an interwoven screen of foliage, more like a green wall constructed for some histrionic purpose than a natural growth. Was it to hide away some

drama that it arose there, so sheer and so thick? Or was it the backcloth
of some immortal mime? Which was the stage and which the audience?
There was not a sound.                                        (130)

Like Fuchsia unsure of what to do with the figments of her imagination, Titus has yet to learn that, on the stage where he materializes his
imaginings, he is both creator and spectator. Unlike Fuchsia's creations,
however, the product of his inner world will take on independent life,
just as Peake's did.

   To enter the forest theatre, Titus has to part the 'screen of foliage';
predictably, it is an effort. In the following quotations I have italicized the
words that also occur in the poem quoted earlier about Peake's effort to
create: 'Titus, *wrench*ing two *boughs apart*, thrust himself forward' (130).
Nor is this achieved without suffering, for 'a branch swung back and
switched him across his cheek, and in the pain of the moment he fought
*the muscled branches*' (131). Titus's fictional experience mirrors Peake's.

   Once through, with 'his heart beat[ing] loudly as the warm breath of
the silence flowed about him', Titus finds himself on

> the forest floor like a sea of golden moss. From its heaving expanses arose,
> as through the chimera of a daydream, a phantasmic gathering of ancient
> oaks. Like dappled gods they stood, each in his own preserve, the wide
> glades of moss flowing between them in swathes of gold and green and
> away into the clear, dwindling distances.                    (131)

It's like stepping into a dramatically realized dreamworld or, as Titus
perceives it, a 'picture that hung before him. Like a canvas of gold' (131)
in which the Thing is already anticipated in his sense that this is 'the
chimera of a daydream'. It is also like being out in space, or on a low-
gravity planet. The soundless sea of moss proves so 'resilient and springy'
that each step he takes is amplified into 'a higher tread and … on landing
it was the easiest thing in the world to float off into the next movement'
(131). Peake accumulates no less than four concurrent similes as he
attempts to express the experience in its rich complexity. The conjunction of sea and space, the stage or 'cyclorama' (133) and the painting are
all familiar to us from *Drawings*. This world that Titus has entered replicates the world of Peake's imagination.

   The silence and apparent endlessness of the wood suddenly inspire
Titus with loathing. At the same time, 'it was as though he were being
drawn towards some dangerous place or person, and that he had no power
to hold himself back' (132). As in myths and classic tragedies, no matter

how hard the hero tries to avoid his destiny, his struggles merely bring him ever closer to it. Filled with Fear (Peake's capital), Titus commits himself: he turns from the fringe of the forest and 'bound[s] into its gold heart with all the speed' (132) he can muster. Naturally, this leads him straight towards 'something for which he had unconsciously pined' (133): the Thing, who floats through the air with the agility of a 'lyric swallow' (416) and the grace and arrogance of a swan on water. She is the embodiment of his heart's desire, the realization of his dreams, 'for in the air with which [she] moved through space was a quality for which Titus unknowingly hungered' (134). The sight of her calms him: beauty banishes fear. He feels 'a peculiar thrill which seemed to grow in intensity rather than quieten, until it had become a trembling globe of ice under his ribs' (133). Love is born. He becomes obsessed by the Thing, 'for what haunts the heart will, when it is found, leap foremost, blinding the eye and leaving the main of Life in darkness' (TG136–37; Peake's capital). At first Titus thinks he is dreaming, a state close to that in which the creative artist views the products of his imagination. So powerful is this experience that it takes him the rest of the novel to come to terms with it.

THIS ANALYSIS OF PEAKE'S creative process and the passages illustrating it begin to answer my opening question. What makes Peake's fiction so memorable derives from what he makes us hear and feel; with that information, we assemble a Gormenghast of our own in our mind's eye. Thus we are led to replicate Peake's own process, just as the text itself rehearses it. Reading becomes a creative experience, with its own energy and sense of exhilaration.

In Peake's writing, there is remarkably little to instruct the eye. Despite the unfamiliarity of the setting, he does not tell us if the Tower of Flints is round or square, or whether the arches of Gormenghast are roman or gothic. (Hence no visual representation of his world, such as a television adaptation, can please everyone.) What readers 'see' in Peake's descriptions they create in their own minds from language that relates more to sensation than to sight. Faced with her father perched like an owl upon the mantelpiece, Fuchsia, 'standing below him with her hands shaking as they grip the marble of the mantel, tilts herself towards him' and exhorts him to look at her. 'Her strong back is hollowed, her head is thrown back and her throat taut' (TG365). Where another writer might have highlighted the curves of her body for the pleasure of the reader's eye, Peake's terms – 'shaking', 'grip', 'tilt', 'hollowed', 'thrown', 'taut' – are all sensation, not sight.

Light itself he expresses physically rather than visually: in the Hall of Bright Carvings, 'the sunlight squeezed itself between the thin cracks of the window blind' and 'the thin bands of moted light edging their way through the shutters barred [Rottcodd's] dark head with the brilliance of the outer world' (TG19). Later, 'the sunlight, as Mr Flay strolled on, still had one finger through the kitchen window' (TG40). A powerfully 'visual' scene, such as Steerpike's view of Flay going down a corridor illumined only by the occasional candle, involves more hearing and feeling than actual seeing:

> At times, when the candles were thirty or forty feet apart, Mr Flay would be lost to view and only the sound of his feet on the flagstones would guide his follower. Then slowly, as his erratic shape approached the next guttering aura he would begin by degrees to become a silhouette, until immediately before the candle he would for a moment appear like an inky scarecrow, a mantis of pitch-black cardboard worked with strings. Then the progression of the lighting would be reversed and for a moment immediately after passing the flame Steerpike would see him quite clearly as a lit object against the depths of the still-to-be-trodden avenues of stone. The grease at those moments shone from the threadbare cloth across his shoulders, the twin vertical muscles of his neck rose out of the tattered collar nakedly and sharply. As he moved forward the light would dim upon his back and Steerpike would lose him, only hearing the cracking of his knee-joints and his feet striking the stones, until the ensuing candle carved him anew.                                                              (TG42)

Perspective is rendered and distance is measured by sound and sensation, as in those 'depths of the still-to-be-trodden avenues of stone'. Appearance depends on striking physical images like the 'mantis of pitch-black cardboard worked with strings'. Even the light of the candles *carves*. The visual references are comparatively weak and vague – 'guttering aura', 'a lit object', 'the grease shone' and 'the light would dim'. Readers who come away from this passage with a memorable visual image of it have unconsciously performed Peake's 'vast alchemy' and transmuted their impressions from one perceptual mode to another. It is a powerful process.

The power of this process fuels Peake's work. But it does not explain what fired his imagination. It will take several more chapters to discover the feelings that the voice of his heart expresses, to unite form and content. For Peake, living, imagining and creating flowed seamlessly one into the other. To imagine was to create. It was part of the miracle of being alive. And what he created would be, he always hoped, another miracle. It made him a prolific artist rather than just a dreamer.

# Solitude

Alone in that vast circle of ocean, any point of whose circumference might form the centre of another circle as vast and as unbroken, stood that crew of [the *Conger Eel*], sat Slaughterboard, stood Smear. They formed their own Universe. Untouched by the workings of other minds, solely dependent upon themselves, they formed a cosmos of existence, a reality that moved and thought between the sea and the sky. A silence more insistent than the monstrous beating of a drum welled into a kind of atmospheric pain.

('Mr Slaughterboard', PP79)

Alone as the last man to be left alive in a great city when even God had died. (MP228)

PEAKE CONCLUDES HIS INTRODUCTION to *Drawings* with a most revealing statement, not of method, but of belief about the role of the artist:

As the earth was thrown from the sun, so from the earth the artist must fling out into space, complete from pole to pole, his own world which, whatsoever form it takes, is the colour of the globe it flew from, as the world itself is coloured by the sun. (D11)

Of the many avenues of investigation that this double comparison opens up, I shall examine but two: the significance of space, and Peake's view of himself as a god-like creator. They will lead us to the theology that lies behind his works and the existential solitude that characterizes them.

First of all, this passage sheds fresh light on the correspondence of inner to outer space that I was uncovering in the previous chapter. It makes sense that Peake should speak of 'the imagination's heart' being 'constellation high' and refer to the 'firmament' of the imagination, when he conceives his creative activity in an astronomical perspective. This clarifies the surprising scale of awareness that he attributes to his characters. To Titus, for instance, 'it seemed that the earth wandered through his skull ... a cosmos in the bone; a universe lit by a hundred lights and thronged by shapes and shadows' (TA258). The infinite immensity of the universe has its counterpart in the infinite immensity of Peake's inner world. And that, in turn, has its counterpart within the inhabitants of the worlds he creates.

The passage also tells us that Peake saw his activity as analogous to God's: he creates living worlds by breathing life into the empty space of the inert page or canvas. Moreover, just as God's creation reflects Him, so the 'native forms and denizens' of Peake's worlds 'have their roots in [his own] experience'. They have 'the colour of the globe [they] flew from' (D11). His claim that the artist 'must fling out' his created world expresses not just the effort of creation (likened to the cosmic force required to wrest the Earth from the sun) but also, in that 'must', a sense of obligation or necessity. His works, shining with his unique colours, confirm his existence just as much as God reveals His through His creation. To create is to be. The alternative, as we saw in the previous chapter, would be suicide.

In his attitude towards drawing, Peake was repeating the theology he was brought up in (although he no longer subscribed to it, treating it with irony and parodying its hymns). He was descended from three generations of Congregationalist missionaries for whom man existed primarily to learn the will of God and to carry it out, seeing His hand in all His works. Although God created man free, He expects absolute submission to His direct will. Putting the artist in the place of God, Peake echoes this doctrine in his instructions to students. Their creations should express their will: 'do exactly what you want with [your drawing], so long as you are absolutely certain of what you *do* want,' he tells them (CLP17); then, 'when you know what you *want* to record, begin' (3; Peake's emphases). He would have them 'leave the spectator no option but to see' what they have chosen: the viewer of their works should have no choice (4). So the works of God and artists alike should reflect the will of their respective creators. Ideally, those who view Peake's graphic art and read his prose and poetry should see only what he wished them to see. In practice, as man is free, neither God nor Peake can oblige viewers or readers to recognize their hand in all their works, nor for that matter do they spell out exactly how those works should be interpreted.

Peake's invented characters enjoy the same freedom as man. While he was writing *Gormenghast*, he told Maurice Collis that 'like the human race, one's characters must have free will, without undue interference from the Authorjehovah' (MPR 19 (Summer 1985), 15). Thus Peake enjoyed two perspectives, that of the creator (with and without a capital letter), and that of the creature or created work. The two views form 'an astral and at the same time a solar province' (G49). There are in fact three perspectives in Peake's work, each with its own source of illumination: the divine (astral), the human (solar) and – as we shall see later – the misguided character's, lit by the borrowed light of the moon (hence sub-lunary). That Peake can easily switch between these views has profound effects on his art, including his use of perspective.

On the other hand, this passage implies a departure from the theology of previous generations, for whom God's presence had infused all things, man and nature, His work and their works, for it implies that God is absent from His creation. Here Peake is representative of his time. It is a change that came gradually over Western culture, starting with a few thoughtful writers in the nineteenth century and becoming endemic in the twentieth. God's absence obliges the artist to create his own worlds in which, through word and image, that lost harmony between man, nature, and their creator may be renewed.[1]

The absence of God (and, for some, His 'death') left a feeling of inner emptiness which was epitomized in twentieth-century literature by T.S. Eliot's 'hollow men' who lean together, their heads 'filled with straw' (NAEL 2: 2383–84). This no doubt contributed to Peake's sense of having the whole universe beneath his ribs. The hollow spaces that we noticed earlier – the 'hollow halls' beneath Gormenghast, for example – were but a foretaste of it; the motif of inner hollowness recurs throughout his work. A simple example, associated with pleasurable solitude, can be found in Titus's sensations as he paddles his canoe over the flood:

> And then a qualm, empty, cold and ringing, as though he was himself a hollow bell, stirred in his bowels like a clapper. An exquisite sense of loneli-ness grew beneath his ribs, like a bubble of expanding glass.          (G439)

---

1. This change has been chronicled and analysed by numerous critics, notably J. Hillis Miller.

But hollowness as a consequence of God's absence may also express loss of moral restraint. Peake's most dramatic example comes at the end of his novella, 'Boy in Darkness', in which an evil Lamb prepares to transform the Boy (whose name proves to be Titus) into an animal. Diverting its attention with a simple stratagem, Titus grabs a sword and brings the edge (naturally) of the 'long, thin deadly yard of steel' (221) down on the creature's head, splitting it in two – yet 'there was no blood, nor anything to be seen in the nature of a brain'. So he slashes at the body; there too he finds nothing but 'complete emptiness devoid of bones and organs' (224). The separation of body and soul produces ultimate hollowness. In Peake's horror story, 'Danse Macabre', a couple witness their own evening clothes waltzing together, headless, handless, footless – for they are dead.

This feeling that God has withdrawn from His creation, distant from the heart and soul of man, has far-reaching effects. Peake maintained that 'Man has always needed the supernatural in the form of one kind of god or another … something to worship – and at the same time something to fear' (notes on *The Cave*). The three acts of *The Cave*, which dates from the mid-1950s, starkly illustrate this thesis: primitive man worships the Moon and fears wolves; medieval man worships God, fearing witchcraft and the fires of Hell; modern man worships the hydrogen bomb and fears loneliness. One character exclaims, 'Lonely world. I wish there was a God!' and his mother asks

> What is as terrible as loneliness? It is something to fear. It is a skeleton. It is part of us all. Compared with it wild beasts are nothing, nor the wrath of God. Even the bomb is a deliverance from fear. (Act III)

This sense of man's solitude in the absence of God, of his 'essential isolation' (G333), is the most pervasive theme of Peake's work.

It is a defining characteristic of his graphic art: very few of his paintings and almost none of his drawings depict groups of people. His second commission as a war artist, to portray bomber aircrews before and after their missions, produced disappointing works. He was not inspired by them as he was by the glassblowers. On the occasions when he does depict a group, they tend to be just heads, or heads-and-shoulders, floating in a vague sea, not anchored in a social situation. The vast majority of his drawings depict single figures. In fact it is a hallmark of a work by Peake that the subject is isolated, often with no background or context at all, and depicted with great economy of line. He concentrated on outline, posture and physical expression, 'that movement of the arm that hinted

Peake's drawing for the front cover of *The Dickens World*
by Humfrey House (Oxford Paperbacks, 1960).

fear: that gesture that spelt amazement' (CLP1), eschewing most of
the conventional external indicators that tell us how to 'read' a picture.
Through 'the story that is told by the tilt of a hat, the torn sleeve, the
stare that is out of focus, the humped shoulders' (LF55), he sought to
convey his sense of a person and their inner world. And in this he was
particularly successful.

  For his illustrations to famous texts like *The Rime of the Ancient
Mariner*, *Alice in Wonderland* and *Treasure Island*, Peake selected scenes
and moments that enabled him to show people in isolation. Only two
of the 30 drawings he made for *The Swiss Family Robinson* include the
complete family. His *Rime* depicts more than one human figure in only
two illustrations out of eight, compared with 36 out of 42 (i.e. seven out
of eight) in Doré's interpretation, which yet had a powerful influence on
him. Peake's *Alice* is full of detached figures, who are generally not worked
into a setting in the way that Tenniel's are. Even when interpreting works
by others, Peake remained faithful to his world-view.

This world-view no doubt contributed to his greater success as a writer than as a painter. In the depiction of character, absence of background is more easily achieved (and generally more effective) in a novel than it is in an oil painting, where convention requires that no area of canvas remain uncoloured. In this respect, drawing is closer to the novel than to painting: the draughtsman need put in only what he chooses by way of background. On the other hand, to depict a person's facial expression at the same time as the position of their feet, the artist, whether drawing or painting, is obliged to draw the whole person, head, body and legs. The writer knows no such constraint: 'Fuchsia stamped her foot and peered into the poor old nurse's face' (TG70). The reader fills the gap between foot and face. In short, narrated space permits greater isolation of the subject than the visual arts. This may be one of the reasons why Peake found oil painting so difficult, 'the medium in which he was least sure', as his wife observed (Gilmore 64). So I disagree with reviewers and

Image courtesy of Chris Beetles Gallery

'Pensive': expressive gesture in a brush portrait.

Linking body and leg: Peake's sketch for a character
'with thin legs and nankeen trousers' in *Bleak House*.

'Mid-European': expressive gesture with pen
and ink, sketched in a London bar.

Tenniel's illustration of the Duchess with
her baby in *Alice in Wonderland.*

students who assume that Peake writes like a painter; for me, he draws
like a writer.

His fiction is remarkable for the almost complete absence – and sometimes active rejection – of *society*. Peake generally depicts the individual
in isolation. On occasions like the Earling in *Titus Groan* or Titus's tenth
birthday masque in *Gormenghast*, it comes as a shock to realize that in
addition to the Groan family and their small circle of retainers there is a
teeming populace in the castle. Most of the time, these people are unseen
and (perhaps more significantly for Peake) unheard, like the Bright
Carvers, an 'all-but forgotten people … remembered with a start, or with
the unreality of a recrudescent dream' (TG17). Their counterparts in
*Titus Alone*, a social context more similar to our own than Gormenghast,
are the displaced persons who congregate in the caverns beneath the river.
Peake focuses on the individual, often solitary by choice, and offers only
fragmentary glimpses of society, with little sense of social cohesion.

Duchess and soon-to-be-pig baby from Peake's
illustrations to *Alice in Wonderland*.

From Peake's *Treasure Island*, the illustration for Part III, 'My Shore Adventure'.

His fundamental concern is with the individual's response to being alone in the world. For himself, of course, solitude is what he thrived on, for it enabled him to concentrate on 'the blindingly exquisite fish' (AW 5) of his imagination and transfer them onto paper or canvas, but he could also feel lonely and want the company of others. While isolation may be the desired condition for creating works of art, loneliness is the dreaded consequence of it. So just as Peake's work aims to achieve balance between classic and romantic, passion and feeling, heart and intellect, it also seeks a balance between enjoying solitude, coping with the feeling of loneliness that it engenders, and satisfying the need for companionship. In the end his writing covers a whole conspectus of responses to solitude, ranging from celebration to deep despair, and from passive acceptance to active attempts to resolve the problem of loneliness.

The most extreme response is solipsism, celebrating solitude to the point of denying that anything or anyone else exists. It is embodied by the ancient philosopher who makes a brief appearance in *Gormenghast*. For him the only reality is 'Death's amazing kingdom, where everything moves twice as fast, and the colours are twice as bright, and love is twice as gorgeous, and sin is twice as spicy' (G 76). However, solipsism is a vulnerable stance, liable to challenge at any moment. The reality of other people and pain in this world is forced upon the philosopher by a young man who sets fire to his beard.

In affirming that 'there is nowhere else' (G 510) but Gormenghast, the Countess adumbrates Peake's second response to solitude: embracing it to make it a way of life. She plans to pass this attitude on to Titus. He should 'take care of himself and … live his own life as far as it is possible', going 'his own way among the birds and the white cats and all the animals so that he is not aware of men' (TG 399). Locked in her own world of birds and cats, she fails to do so. Titus turns his back on the castle and goes off to prove the existence of elsewhere, seeking his own, more balanced solution to the problem of solitude.

The one character who achieves the Countess's ideal is Rottcodd, the curator of the Hall of Bright Carvings that no one ever visits; he features in the opening and closing chapters of *Titus Groan*, thus framing the novel. He spends every moment of his life in his gallery, either dusting the pieces of sculpture or sleeping in his hammock. He does not even leave to eat or drink: his meals are sent up to him by means of a 'miniature lift from the kitchen, forty fathoms below' (TG 500). Peake declares this to be 'an ideal existence' (18), for it is dedicated to 'enjoying the solitude for its Own Sake' (19; Peake's capitals).

How Rottcodd is fed and watered is clearly important; throughout his work Peake associates solitude with eating and drinking, sometimes through metaphor but most often literally. In *Titus Alone*, for instance, Muzzlehatch confesses that he swapped his relationship with Juno 'for solitude which I eat as though it were food' (TA107). And another character in the same novel admits

> I used to dread the nights I spent alone, but after a while … I looked back upon those solitary evenings as times of excitement. It has always been my longing to be alone again and drink the silence.          (TA116)

For Peake solitude is as necessary to the soul as food and drink is to the body. However, feeding the recluse poses problems: the presence of other people precludes solitude. To resolve this, some of Peake's male characters have recourse to an animal companion. Captain Slaughterboard's Yellow Creature, for instance, ingeniously cooks up delicious meals for them both. Rottcodd's situation is ideal because his meals come by lift from a remote kitchen.

Another 'character' who enjoys perfect solitude at the same time as being provided with food is the tiger in 'Aqueous Ecstasy' (Peake's capitals) on the first page of *Rhymes without Reason*. Lying on his back in the midst of a golden ocean, he is fed with fish by a pelican that perches on his paws. This enviable situation came about because the tiger did *not* eat the pelican one day; out of gratitude it feeds the tiger. The tiger obviously doesn't know that the pelican has fish to spare anyway, since its beak can hold more than its belly can. The same ambiguous association of motifs can be found in the picture of a young man who seems to enjoy letting crows steal buns from his tea table – or does he enjoy lying there because they are bringing them to him? At any rate, the scene is bathed in glorious sunshine which 'falls on everything it can' (RWR12–13).

The supply of food and drink is not the only problem in a life of perfect isolation. There is also the risk of being forgotten, of disappearing from the record, as it were. In the first chapter of *Titus Groan* Rottcodd receives 'an interesting titbit' (18) in the shape of news of the birth of Titus; thereafter he is left in solitary peace for a whole year. Then, one day, he is disturbed to realize that his lunch has not been sent up and the castle is empty. Through the window he sees the assembled inhabitants of Gormenghast returning from the Earling; he deduces that the Earl has

'Upon my golden backbone / I float like any cork':
the tiger being fed by a pelican in *Rhymes without Reason*.

died and the one-year-old son succeeded him. With a pang it occurs to Rottcodd that 'no one had thought fit to tell him! No one! ... He had been forgotten.' He is honest with himself, although 'it was a bitter pill for him to swallow'; he can but recognize that 'he had always wished to be forgotten. He could not have it both ways' (501). He is unique among Peake's characters in enjoying extreme and lifelong solitude while fully assuming the risk it involves.

Unless they withdraw to some totally secluded and inaccessible spot, persons who dedicate their lives to the enjoyment of solitude are always liable to interruption. Irma Prunesquallor, for instance, comes and bangs on her brother's study door whenever he retreats there. So there always lingers, at the back of Rottcodd's mind, 'the dread of an intruder' (19). He discourages visitors as much as he can by adopting an aloof and even nervous manner. Like all male ascetics and hermits who attempt to withdraw from the world, he feels that women are his greatest threat: 'the ladies held a peculiar horror for him' (18). In Peake's world, women have an anomalous status: men seek them out to cure their loneliness, but also resent them because they make solitude impossible.

Gormenghast's prototypical Poet voices this male predicament from the point of view of the creative artist. Through the window of his garret, he declaims verses that celebrate solitude while bemoaning its effects:

> When I'm all alone, my glory
> Always fades, because I find
> Being lonely drives the splendour
> Of my vision from my mind.
>
> (TG141)

It's a catch-22 situation: the solitude required for inspiration causes lone-liness, which drives the inspiration away. Climbing past the window, Steerpike overhears the haunting refrain inviting 'Beauty' to come and share the Poet's loneliness:

> Come, oh, come, my own! my Only!
> Through the Gormenghast of Groan.
> Lingering has become so lonely
> As I linger all alone!
>
> (141)

Unaware that the invitation is a purely rhetorical, poetic gesture, Steer-pike reveals his presence (though heaven knows, he is no beauty). This results in 'an inconceivable commotion. Every sort of object suddenly began to appear at the [Poet's] window, starting at its base and working up' to form a 'fantastic pagoda' (142) which overtopples into the abyss below. The Poet's compulsive desire to block out the unexpected witness of his recitation at the cost of all the furnishings in his room shows that at heart he dreads intrusion quite as much as Rottcodd does. And loneliness is inseparable from solitude as a source of poetic inspiration.

The eponymous writer of *Letters from a Lost Uncle* is another artist who craves solitude. The most antisocial of all Peake's characters, he first runs away when he is less than a week old (!), only to be brought back home 'and strapped down in a cradle' by his parents. He avoids school by drinking ink, so that he is confined to his bed until he reaches school-leaving age. Then he runs away again 'but [gets] tired of being hungry' so he returns home and eats his way through the larder. This time he is ill until his wedding at the age of 22. In other words, since he cannot get the solitude he wants by running away, he obtains it by inappropriate eating and drinking!

Abandoning his wife and rejecting human society altogether, the Uncle takes ship for the tropics and on an impulse begins his adventures by jumping overboard with a table as makeshift raft. But his long-sought mid-ocean solitude is brief, for he needs food and drink. On the beach of his first landfall he encounters a turtle that he names Jackson and adopts as his 'retainer' (that is, luggage bearer and, more significantly, cook) 'and possibly as a friend' (39). In this way he gets his food prepared for him, and company, with minimal erosion of his solitude.

Like the Poet's verse and practically all Peake's works, *Letters from a Lost Uncle* contains a self-referential level; through meta-text or subtext, they refer to the problems of creating works of art. The Lost Uncle's letters, which are reproduced in facsimile, recount and illustrate his quest for the White Lion of the Snows, the ultimate in animal isolation, its very habitat being unknown. Jackson uses this as an opportunity for surreptitious revenge, spilling gravy and dishwater over the pages, particularly when the White Lion is mentioned. Used as an easel, Jackson moves at all the wrong moments. The overall message is clear: although the artist prefers solitude above all things, loneliness drives him to seek companionship, which inevitably makes solitude, particularly for writing and drawing, difficult to obtain. Worse, the partner may be jealous of the artist's work. However, having one's cake and eating it by taking an animal companion is possible only in fantasy, as Peake knows only too well.

In fact, he literalizes the metaphor of solitude-as-food-and-drink in Fuchsia's favourite poem, 'The Frivolous Cake', a delightful piece of nonsense verse that Steerpike discovers in her attic (TG84–85). It tells of a sea-going cake in love with a 'dinner knife fierce and blue' that swims in its wake 'like a swordfish grim'. Followed by its love the 'freckled and frivolous cake' sails wherever it likes 'in a manner emphatic and free'. Were the knife to catch up with the cake, the cake would lose not only its freedom but also its life, consumed in the consummation of their love. Luckily, 'the sensitive steel of the knife can feel / That love is a race apart' – and the pun in 'a race apart' suggests that the knife is prepared to prolong its amorous pursuit of the cake indefinitely rather than close with it. So they continue their ocean voyage, with the knife winking 'his glamorous indigo eye / In the wake of his future wife' while 'The tropical air vibrates to the drone / Of a cake in the throes of love'. This strangely ill-matched couple achieve another version of Peake's ideal; by remaining apart they preserve both their solitude and their love for each other.

As a cure for loneliness, marriage works no better than any other form of companionship. In Peake's fiction, marriages are invariably broken. Even the couple in 'Danse Macabre', who obviously love each other dearly, have separated because the husband is sadistic (fulfilling the implicit threat of the knife in the poem): 'the more the love, the more the wish to hurt' (PP140). They are reunited only in death in the last sentence. In fact marriage may even cause a fresh sense of solitude and in *Gormenghast* Peake tells us why: a spouse is liable to 'raise those formidable earthworks that can so isolate the marital unit from the universe' (G338).

He illustrates this in the comic mode with the 'romance' of Bellgrove and Irma Prunesquallor. When Bellgrove gets promoted to headmaster, he discovers that

> he had forfeited his room above the Professors' Quadrangle which he had occupied for three quarters of his life. Alone among the professors it was for him to turn back … to return alone to his Headmaster's bedroom.
>
> (G119–20)

This new isolation makes him think of getting married. Irma's experience is comparable. After spending all her life with her brother, she discovers the pleasure of company – and flattery – when Steerpike moves in with them. On his departure, she feels the loss and resolves to find a husband. How Irma and Bellgrove persuade themselves, and each other, that they are in love is one of the comic highlights of *Gormenghast*. Theirs is one of only two weddings in all Peake's work – and it is celebrated hors texte. From that point on, their relationship can only deteriorate. In a pathetic scene close to the end of the book, Peake depicts them staring in mutual disappointment at a patch of wall in their loft from which a piece of plaster has fallen and 'left a small grey pattern the shape of a heart' (G451). Two solitudes side by side, they are as lonely as ever; the heart is but a shape without feeling and their colourful marriage has turned depressingly grey.

The story of Fuchsia forms a counterpart to this in the tragic mode. In a castle community singularly devoid of women, her isolation is acute – but not always unwelcome. She has no friends of her own age, neither girls – it seems there is not even a school for girls in Gormenghast – nor boys. 'Who is there anyway who isn't old?' she observes gloomily to herself (TG304). So she usually spends her days quite alone, often resorting to the attics above her bedroom. There she can read her books and dream and watch her imaginary characters act out their stories, as we saw in the previous chapter. She greatly enjoys this solitude for it frees her to 'taste the pleasure of her isolation' (81–82). But Steerpike climbs in through the window and eats the picnic she has left there, robbing her simultaneously of food and solitude. She experiences this invasion of her privacy, this intrusion into the very place where she thought no one would come, since no one else knew of it, as tantamount to rape. Thereafter the attic no longer sustains her. She takes to wandering in the woods instead, with 'so lonely a feeling that tears were never far distant' (271), for the attic and its solitude had been her companions in life. Her depression is heightened by the absence of any social network or support group – she has but the doctor to confide in – and by the events that follow on remorselessly: the burning of the library, the madness and then the disappearance of her father. Everything conspires to make her vulnerable to the blandishments of the scheming Steerpike.

To gain power over her and, through her, over the castle itself, Steerpike courts her and pretends to fall in love with her. Much to the reader's relief his plan to ravish her is foiled at the last moment. Discovering the truth about him, Fuchsia falls into depression again, repeating the previous pattern. This exacerbates her sense of isolation and, like her father, she finds herself entertaining thoughts of suicide. The loss of her solitude and of her companionable loneliness, followed by betrayal by the man who robbed her, precipitate her accidental death.

With the death of her father Peake develops another aspect of solitude: all the main characters in Gormenghast are isolated not only by personality but also by their unique social status. Among them, Lord Sepulchrave is pre-eminent in more senses than one, for he illustrates the destructive effect of isolation and loneliness on the personality. Despite the public appearances he has to make each day in fulfilling the requirements of the castle ritual (rather than merely once a year like the Poet), he is very much alone, not only in his role as the figurehead of Gormenghast but also in his private life, for he has no peers, his sisters are half-witted, and (predictably) he is estranged from his wife. The only person in the whole of Gormenghast with whom he can converse 'upon the level of his own thought' is the Poet. But 'in the Poet there was an element of the idealist, a certain enthusiasm which was a source of irritation to Lord Sepulchrave, so that they met only at long intervals' (TG205). He retreats into his library and reads, takes laudanum, sinks into melancholia and, after the loss of his library, succumbs to madness.

As Lord Sepulchrave's control over his mind weakens he clings to the castle's ritual with 'a fervour quite unprecedented' (329), which is typical of persons suffering from excess of solitude. It provides him with 'escape from himself' (205). As long as ritual and routine, no matter how absurd, are freely chosen and imposed by strict self-discipline, they can save a person's mind. In a character like Lord Sepulchrave, who is 'a victim of chronic melancholia' (205), the act of relinquishing autonomy and giving himself up to the ritual is literally fatal.

With Mr Flay, who is banished from the castle by the Countess for flinging one of her cats at Steerpike, Peake explores isolation as dire punishment. In saying 'the Castle throws you out' (TG378), she pronounces a sentence of death; for her, life outside the castle is impossible. Against all expectation, however, Flay manages to survive with Crusoesque ingenuity in the wilderness. At first 'the horror of his ostracization [is] too close for him to grasp'. He can feel 'only the crater-like emptiness' that Peake qualifies as 'loneliness without pain' (TG414). It takes him months to gets used to the change:

> Hours of solitude in the woods were apt to detach him from the reality of any other life, and he would at times find that he was running gawkily through the boles in a sudden fear that there was no Gormenghast: that he had dreamed it all: that he belonged to nowhere, to nothing: that he was the only man alive in a dream of endless branches.        (TG442–43)

In the end, though, he adapts and becomes almost happy in his extreme solitude. It is, after all, the essence of the human condition.

Peake was well aware that isolation is not, of itself, a good or a bad thing for the human mind. When it is self-imposed, it may be just the diet that the artist, the mystic, or simply the solitary nature, needs and thrives on. When not desired, however, it can leave a person disoriented and panic-stricken; social exclusion, as with Flay, or solitary confinement, can be highly destructive of the personality. Starved of social contact, the mind, unlike the body, may never recover. Peake covers the whole range.

There are numerous instances of enforced isolation in the Titus books, starting with Flay locking Steerpike in the octagonal room. He soon escapes (making his memorable climb up the wall) and takes a terrible revenge on the Twins. Being the younger sisters of Lord Sepulchrave, and dim-witted into the bargain, they are neglected by the Castle. This makes them perfect victims for Steerpike: on the pretext of protecting them from 'Weasel Plague', he locks them up. As they starve to death, they go mad, but they die laughing at the booby trap they have rigged up for him. Solitary confinement is conducive to such laughter. When Titus is imprisoned in *Titus Alone*, an inmate known as Old Crime, who has spent so long in jail that he believes that it protects him 'from the filthy thing called Life' (TA73; Peake's capital), attempts to come up through the floor of Titus's cell. Preparing to repel this intruder, Titus feels 'a kind of mad laughter' (71) rise within him. Madness as a result of social exclusion is echoed in the refugees in the Under-River and again in the shadowy figures who are incarcerated in the cells of the scientist's 'factory'. With each evocation, the characters become less clearly defined and the details of what they are subjected to more vague; by leaving more to the imagination, Peake makes their situation more horrific. The final cry over the factory intercom expresses the refrain of them all, 'I want to live!' (204).

This cry echoes Titus Groan's basic feeling throughout his youth in Gormenghast. He experiences his whole existence there as a suffocating seclusion, cutting him off from life itself. The strictly predetermined social role in which he is confined is aptly imaged at his christening: he is enclosed first in 'a small velvet cylinder, or mummy' (TG370), then between the pages of the book of Gormenghast law, both literally and then figuratively. The law dictates every minute of his life, and for every infringement or attempt at deviation from the strict line, he is incarcerated in the Stone Fort. This has no ill effect on him, however, perhaps because in this respect Titus is closer to Peake than any other character: he thrives on solitude.

The occasion of his tenth birthday masque is an instance of positive incarceration for Titus. To prevent him from seeing the preparations, he is 'confined for the entire twelve [daylight] hours in a great playroom quite unknown to him' (G319). It bears a strange likeness to Fuchsia's attic, for it is filled with old 'toys of weird and ingenious mechanism ... and ladders leading to dizzy balconies' (319). From Titus's point of view 'this was a strange way to treat a boy on his tenth anniversary; to immure him for the entire day in a strange land' (319), but it is implied that the experience will 'appeal to his imagination' (318). It is in fact the first step of a sequence that replicates Peake's own creative process. Assured that this confinement aims to make his birthday surprise all the more enjoyable, Titus takes it as patiently as he can.

Up in the playroom, the 'strange land' of the imagination, he has silence and solitude, 'save for those times when his meals were brought in on the golden trays of the occasion' (319). At the end of the day, he is blindfolded and carried to the masque in 'a light basketwork palanquin, or mountain-chair' (320).[2] Like Peake, Titus cannot see the 'work' that is in preparation; he makes a 'blind journey' (323), during which Peake emphasizes what Titus can and cannot hear:

> The silence about him was like something that hummed against his eardrums. This was another kind of silence. This was not the silence of nothing happening – of emptiness, or negation – but was a positive thing – a silence that knew of itself – that was charged, conscious and wide awake.
> (324)

This corresponds to the state in which Peake tunes in to his imagination, preparatory to producing a work.

For the performance, Titus is installed in a horsehair armchair on a platform, as in a box at the theatre, overlooking a natural, moonlit stage (rather like Fuchsia in her attic). When the curtain rises – or rather, the scarf is removed from his eyes – he sees

2. Those who like biographical sources for fiction will note that it was in just such a chair that Europeans were carried up to Kuling, the mountain village where Peake was born. Cf MPMA 23, 24 and 105.

stretched, as it were, across the area of his vision, a canvas – a canvas hushed and unearthly. A canvas of great depth; of width that spread from east to the west and of a height that wandered way above the moon. It was painted with fire and moonlight – upon a dark impalpable surface. The lunar rhythms rose and moved through darkness. A counterpoint of bonfires burned like anchors – anchors that held the sliding woods in check.                                                            (325)

Here we have the creation of Peake's ideal work of art, which Titus (surprisingly) perceives as a painting: when the order is given for the cannon to be fired, it comes to him as 'a voice out of the paint' (325). (In *Mr Pye* the same combination of motifs – a waterside bonfire at night, illumined by a moon 'as big as a dinnerplate' (G326 and MP93) – inspires in Thorpe a comparable ideal work, 'dynamic, vital, savage, frozen into geometry, … a painting unlike any other painting – yet in the tremendous tradition of the masters' (93).) At this signal, 'the picture, as though at the stroke of a warlock's wand, came suddenly to life' (326). Thanks to the imagination working in solitude, Peake creates a work within which a work of art takes on independent life, beneath the light of the moon.

For Peake, the difference between positive and negative solitude lies in the degree of personal choice: freely chosen solitude amplifies freedom. As a young Earl, Titus gets no positive solitude until he is seven years old and makes his first forbidden excursion beyond the confines of the castle. On Gormenghast mountain he realizes 'in full what it was to be alone. The solitude was of a kind he had never experienced before' (G101). Moreover, looking back at the castle and seeing it from a distance for the first time gives him a new perspective on his life. This is reinforced at once: he glimpses the Thing, that 'figment from a rarer and more curious climate than Titus had ever breathed' (G134). If she can live outside Gormenghast, without the yoke of ritual and tradition, then he can too. In other words, he gains 'an awareness of liberty' (G403), of being responsible for his own future, which is something that ritual and tradition completely forbid him. It takes him 10 years and the remainder of the book to realize the significance of this new perspective and ultimately appropriate that freedom for himself.

We half expect Peake to make the Thing a companion for Titus, but when he finally sees her again, in Flay's cave, the bird she is cooking over a small fire is for herself, not for him. Moments later Peake burns her up with a fateful bolt of lightning. This confrontation between the reality of her existence and the figment that Titus has been dreaming of, closely followed by her annihilation, brings about what Peake calls 'the death of his imagination'. It is simultaneously the birth of a new Titus who is 'free for the first time', having learned 'there were other ways of life from the ways of his great home' (G424). In short, without the Thing 'he would never have dared to do more than dream of insurrection' (G506). His need for solitude proves to be a liberating force, driving him to self-discovery and setting him on a path of self-realization. By the end of *Gormenghast*, he is ready to throw off the shackles of ritual and tradition and 'ride out of his world' to enjoy freedom – and self-imposed solitude.

Set in a city, that godless man-made world in which the individual is more lonely than ever before, the next volume is all about living alone and assuming the consequences of choosing solitude. Every time Titus gets into trouble – which is often, for he has neither the social skills nor the official papers that would make him acceptable – people attempt to help him, and he throws them off in the name of his right to be alone. Imprisoned, he rejects Old Crime's offer to initiate him into the carceral community: 'Leave me alone,' he cries, 'leave me alone!' (73). The difficulty lies in creating positive consequences to rejecting society.

Titus's first helper is Muzzlehatch, who some years earlier renounced his relationship with Juno (the mother-goddess figure in the novel) in favour of his solitude; he now keeps a private zoo in lieu of human company. But with Muzzlehatch Titus feels as restless as a caged animal and proudly rejects his assistance. In no time he's arrested for vagrancy; Juno rescues him and he becomes her lover, but he soon starts to feel like a pet of hers, and his need for solitude and independence makes him leave her too. Finally he falls into the clutches of a girl called Cheeta (another potential 'animal' companion); he rejects her as well and in revenge she tries to drive him mad with a midnight masquerade, parodying not just the birthday masque but Gormenghast itself. She fails because her vast puppet show serves only to reinforce Titus's sense of himself. He realizes that he has all that he needs within himself; he even hears his dead sister's voice assuring him, 'You are not alone' (235). Cheeta, on the other hand, whose inner resources are minimal, is driven mad by the failure of her plans and the realization that she is 'irrevocably alone' (252).

In the final pages, Peake depicts Titus's budding acceptance of his essential solitude with numerous allusions to the astral and solar provinces. Titus escapes by plane from the masquerade on which 'the stars shone down' (218), but he uses the ejection seat, repeating the basic pattern of the three books. Descending by parachute, he forgets his loneliness for a little while, 'which was strange, for what could have been a lonelier setting than the night through which, suspended, he gradually fell?' (260). Back on earth and 'really alone' (261) he rejects the possibility of returning to Gormenghast and becomes an eternal outsider.[3] Peake planned further volumes in which, like the Ancient Mariner at the end of Coleridge's *Rime*, he was to be forever wandering (Gilmore 105–06).

Two late works highlight Peake's feelings about solitude and underline the connections between the motifs I have been exploring. Both *Mr Pye*, a comic fantasy novel, and 'Boy in Darkness', a sombre fantastic novella, concern people who, instead of embracing the freedom offered by solitude, try to oblige others to join them in the hope of alleviating their loneliness. In this they move in the opposite direction to Titus.

A bachelor of independent means, Mr Pye finds his solitude unbearable; he feels

> intensely lonely. Lonely as a gull among rooks. Lonely as a child among old men. Lonely as an old man among children. Lonely as a new boy in a great school. Lonely as the soul that has lost the body that gave it shelter. Lonely as the body when the soul has fled. (MP138)

He invents a god to share his solitude, calls him the Great Pal and chats with him all the time. Not content with this, he sets out to convert the islanders of Sark to his new faith, but his project is at variance with the universe. His planned mass conversion, crowning his crusade at a midnight picnic, is disrupted by the arrival of a drifting dead whale whose smell is as high as Mr Pye's aspirations. Mortality – the very fact that we inhabit bodies – is the insuperable obstacle to the spiritual union that he envisages. Then his own body betrays him: wings grow on his shoulders. To make them go away he turns to evil, and horns sprout from his forehead. The Sarkese react as though he were the devil itself and hunt him down. He escapes by miraculously taking flight from the Coupée. In the last glimpse of him 'there was pathos – for he looked so solitary – adrift in the hollow air' (254). Obliged to 'live up to his pinions' (146), Mr Pye ultimately finds himself more lonely than ever, for now there is nowhere on earth for him to live.

'Boy in Darkness' tends towards hell rather than heaven; in fact it contrasts with *Mr Pye* in almost every respect. It opens with Titus sneaking

---

3. Colin Wilson's book, *The Outsider*, was published in 1956 while Peake was writing *Titus Alone*.

out of his castle home to escape the daily grind of social obligations and be alone for a while. Soon he falls into the clutches of a man who has turned himself into a Lamb of pure white wool, the opposite of Mr Pye the satyr. This evil Lamb wants to reform people too – but in a physical rather than a spiritual sense, for he changes them into the animals that he perceives within them. Titus is next in line for 'conversion'. As we have seen, he kills the Lamb; 'lost and weary' he is 'carried back to his imme-morial home' (BiD224).

These stories tell us more of Peake's hopes and fears. In *Mr Pye* he trusts that God still exists, for all His infinite distance, and that miracles can still take place – for otherwise how could Peake, as a creator, aspire to work miracles too? In 'Boy in Darkness', on the other hand, God's absence has left man alone to face his animal nature – the beast within – and the chthonic powers of darkness (themes that I shall develop in later chapters). Furthermore, the two stories connect food and drink and man's solitude. Mr Pye wines and dines the Sarkese at his midnight picnic, and the blind Lamb calls for a feast at which he will reshape the Boy. The scenes are loaded with religious symbolism; both celebrate the conversion of the participants to a new life, and thus point to the desire behind Peake's metaphor. Just as the communion service used to unite the participants both with one another and with God as they partook of the bread and the wine, so the serving of food and drink in Peake's work aims to heal the loneliness of the individual soul by creating community, even with animals. The desacralized eucharist lies behind the ceremonial repasts, such as the christening and the dark breakfast, that structure *Titus Groan* and *Gormenghast*.

Considering the spiritual dimension of these stories helps us to under-stand why the theme of *change* is so important for Peake. In a poem about walking down a country road, he describes an experience that Sweden-borg (and after him William James, in *Varieties of Religious Experience*) called a 'vastation'. Suddenly he felt that

> For all the comfort of the elms, the banal
> Normality of houses with their garages, the apparent
> Changelessness of the ploughed field on my right –
> All was in danger.
> A marble spinning through the universe
> Wears on its dizzy crust, men, houses, trees
> That circle through cavernous aeons, and I was afraid.
>
> (SP36)

Without belief in the presence of God's guiding hand, the world seems terrifyingly vulnerable. Rottcodd has a similar experience on the day of the Earling when he finds himself entirely alone in the great castle. The portentous silence tells him that something is wrong; 'he became aware of a sense of instability – a sensation almost of fear'. It was

> as though some ethic he had never questioned … was now threatened. As though, somewhere, there was *treason*. Something unhallowed, menacing, and ruthless in its disregard for the fundamental premises of *loyalty* itself. What could be thought to count, or have even the meanest kind of value in action or thought if the foundation on which his house of belief was erected was found to be sinking and imperilling the sacrosanct structure it supported.                                              (TG500)

Disbelief threatens the foundations of the world itself.

Peake uses terms like *insurrection* and *treason* to qualify what is actually a question of belief, as confirmed by the word *sacrosanct*. Gormenghast stands for the immutable credo of previous generations, perpetuated through education. Right at the beginning of *Titus Groan*, Flay intones, with slow emphasis, 'No *Change*, Rottcodd. No Change!' (23; Peake's capitals and italics). To ensure that the castle's ethos is handed down intact to the next generation, 'it was for the professors [of Gormenghast] to suffer no change' (G119). An upholder of the faith like Rottcodd experiences 'disregard for the fundamental premises' of the castle in much the same way that traditional Christians experienced the scepticism of their children in the twentieth century.[4] The dynasty of the Groans is as old as Christianity itself. Titus is the seventy-seventh Earl; twenty-five years per generation would make the line 1900 years old at his birth. Writing in 1940, Peake began with Titus aged 40. Like mid-twentieth-century Christianity, Gormenghast is in the grip of beliefs that cannot be questioned and age-old rituals 'ankle-deep in stone' (G7) whose original significance has long been lost. These are the shackles that Titus revolts against.

The disloyalty that Rottcodd senses in the infant Titus – he is but one year old at his Earling – comes from the fact that he represents change

---

4. During WWII, the word 'doctor' was written on the windscreen of Peake's father's car; seen from inside it read 'rotcod'. The character who bears the name may well reflect the attitude of Peake's father, who had been a medical missionary.

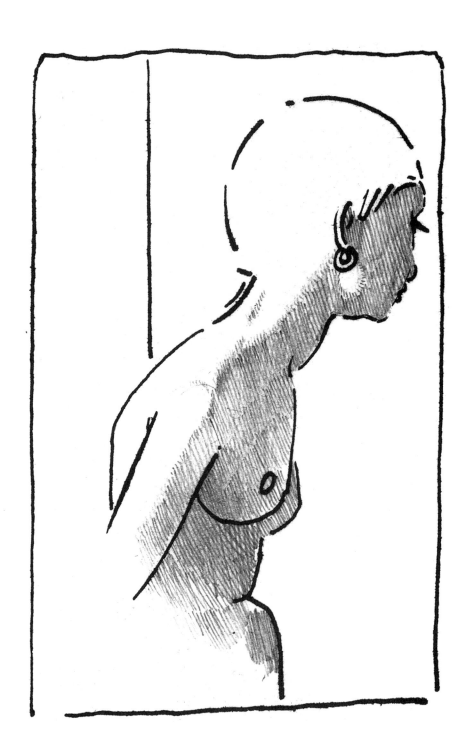

itself. The story begins with his birth because before that there would have been only changelessness to describe. The books grow with him: *Titus Groan*, covering his first year of life, alternates between long descriptive passages and brief moments of action; *Gormenghast*, covering ages seven to seventeen, is more evenly balanced, whereas *Titus Alone* is nearly all action and correspondingly little description. Peake's 'other worlds imprisoned yet breathing among the network of a million commas, semicolons, full stops, [and] hyphens' (TG305) enable him to express Titus's rejection of the faith of his parents and his exploration of freedom and solitude in a world from which God is absent.

This chapter opened with Peake's metaphor of the created world illumined by the light of its sun-cum-creator. (The *sun* can of course also be the Son, as in many traditional writers.) We might close with this notion, just as *Titus Alone* ends with Titus heading east because 'it was out of there that the sunbeams were pouring' (261). Because the direction and quality of the light falling upon an object produce highlights and shadows, Peake instructs his students to 'pay particular attention to the edges of shadows' (CLP8). A cube, for example, casts shadows with 'sharp and distinct' edges; there is 'no gradation'. Conversely, 'the shadow graduates around [an] egg' because it 'has no sharp edges' (5). Shadows result from the shape of objects. Among modern works of literature, Peake's are identifiable by their characteristic play of light. When *Titus Groan* and *Gormenghast* were dramatized for television, viewers familiar with the books complained that the adaptation lacked shadow. Rather as the works of the Bright Carvers 'exuded a kind of darkness for all their colour' (TG16), so the form of Peake's worlds, 'swung out of sunlight into cosmic shade', produces chiaroscuro effects. The particular highlights and shadows that we perceive result from the light and love that their 'Author-jehovah' cast upon them. 'There are no accidental shadows' (CLP5).

*Facing page:* The edge of shadow defining shape in a figure study.

# Islands

> Lady I become
> Each day, each hour of this little journey
> We make together, less alone, although
> You will always be far and islanded.
>
> (RoB31)

> Each one of us an island, floating free. (*Cave*, Act III)

> We get our thoughts tangled in metaphors and act
> fatally on the strength of them.
> (George Eliot, *Middlemarch*, Ch. 10)

THROUGHOUT HIS WORK, PEAKE consistently uses the island, along with its specific physical features such as beaches and cliffs, as an image of solitude. Islands, generally with a sole human inhabitant, are central to many of his works: *Captain Slaughterboard Drops Anchor*, *Rhymes without Reason* and *Letters from a Lost Uncle*. The island of Sark is the setting for *Mr Pye*, and it has generally been assumed that the maritime imagery in Peake's work derives from his love of Sark. However, his earliest known poems, 'The Touch o' the Ash' and the recently recovered 'Vikings', are both set on the sea, and they were composed before he discovered Sark, so the source lies earlier than that. Literal and metaphorical islands crop up constantly throughout his prose and verse; the associated seascape figures in many of his drawings and illustrations. On Peake's map of the world there are archipelagos perhaps, friendly isles but no society islands. The isolated island stands for the condition of mankind, marooned by God on this planet.

For Peake, man's great solitude begins at birth, when a little island first separates from the maternal continent. The newborn child, he writes,

> Like madagascar[1] broken from its mother
> Must feel the tides divide an africa
> Of love from his clay island, that the sighs
> Of the seas encircle with chill ancientry;
>                                        (Gb4)

The experience of separation from the mother at birth has profound effects on the human psyche. Peake's sense of isolation will have been exacerbated by the Congregationalist theology of his parents, which denies the existence of a self separate from God. Yet Peake did feel himself to be separate; as a twentieth-century artist he could hardly fail to do so. Thus the universal sense of separation from the mother and a personal sense of separation from God combine in him to form a constant desire for a return to union with the whole.

That every person is an island is a metaphor that Peake lived by, 'something on which whatever he believed was founded and through which his every concept filtered' (TG500); it lies so deep that it is more often presupposed than explicitly affirmed in his work. For instance, islands are not mentioned in a poem like 'O this Estrangement Forms a Distance Vaster' (Gb10), but 'the great seas' and the 'tract' of water between the lovers implies that one of them at least is an island. We could define his belief as the opposite of John Donne's, so famously proclaimed in Meditation 17. For Peake, each of us *is* an island, 'entire of itself', detached from the continent that bore us, and separated from the mainland by a 'wild strait' (Gb4), or even a whole ocean.

A person's island constitutes their world, their life, their *all*, and the infinite ocean that surrounds them contains everything else, including the mirror opposite of life: death, non-being and nothingness. For Peake, a scene reflected in still water recalls death because the image is unselective, unthinkingly repeating everything above it. It's like the heartless imitative

---

1. Madagascar is where Peake's grandparents and several of his aunts and uncles spent their missionary lives – it was the family island, so to speak. Another good reason for choosing it here (rather than Sark, which is what we might have expected) is Madagascar's geographic isolation: it separated from India nearly 90 million years ago; separation from Africa took place even earlier, 160 million years ago – 'chill ancientry' indeed.

painting that he calls 'mimic' art (CLP4) which is suicide for the painter. In the 'picture' that Titus sees at his birthday masque, the mirroring water is 'nothingness, a sheet of death' and at the same time 'everything' (G326). This gives rise to the metaphors with which Peake ended his radio talk on what it is to be an artist:

> As I see it, life is an effort to grip before they slip through one's fingers and slide into oblivion, the startling, the ghastly or the blindingly exquisite fish of the imagination, before they whip away on the endless current and are lost for ever in oblivion's black ocean.                    (AW5)

As an island in a sea of nothingness, he saves the vital fruit of his imagination from the dark void of unfulfilment.

The castle of Gormenghast, 'the great stone island of the Groans' (TG414) set in 'a sea of nettles' (G7), and its inhabitants provide Peake with the means to explore this metaphor in some detail. The Countess herself is much like an unvisited island, with a sea of white cats about her feet – their very purring is 'a heavy, deep throbbing, a monotonous sea-like drumming of sound' (TG45–46) – and birds are forever landing on her, even nesting in her hair. For her, there is but nothing beyond the margins of the castle. When she exiles Flay, she is sending him out into oblivion, a sea of negation.

So it is not by chance that Barquentine drowns in the moat, or that Fuchsia (as well as countless other nameless characters and at least half the animal population of the region around the castle) dies by drowning in the flood that turns Gormenghast into a literal island. In fact, any step on the journey towards death – loss of confidence in life, loss of reason – is a step towards or into the surrounding water. Fuchsia was already drowning long before she fell from her window ledge: after her discovery that 'her first and only affair of the heart had been with a murderer … a depression of utter blackness drowned her' (G395). After her death, 'the tides of the loneliness that had surged over [Titus] drowned him in seas that knew no fear of the living' (G461). Before Steerpike dies in the flood water, 'an arrogant wave had entered him and drowned his brain in black, fantastic water' (G496). Drowning supplies Peake with a metaphor for how events in the surrounding world can overwhelm his characters like a tidal wave, carrying them closer to ultimate oblivion.

Islands and the sea-coast landscape abound in *Rhymes without Reason*. Of the 16 illustrated poems in the first edition – later ones contain only 13 because some of the original artwork was lost – four have marine settings, three of them depicting islands. The illustrations to five other poems show marine settings even though the words do not require them or even seem to imply them. For instance, in 'The Sunlight falls upon the Grass', we might expect to see the table, laid with currant buns for tea, in an English garden – but no, it stands beside a yellow beach, with

'The Sunlight falls upon the Grass' from *Rhymes without Reason*.

rocks and islands in the distance. The giraffe who is glum because, by the time its laughter has climbed up to its face, it has forgotten what the joke was, belongs to the African savannah, but in Peake's illustration it sits with its back to the sea; so does the elephant who predicts that its ears will be cut off by pirates. The wonderfully ugly-faced hippopotamus is standing in the shallows of a seashore, as is the strange group that figured on the original dustwrapper: a man in pinstripe and bowler hat, a horse, a bird and a fish, all holding up a sheet that bears the title of the book (cf MPMA 130–31). As none of these creatures (except for the fish) is normally associated with the sea or beaches, the setting serves to enhance their isolation and their sense of desolation or helplessness.

The significance of the island metaphor for Peake is confirmed by his lifelong love for Stevenson's *Treasure Island*, with its memorable maroon, Ben Gunn. If every person is alone on their island, then we are all maroons. In the sketch called 'The House of Darkstones' that triggered off the story of *Titus Groan*, two characters meet 'on the beach of an island. … Lord Groan had been marooned and Mr Stewflower had been living there alone' (PP107). Peake compares Gormenghast itself to 'an island of maroons set in desolate water beyond all trade routes' (G99), and he literalizes the simile when the flood has surrounded the castle: it 'had become an island. Gormenghast was marooned' (G429). As soon as Irma Prunesquallor begins to harbour tender feelings for Steerpike, her brother senses a new emotional distance in her and exclaims, 'Am I to be marooned for ever?' (TG188). In the event, it is not Steerpike's arrival but his departure that causes her to 'maroon' the doctor by marrying Bellgrove. Along with the island, the figure of the castaway as its sole inhabitant (whether by choice, like the hermit who looks after Keda, or by force, like Flay in his exile) stands for the individual's essential isolation. What a shame that Peake was commissioned to illustrate *The Swiss Family Robinson*, rather than *Robinson Crusoe*!

Every facet of the relationship of an island to the surrounding sea provides Peake with metaphors for man's condition and each person's way of life. The tide, which rhythms the life of an island quite as powerfully as night and day, is a favourite image. For instance, the beggars at the foot of the walls of Gormenghast squat in dust 'like a dead, grey sea. It was as though the tide were in – a tide of soft dust' (G279). The outgoing tide is more poignant, characterizing separation and decline. In *Titus Alone*, Juno 'slipped away from [Muzzlehatch] like a ship on the ebb tide' (107), and both the old widow in *Rhymes without Reason* and Nannie Slagg

complain to their respective doctors, 'I ebbs and I flows, sir' (TG462).
Lord Sepulchrave loses his sanity on the outgoing tide:

> His every breath a kind of ebb that leaves him further from himself, he
> floats rather than steers to the island of the mad – beyond all trade routes,
> in a doldrum sea, its high crags burning.                          (G8)

The same thing is implied in a nonsense poem in which a woman rolls

> her eyes aside
> As though she were not able
> To quell an inward rise of tide
> And feared to slip her cable.
> (BN23)

The tide rises and falls on the beach of an island. Now we have already
observed the importance of the *edge* for Peake, as the border between light
and shade or, more symbolically, between life and death, so the edges
of his islands are highly significant places. On the first page of *Captain
Slaughterboard Drops Anchor* 'the bright blue ocean' is speckled with 'little
green islands with undiscovered edges', each inhabited by a single fantastical creature. Since a visitor to an island first makes its acquaintance,
so to speak, on the beach, those 'undiscovered edges' are the inevitable
meeting place; the beach is the threshold to a person's world.

Peake likes to orchestrate first meetings and surprise encounters on
shores and beaches: Lord Sepulchrave is delighted to meet Mr Stewflower
on the beach of what he thought was 'a companionless island' (PP107), and
the Lost Uncle, who spends much of his time on an enormous ice
floe, picks up Jackson on the beach of his first landfall. The eponymous
Mr Pye meets Miss Dredger the moment he steps off the boat in Sark's
harbour; they spend the rest of the novel singing 'Pull for the shore,
sailor' to each other, as though to repeat and reinforce the impact of that
first meeting. In the lines of verse that 'the dark man' insists on reciting
at the cocktail party in *Titus Alone*, the shore 'is such a place, / As I, my
love, have long been looking for. / Here … we can fly / Our kites of love'
(TA41). For Peake, the shore is pregnant with possibilities of meeting and
therefore love, be it only Platonic.

However, the beach also provides the setting for the opposite kind
of encounter. All the killings in the Titus books take place in shallow
water, literally or metaphorically. Even the Thing – struck by lightning
– dies knee-deep in water. In *Titus Groan*, the duel between Swelter and

Flay climaxes with them too knee-deep in rainwater. Keda's rival lovers, Braigon and Rantel, fight in a hollow, 'a basin of grass' where they walk in 'pools of [their] own midnight' (TG281). In *Gormenghast* Steerpike drowns Barquentine in the moat, and then flounders to the edge, where he lies 'like a fish thrown up by the sea over whose minute and stranded body the great cliffs tower, for the walls of Gormenghast rose high above the moat, soaring like cliffs themselves into the upper darkness' (277). Titus kills Steerpike half in and half out of the flood water, at the foot of those same cliff-like, ivy-covered walls. The corresponding duel between Titus and Veil in *Titus Alone* takes place in ankle-deep water in the caverns of the Under-River. In addition, all these protagonists use sharp-edged knives or swords (or a cleaver for Swelter, of course); only Steerpike has to abandon his swordstick at the last to drown Barquentine by hand. (These scenes hark back to the illustrations of pirate fights by Stanley L. Wood that Peake admired so much as a boy (BI).) When men fight for their lives like this, they are metaphorically invading or defending an island.

The opening of *Gormenghast* expresses all the expectations that beaches arouse in Peake:

> About the rough margins of the castle life – margins irregular as the coast-line of a squall-rent island – there were characters that stood or moved gradually to the central hub. They were wading out of the tides of limitless negation – the timeless, opaque waters. Yet what are these that set foot on the cold beach? Surely so portentous an expanse should unburden itself of gods at least; scaled kings, or creatures whose outstretched wings might darken two horizons. Or dappled Satan with his brow of brass. (G14–15)

These characters 'wading out of the tides' of Peake's imagination and up the 'portentous expanse' of the beach remind us of that moment when he is about to produce a drawing and wonders 'What should we hope for as the curtain rises and lays bare the gratuitous stage?' (D7). With gods, 'scaled kings', winged creatures and 'dappled Satan', he suggests that his novel could take on the dimensions of myth and the stature of epic, a miracle of creation.

This clarifies a puzzling phrase in *Titus Groan*: as Fuchsia enters her second attic, where the creatures of her imagination act out their stories, she feels 'a forsaken shore spread through her' (80). Here the 'shore' is Peake's shorthand for her feeling of loneliness combined with the hope, or expectation, of meeting someone, if only in imagination. This is confirmed by the opening lines of the Poet's complaint: 'Linger now with me, thou

'I *wish* I could remember / The *cause* of my distress'.
The walrus on his little iceberg, from *Rhymes without Reason*.

Beauty, / On the sharp archaic shore' (TG140), and Titus's explorations in search of love 'from the gold shores to the cold shores' (TA9).

There is nothing fortuitous about the characteristic shape of Peake's islands; he always drew them with a central monolith of rock. Sometimes this single block is surrounded by a sandy beach (a pattern he parodies in the women's hats in *Rhymes without Reason*) and sometimes there is none. He seems never to have drawn the Pacific atoll kind of island that's all beach and no central rock. The rock is a person's core identity, and the presence or absence of a beach reveals their degree of openness to others. All the islands depicted in *Captain Slaughterboard* have beaches, as do many of them in *Rhymes without Reason*. They all involve encounters.

An island without a beach is a particularly solitary place: if a visitor cannot land, there can be no meeting. An illustration in *Rhymes* provides a simple example: without knowing why, a walrus weeps atop a miniature iceberg-island whose sides fall straight into the sea. Around there are but circular ripples, caused by the tears that roll down his moustache and plop into the water. We can guess why he is crying: he has no partner, nor even space for one on his little iceberg. He seems to have no food either; there's not a fish in sight (and yet fishes pop up in all sorts of unexpected places in all Peake's illustrated works), no land, not even another iceberg. When his melts, will he survive the long and lonely swim? The sepulchral, ink-black Arctic Ocean about him seems to spell oblivion.

For Juno and Muzzlehatch, who were lovers 20 years before Titus enters the story, the absence of a beach accounts for the failure of their relationship. Together they 'had travelled to outlandish islands' but their journeys became an agony for them both; 'they broke against one another like waves breaking against headlands' (TA89). Without a beach people are condemned to separateness, and a headland suggests unwillingness to open up.

Other features of Peake's islands confirm this opposition: whereas gently sloping shores evoke the possibility of relationships, and therefore a degree of vulnerability, vertical rockfaces, such as cliffs, pinnacles and precipices, go with the rejection of others, a hardening of the heart. Founded on the bedrock of identity, they affirm determination to remain faithful to principles, or a personal code of conduct, whatever the social cost. Peake's most prickly character, the Lost Uncle, is a typical case. He draws himself attempting to sketch an impressively needle-pointed iceberg, using Jackson's back as his easel, 'but he kept moving just when I got my pencil on the paper,' he complains. 'Sometimes I wish I was on my own' (59).

That single monolith may be a crag, from which it is difficult to climb down, both literally and figuratively.[2] Muzzlehatch's face aptly 'illustrates' this; Titus wants to thank him for rescuing him from the river,

> but on gazing at the craggy face he saw that his thanks would find no answer, and it was Muzzlehatch himself who volunteered the information that he considered Titus to be a soft and rancid egg if he imagined that he, Muzzlehatch, had ever lifted a finger to help anyone in his life, let alone a bunch of rags out of the river. (TA26)

Muzzlehatch's toughness and obstinacy is expressed in the landscape of his face. At a glance Titus knows that he is a person who will not back down. And he does not hesitate to say so:

> You are too vast and craggy. Your features are the mountains of the moon. Lions and tigers lie bleeding in your brain. Revenge is in your belly. You are too vast and remote. Your predicament burns. (143)

These are all loaded terms, as we shall see; the *predicament* is whether or not to affirm oneself, based on moral rights or principles. It's a choice between admitting defeat and taking a desperate stance.

Figures perched on precipitous crags and pinnacles feature in many of Peake's drawings (cf MPMA 59 and 107), and the crag concurs with characters who believe that unbending pride and self-respect are expected of them. Bellgrove sees himself 'as the proud eagle, landing with a sigh of his wings upon a solitary crag' (G239). Commenting on his 'full-length self-portrait' the Lost Uncle is careful to point out that 'in the distance is the crag which I climbed before I lost my leg. No one else knows the way up' (4). Climbing a crag involves a balancing act, with the risk of falling into a quagmire at its foot, which probably gave rise to the punning name of 'Craggmire, the acrobat' glimpsed briefly by Steerpike (G17). I have no doubt that it also gave rise to the name of that comic gentleman, the Honourable Peter Cragg, who believes himself engaged to the island's whore in *Mr Pye*. Being an *honourable* man – he is given his title in full at every mention – he backs down gracefully. But these are all light-hearted instances; the crag has a far more serious function than this in Peake's topography.

------

2. For Peake, the crag will have been associated with his climbs on the cliffs of Sark – see *Vast Alchemies*, pp. 66–67.

Take the moment when Titus, standing on the lid of his desk in class, has mistakenly cried 'Shut up!' to Steerpike himself:

> To apologize would be to submit.
>
> He knew in the darkness of his heart's blood that he must not climb down. In the face of peril, in the presence of officialdom ... he must not climb down. He must cling to his dizzy crag until, trembling but triumphant in the enormous knowledge of his victory, he stood once more upon solid ground, secure in the knowledge that as a creature of different clay he had not sold his birthright out of terror.
>
> But he could not move. ... To cling to his crag was enough.     (G310)

Titus knows that he will, ultimately, climb down. Defying Steerpike is not, at this point, a matter of life and death.

For his foster-mother, Keda, on the other hand, the crag is a matter of life and death. She has been contemplating suicide 'with a blade' (TG357) until she looks again at 'the blasphemous finger of rock' that has loomed over her return from her wanderings. She asks the hermit who is caring for her what 'that thin and dreadful crag' means; he answers, 'If it is dreadful to you, Keda, it means that your death is near' (TG358). From that moment she knows how and where she will commit suicide after giving birth to her child, the future Thing. There will be no climbing down for her.

Describing her suicide, Peake underlines that Keda's crag (as it must be called in all future guidebooks to Gormenghast mountain) overlooks 'a heart-shaped gulch' that lies 'sunk in a sea of shade' (443–44), for the sun is setting; 'as at the stroke of a warlock's wand' (444) the sky above is suffused with its rosy light. From his cave Flay sees her 'tiny, infinitely remote figure' with her carvings, her white eagle and her yellow stag, hanging round her neck, move 'across the sun towards the crag's black edge' and throw herself off, 'most fabulously lit by the moon and the sun' (447). Although she actually falls into the 'sea of shade' below, the reader is left with the impression that she merges with the cosmos.

In the parallel scene in *Titus Alone*, soon after Muzzlehatch's zoo has been wiped out by the scientists, he climbs, with his car and his pet monkey, to watch a fabulous sunset from the edge of a precipice. In the sky 'a thousand animals of cloud streamed through the west ... changed shape before his gaze, melting from species to species' (156). Muzzlehatch rises to his feet. 'Beast after beast of the upper air recalled some most particular one of feather, scale or claw, ... of beauty or of strength' from

A solitary figure on a cliff edge drawn by Peake to decorate *Quest for Sita*.

Keda atop her crag. A much enlarged pencil
sketch from the MS of *Titus Groan*.

his lost zoo. Aware of 'an inner predicament from which he had no right, no wish to escape' (157), he decides not to commit suicide, although he clearly contemplates it, standing for a moment 'within an inch or two of the swallowing edge' (159). He chooses rather to punish the destroyers of so much beauty. He turns to

> his crazy car. He released the brake, and brought her to life, so that she sobbed, like a child pleading. He turned her to the precipice, and with a great heave sent her running upon her way. As she ran, the small ape leaped from his shoulders to the driver's seat, and riding her like a little horseman plunged down the abyss.                                                (158)

He sends his anthropomorphic and specifically female car over the edge, and his monkey stands in for him as its driver. True to his principles, Muzzlehatch chooses life, and action in revenge – for which he ultimately pays with his life.

Taken on the brink of a crag or a precipice, these life-and-death decisions – responses to an inescapable 'inner predicament' – illustrate once again Peake's symbolism of the *edge*. Every instance is a statement of identity. A carnal character like the obese Swelter trips, overbalances and is reduced to bubbling blubber, for instance. The little man called The Fly, who causes Deadyawn's death in *Gormenghast* by skidding on the polished floorboards of a classroom, throws himself out of the window through which the boys have been playing their dangerous acrobatic game, and dies like a squashed fly on the flagstones of the courtyard far below. Complex characters like Steerpike go over the edge and survive: he escapes through the window of a locked room and resolves his predicament by climbing *up* the castle wall rather climbing (or throwing himself) *down*. (When Titus is lost in the hollow halls, he too realizes that salvation lies in going up.) Mr Pye anticipates his final flight from the Coupée by looking out through 'a square window' cut in a cliff. Gazing 'down a sheer wall of sickening rock', he comments, 'What a place to take off from' (188), revealing that he too is thinking *up*. In the case of Keda, who in her own mind is also going up, towards heaven, rather than down into the sea of shadow, Peake emphasizes the *beauty* of the edge, just before she leaps: 'At the edge of age, there was a perilous beauty in her face as of the crag's edge that she stood upon' (TG446). With Muzzlehatch, Peake shows that when there is action to be taken on this side of the edge, the predicament can be addressed without going over. In other words, every island has its precipitous monolith, and (rather as in Webster's plays) the decision that characters take on the lip of the abyss defines who they are.

The same applies to Peake as he creates his works: he is constantly on a razor's edge from which he and his work may topple – from which they *will* topple if he succumbs to 'mimic' art (CLP4) – or from which they may ascend to the pantheon of masterpieces. This thought lies behind his claim in *The Craft of the Lead Pencil* that 'drawing should be an attempt to hold back from the brink of oblivion some fleeting line or rhythm, some mood, some shape or structure suddenly perceived, imaginary or visual' (1). And just as 'the demarcation line where the planes unite at their varying angles' divides light from shadow, life from death, so it also 'divulge[s] the texture of the surface' (8), the quality of character, if only in metaphor. Fuchsia discovers 'the natural edge of her own intellect' (G357) in taunting Steerpike, whereas he 'live[s] too much upon the edge of instancy for introspection' (G362). Ultimately, the *edge* is a touchstone by which Peake assesses everything, real and imagined, even time itself.

It's in his poetry that Peake expresses most clearly the link between the 'brink of oblivion' and time. For him, the present moment, the *now* that we live, is a lifelong, 'whetted edge' balanced between past and future:

> In crazy balance at the edge of time
> Our spent days turn to cloud behind today –
> And all tomorrow is a prophet's dream –
>
> (SP9)

It was this thought that caused Peake to feel a sense of panic and fear while walking along a country road. The apparent changelessness of the world masks continuous flux. Suddenly he realized that, standing 'Upon the surface, the edge of a planet / That runs around the sun' (SP36), he was in danger. This makes his heart beat fast, bringing us back to those heartbeats with which we began:

> O heartbeats, you are rattling dice –
> My rattling dice –
> Proclaim the edge of precipice,
> At whose hid boulders, stands a soundless sea –
> Then dice
> Endanger me,
> And spice
> My days with hazards of futurity.
>
> (10P)

This view of himself unites the main motifs that I have been studying so far and supplies Peake's image of man: the vital pulse of life beating in the heart, balanced on the crag of a solitary island.

T HE NEED TO LOVE and be loved renders the loneliness of Peake's maroons unbearable. Like Juno in *Titus Alone*, they find it intolerable that others 'should be so single; so contained, so little merged into [their] own existence … an island surrounded by deep water' (TA98) and therefore inaccessible to their love. So (to borrow the closing words of *Titus Groan*) love itself cries for insurrection, for revolt against the human condition. Those who refuse to accept their loneliness seek another castaway to share their solitude with. For this they need a means to cross the water between them. The alternative of inviting someone else to come and join them on their island presupposes not only that they can communicate their desire across the sea, but also that the other can cross the water, and – an aporia that affects both solutions – that two human beings can actually share the same island. Peake faces this problem squarely in his poetry, but resorts to fantasy in works like *Captain Slaughterboard Drops Anchor*, turning one of the maroons into an anthropomorphic animal. The closer his narratives approach what we might call 'real life' the more insuperable the problem becomes. So a story like 'Same Time, Same Place' begins with the drab reality of everyday life, enters a fantastic world of chimeras (or human–animal hybrids), and then returns to stark realism all within a dozen pages or so. *Mr Pye* begins just as realistically and ends with a literal 'flight' of fancy. Peake's work has proved resistant to genre analysis because it changes page by page as he varies his solutions to the human condition.

Exploring the seas in search of another island-cum-partner requires a map or chart. From the illustrations, Captain Slaughterboard proves to be a regular collector of islands: a 'map of some of the islands [he has] discovered so far' (36) is tacked up on the deckhouse wall. In the opening scene, he has left a message instructing his crew not to interrupt his nap, 'unless it's important you dogs!!' (11). One of his sea dogs wakes him when land is sighted, so finding a new island must be important – and indeed on hearing that it 'looks kind of pink' (11) the Captain jumps up in enthusiasm. In seeking new islands he was looking for a potential life partner quite as much as the Yellow Creature was looking to solve its problem of loneliness: 'You see, nearly all the other creatures [on its island] were purple' (23). No wonder they smirk with mutual satisfaction in the final pictures.

In the silent, hollow halls beneath Gormenghast Flay hears the mad laughter of the incarcerated Twins. Realizing that they are dying, he is filled with 'blind pity' and does 'all in his power to locate the suffering creature' (G301). (The word *creature* is singular here because Flay assumes that the 'double note' (300 and 302) of the Twins' almost identical voices must issue from a single throat. Elsewhere Peake uses 'double note' for the sound of the beating heart, along with 'double-thud' (G85) and 'the double-throated chord of loving' (Gb4). The Twins' ultimate cry of despair is unquestionably the voice of the heart.) Like Captain Slaughterboard in search of his 'creature', Flay starts to map 'the hollow expanses [of] the uncharted labyrinth' (G298). Eventually he produces 'a great sail of paper that not only covers the table, but descends in awkward folds and creases to the floor on every side' (G335). Yet still he can find 'no other frontier points between his world and theirs' (298) other than the original wall where he heard them. In his case, the map proves as useless as the lowered sail of a ship – but not for lack of effort.

Peake constantly seeks ways to cross the frontier that separates one person's world from another's. His brief 'Adventures of Footfruit' is about just such a journey 'over the border' and back (BN82–87). John Donne, at least, had a simple solution: while affirming that 'no man is an island' he implied that we are indeed islands, but all interconnected at a deep, underwater level. Peake would have preferred us to be joined *above* the waterline by a geographical feature that would enable us to cross dry-shod to another's island and share it with them. In *Titus Alone*, for instance, Juno regrets that between her and Titus 'there was no isthmus leading to her bounty; no causeway to her continent of love' (99). Of course, an island that is joined to a continent by an isthmus is no longer an island, merely a peninsula, but such logical considerations are irrelevant here, for we are dealing not with the physical geography of the 'real' world, but with psycho-geography, the landscape of the emotions.

'Name an isthmus!' (G115) booms the voice of Bellgrove in the Gormenghast classroom as he awakens from his mid-lesson doze. For Peake, to name an isthmus is to name a bond as close as motherhood or life itself. On the following page Shred affirms that 'Life itself is an isthmus' between birth and 'death's continent' (116). Against all rational hope, Peake wanted an isthmus, a slim land bridge that would join an island to a continent or turn two islands into one. And in Sark, he found just that, for it is shaped like two islands: Big Sark and Little Sark are joined together by the narrowest of threads, the Coupée, a knife-edge of rock, three hundred feet high and just wide enough for a footpath along its crest.[3] In Sark he saw a tangible model of how two people might be joined together in a bond of love as physical as the umbilical cord. No wonder he loved Sark so much, for it realized his dream of a symbiotic end to isolation. In his own words,

> it seemed as though two great forces were joined together by the Coupée as though it were the cord that joins the unborn child to its mother, or like that moment called *life* that links the dark domains of the womb and of the tomb. (MP249, Peake's emphasis)

The Coupée joining the two halves of Sark sums up all Peake's metaphors of life on earth, his hopes and fears. Advancing along it he would have a precipice to left and right, down which it would be fatal to fall; before him a narrow path suspended between sea and sky that he walks in the now, linking past (the island behind where he was a moment before) and future (the island in front where he will be in a few steps). As Mr Pye contemplates the Coupée for the first time, he observes that 'this is where the wisdom begins. This is what the soul has need of' (46). It has taken three chapters to bring out the meaning of his claim – and there's more to come. In the Coupée Peake sees the cure for loneliness that his soul desires, the point of balance upon the razor's edge between isolation and togetherness, the *equipoise* that 'wise men crave' (G58).

To illustrate this, we can turn to *Gormenghast*. At the height of the flood, Titus sees Steerpike stealing the new canoe in which he has just paddled for the first time over the 'sepulchral' waters (G440). To bring news of the sighting back to his mother, he has to 'crawl across the Coupée – the high knife-edge' (358), an exploit that greatly impresses the Countess. In fact it precipitates between mother and son the warmest, the most intense and the most genuine interaction of their lives.

Since the Coupée is objective and literal, it cannot solve Peake's predicament, which is subjective and metaphorical. Throughout his work, he seeks ways to link islands and cross rivers, man-made means like fords, stepping stones, causeways (the nearest thing to an isthmus) and bridges. One of the arduous tasks that the exiled and solitary Mr Flay sets himself is to place stepping stones across the local river. Years later, they enable the truant Titus, whom he has spotted by 'sweeping the opposite shore with his eyes' (G136), to cross the river to join him. This is their first

---

3. That, at least, is how the Coupée was when Peake first knew it. The Germans who occupied the island during WWII widened it for vehicles.

meeting since Titus was a babe-in-arms, and the first time that Flay has spoken with anybody since the deaths of Swelter and Lord Sepulchrave, six years before. His stepping stones are the means whereby two very isolated persons get together.

When Titus feels cut off from the people he meets in the new world he discovers, he wonders, 'Were there no bridges? Was there no common land?' (TA32). The bond between Titus and Fuchsia loosens as they grow up; he is about seven years old when she tells him that she loves him: 'a year ago they would have kissed. They had needed each other's love. Now, they needed it even more, but something had gone wrong. A space had formed between them, and they had no bridge' (G397). They are siblings and close to each other; between unrelated people, the gap proves quite unbridgeable, despite their best efforts. Indeed, Peake qualifies the gulf between the sexes as 'wide, dangerous, imponderable and littered with the wrecks of broken bridges' (G249). In the illustration to 'Simple, Seldom and Sad' that Steerpike reads in Fuchsia's attic, 'the landscape beyond [the men] was desolate and was filled with old metal bridges' (TG149). A poem that Peake did not publish in his lifetime describes the difficulties of communicating love in similar terms: 'the brittle bridges / And the little fords that I must cross, or wade / Are tortuous and make my heart afraid' (10P). So even when the bridge exists, it cannot be trusted, being liable to join the other wrecks at the bottom of the gulf.

The obvious means for crossing the water between islands is the boat, and from his earliest works onwards Peake explores all kinds of possibilities, from improvised craft to exquisitely carved vessels. (This is perhaps the moment to recall Peake's extended pun on 'craft' in the Introduction to *Drawings*, noticed in the opening chapter. His works are ships launched upon the waters of the world to make contact with the 'floating population' (TA42) around him.) On the other hand, he generally considers the simplest kind of boat, the raft, not as a means of transport but as another form of island, on which the individual is as isolated as ever: think of Titus aged one at his Earling, or the Lost Uncle in the middle of the ocean on his upturned table. This is summed up in Peake's earliest story about Mr Slaughterboard, who

> had never been on land in his life, and he had no intention of going. The idea frightened him. He had once seen a picture of a woman too. That also frightened him. The land and women seemed somehow to bring him the same feeling of dismay.                                          (PP83)

So when he sees a Yellow Creature on an island and determines to capture it, he calls for a 'Raft!' (rather than the ship's longboat) which keeps his solitude intact.

A table – symbolic of all the shared repasts that we saw in the previous chapter – can function as a boat too. In *Gormenghast* the professors turn their refectory tables upside down 'as though they were boats' and sit in them as if they are 'about to oar their way into some fabulous ocean' (G129) while they intone their dirge. The action is purely symbolic. However, they do get their own boat, a primitive dugout, when the flood comes, and they paddle it with their mortarboards, literalizing the original ceremony. And we might note that in their dugout they argue and bicker: the desire to share an island is all very well in theory, but in practice several people cannot even share a boat in harmony.

Another table used as a boat features in *Rhymes without Reason*: placed legs down in the water, it surges along like a speedboat. On board is a couple who are obviously at cross purposes: while the wife scans the far horizon through her telescope her husband looks over the side, at right angles to her line of view, and sees the islands that she is surely missing. Indeed, he may well be scanning the islands in the hope of finding a better partner!

The boat motif (implicit in 'Pull for the shore, sailor') permeates *Mr Pye*. Inviting Miss Dredger to become his disciple, the indefatigable evangelist asks her to join him in his skiff (MP61). His somewhat ambiguous proposal 'opens a window' for Miss Dredger, giving her a view of 'virgin country with forests and hills' which rapidly begins 'to shrink and dwindle' until it takes the size and shape of Sark, the island she lives on (61–62). Once her sense of being an isolated, unloved virgin has been reinforced, she is ready to throw in her spiritual lot with Mr Pye and row second oar with him.

Among the many boats that Peake deploys (including rafts, kayaks, canoes and a coracle in the Lost Uncle), the two that most clearly symbolize attempts to end isolation and communicate between islands are, predictably, models rather than full-sized boats. The only thing that Barquentine remembers about his wife is that she used to weep while making paper boats which she 'sailed across the harbour of her lap' (G267–68). Her tears express the loveless isolation of being married to Barquentine (the least attractive of husbands), but her frail craft remain timidly in the harbour instead of venturing out towards him. Titus also plays with boats when he is a boy, carving small wooden models and 'naming them as he launched them upon their perilous missions to the isles of blood and spices' upon the castle moat (G342). In contrast to hers, his ships have names and courageously set out for distant islands, anticipating Titus's eventual departure from Gormenghast in search of elsewhere. The association of 'blood and spices' may evoke pirates; it may also suggest that the islands he imagines are people, and more specifically girls of flesh and blood, for Peake grew up in a world where little girls were made of 'sugar and spice and all things nice'. Be that as it may, in the world that Titus enters at the age of 18 or so by travelling down a river by boat, the women turn out to be 'spicy'. We learn that 'between those little feet of [Juno's] and her noble, Roman head, lay, as though between the poles, a golden world of spices' (TA51). (Peake's love imagery often recalls John Donne's.) When Titus argues with Cheeta, he says: 'And yet you said you loved me. That is the spice of it.' The little boy's act of launching model boats anticipates the adolescent's search for a partner to love.

The most poignant evocation of spices, boats, beaches and castaways also comes in *Titus Alone*, when Muzzlehatch is daydreaming. 'Are you still there?' asks Titus, and Muzzlehatch answers, 'I am still here, or some of me is.' He continues:

> 'The rest of me is leaning on the rails of a ship. The air is full of spices and the deep salt water shines with phosphorus. I am alone on deck and there is no one else to see the moon float out of a cloud so that a string of palms is lit like a procession. I can see the dark-white surf as it beats upon the shore; and I see, and I remember, how a figure ran along the strip of moonlit sand, with his arms raised high above his head, and his shadow ran beside him and jerked as it sped, for the beach was uneven; and then the moon slid into the clouds again and the world went black.'
>     'Who was he?' said Titus.
>     'How should I know?' said Muzzlehatch. 'It might have been anyone. It might have been me.'                                    (TA56–57)

Indeed, 'it might have been anyone', any castaway desperate for rescue from his desert island. It's the existential situation of everyone in Peake's world.

In *Titus Alone*, Muzzlehatch is the first person that Titus meets (in another of Peake's waterside encounters) – he and his extraordinary car. It has characteristics of both an animal companion and a boat (rather as Muzzlehatch himself has a rudder-shaped nose!). As an animal, it evokes in Muzzlehatch a response worthy of the Lost Uncle: '"She's a bitch – and smells like one"' (56). As a ship, it has a 'stern' (15) and a 'prow-like bonnet' (18). Riding in the back, Titus finds himself 'clinging to an old brass railing' and gasping at 'the air that ran into his lungs like icy water'. Furthermore, 'it seemed that the car had an existence of its own and was making its own decisions' (18): when parked it has to be moored – Peake actually writes 'lashed' on two occasions (19 and 67). Its will is as unpredictable as the wind; driving it is like sailing a boat. Once Muzzlehatch is at the wheel, whatever plans he may have had are 'no more than chaff in the wind'. Taking Juno home, he finds himself heading instead for yet another beach, a 'wide and sandy stretch of the river where the banks shelved gently into the shallow water' (64). Reclining in his favourite position with 'one eye above the "bulwarks"' (65), Muzzlehatch drives into the shallows. 'Once in the water he acceler-ated and great arcs of brine spurted from the wheels to port and starboard' (64). (Note that although this is a river, Peake writes 'brine'; he has the sea in mind.) However, despite its boat-like characteristics the car is not amphibious and can no more cross the water than Muzzlehatch can regain his previous relationship with Juno, as this episode reminds him:

> those faraway days when they were lovers came flooding back … each one challenging the strength of the dykes which they had built against one another. For they knew that beyond the dykes heaved the great seas of sentiment on whose bosom they had lost their way.          (66)

Driving his boat-like car into the water merely recalls the impossibility of reaching Juno's island and living together as a couple.

Paradoxically, Peake ends up finding the closest link between people in the same place that John Donne did: deep under water. For instance, when Titus and Fuchsia reach out to one another through the narrow window of the Lichen Fort, 'their fingers touching might have been the prows of foundered vessels which grazed one another in the sub-aqueous depths, so huge and vivid and yet unreal was the contact' (G148). The use of 'unreal' is significant; such a meeting could only truly take place before birth or after death, in the boundless ocean of oblivion that surrounds their lives. Yet whenever Peake's characters make love, the breathing of the sea – the advance and withdrawal of the waves – can be heard in the background, recalling this imagined ideal. Incongruous though it seems in the setting of Juno's house, the room where she and Titus consummate their relation-ship has 'the remoteness of a ship at sea' (93) as they 'begin to drown' in each other's arms (94). So when Muzzlehatch peeps into the room he hears 'a long sigh like the sigh of the sea' (96). Later Juno falls for the man she first glimpses in the depths of 'a wide glaze of dew' (TA148) and calls him Anchor. They take a honeymoon suite filled with a pale blue light on the ninety-ninth floor of a hotel; against all probability 'far away there was a murmuring sound like the sound of the sound of the sea' (211). The most tender scenes in *Titus Alone* take place beneath a river, 'whose muffled reverberations were a background to all that ever happened' there (112), and the most attentive husband of the Under-River is called Jonah (121). The same 'murmur of the breathing sea' is heard when the painter and Tintagieu make love in *Mr Pye* (75). For Peake two people making love abandon self and consciousness to sink into the depths of that sepulchral ocean between their respective islands. Not for nothing has the post-coital state long been known as 'the little death'.

Although Peake and Donne seem to be making opposite claims, deep-down they are saying the same thing. The apparent opposition is due simply to the different points of view that they adopt: in this instance Peake looks down on his characters from a height, and sees each one isolated, like an island on a map. Donne, who also uses maps as metaphors, reassures himself (and us) by switching to a cross-section view: seen from the side, an island is clearly joined to the mainland by the seabed. Although Peake does use cross-section views in some of his works (as I shall be mentioning later), he stuck with the bird's eye view as far as man's isolation is concerned. In doing so, he imprisoned himself with his own metaphor.

Consequently, he never finds a way for two people to share one island. Instead, he celebrates the seabed as the place where the solitary individual can find love of a different kind,

> a love that equals in its power the love of man for woman and reaches inwards as deeply. It is the love of a man or of a woman for their world. ...
> The love of the diver for his world of wavering light. His world of pearls and tendrils and his breath at his breast. ... As he holds himself to the ocean's faery floor, one hand clasped to a bedded whale's rib, he is complete and infinite. Pulse, power and universe sway in his body. He is in love.
>
> (TG77)

This rare sense of wholeness, of completion, of oneness with the universe inspires Peake's dream that union might be realized in the future, for 'tomorrow is another day' (TG506). More often, though, we find him lamenting, 'Is there no love can link us – I and they? / Only this hectic moment?' and concluding 'There is no other link. Only this sliding / Second we share: this desperate edge of now' (S&S20). To have realized his dream in this world would have been to deny the metaphor he lived by.

# Animals

'Are you an animal, Mrs Slagg? I repeat are you an animal?
… You are not an animal,' repeated Prunesquallor, 'are
you?'                                                      (TG73)


Slamming the door behind her [Irma] gave vent to the
primeval jungle in her veins.                             (G225)


I think I could turn and live with animals, they are so
                                        placid and self-contain'd,
[…]
They do not sweat and whine about their condition,
They do not lie awake in the dark and weep for their sins,
They do not make me sick discussing their duty to God
[…]
Not one kneels to another, nor to his kind that lived
                                        thousands of years ago.
                        (Walt Whitman, 'Song of Myself', 32,
                    ll. 684, 686–88 and 690; NAAL 1: 2117)


BELIEVING THAT EVERY PERSON is a separate island, Peake constantly
comes up against the stubborn 'fact' that *two* people cannot share
*one* island. However, an animal companion – not just any old domestic
pet, of course, but an anthropomorphic animal, like Captain Slaughterboard's Yellow Creature – would relieve the solitude. Consequently many
of Peake's works feature partnerships between hybrids and humans. The
strange relationship between Titus and the Thing starts to make sense
when viewed in this light. It represents a particular moment in Peake's
thinking, for unlike his belief about islands his attitude towards animals
evolved over the years. The loving realism of his early animal studies is

Image courtesy of Chris Beetles Gallery

Early drawing of a seal.

founded on close observation. The same qualities inspire the slightly anthropomorphosized – and superbly expressive – animal figures in works like Grimm's *Household Tales*, which he executed in the mid-1940s. In the 1950s, however, fantastical human–animal hybrids and chimeras predominate. They reflect an existential question: once the God who set man over the animals is no longer there, what is left of man's status?

Anthropomorphic animals (wearing loincloths or little skirts) readily share their islands with humans in 'The Moccus Book', Peake's first and still unpublished story in illustrated verse produced in collaboration with Gordon Smith.[1] Their spirit of welcome towards a marooned sailor anticipates the Yellow Creature, which figures in both the uncompleted story about Mr Slaughterboard and the illustrated tale that grew out of it, *Captain Slaughterboard Drops Anchor*.

Anxiety about man's animal nature is present from the first lines of 'Mr Slaughterboard': the captain is throwing 'the most nutritious portions of

---

1. As Gordon Smith later claimed authorship of the texts, I have abstained from using them as evidence here. The drawings, though, are definitely Peake's and a selection of them can be seen in MPMA 36–41.

Early drawing of a rhinoceros.

Parmesan cheese to a deep-sea shark' (PP65) and keeping only the rind for himself.[2] He feels a need to placate the most feared fish of the deeps – perhaps because part of him is already animal: 'One of his hands was formed in the shape of an elephant's foot' (69). He is as cruel a character as ever Peake invented, killing members of his crew in the name of art, and sacrificing them to the sea 'to appease [his] conscience – to satisfy [his] soul' (71). He treats his crew like animals, calling his blind servant Smear a 'benighted crab' (69), for instance. He assures him,

> Had you not a little of that stuff within which longs for more than material
> things, do you think that you would be alive now? Toad that you are, you
> have the semblance of a soul.                                        (69)

In other words, had Smear been a truly soul-less creature, Mr Slaughter-board would have had no hesitation about killing him too. No wonder

---

2. This unexpected presence of Italian cheese may well derive from chapter 19 of *Treasure Island*: Doctor Livesey gives a 'very nutritious' piece of Parmesan to Ben Gunn, who craves cheese.

Donkey.

Smear comes running 'like a dog to the whistle' (68) when his captain calls. Considering the crew as animals allows Slaughterboard to share his ship with them, while hating them for their animal nature instead of accepting the animal in himself.

Presumably the Yellow Creature is sufficiently human to be spared, too. Declining to be captured, he – Peake makes the Creature male – makes his own way to Mr Slaughterboard, who is 'enthroned' on a raft, and obsequiously drops on all fours before him, looking up 'as a rabbit will gaze spellbound at a snake' (70). This simile sees the 'kingly' captain as an animal, and not a pleasant one at that. Yet the Yellow Creature is determined to 'follow this grim master into the ends of the world. Why – he did not know. Sufficient that he felt he was in the presence of a Being' (90; Peake's capital). He has found something to worship, but the object is unworthy.

Slightly anthropomorphosized animals from *Household Tales*:
'The cat and mouse in partnership' and
the wolf carrying off the baby for 'Old Sultan'.

Humour often serves to defuse anxiety. As Peake writes in *Titus Alone*, laughter 'takes a sacrosanct convention and snaps it in half as though it were a stick. It lifts up some holy relic and throws it at the sun' (229). So we may wonder whether the Yellow Creature's behaviour is not a parody of man's need to invent gods to worship. This thought is reinforced by the discussions of art and literature that Mr Slaughterboard enjoys with Smear.[3] In the ship's library they read Shakespeare together.

> 'Which is it to be, Captain?' he whispered.
> 'I think *The Tempest*, Mr Smear.'                                    (PP73)

And they proceed to recite their favourite verse, 'Full fathom five' – another evocation of undersea meetings. Peake was assuredly inspired by Shakespeare, and he may have Caliban's besotted admiration for Stefano in mind when he makes the Yellow Creature worship Mr Slaughterboard. At any rate, the pirate song in this story (83) certainly parodies Stefano's 'Flout 'em and cout 'em' song in *The Tempest* (II.iii). The central motif of the island and the nature/nurture debate in that play are germane to Peake's preoccupations too, but he does not pursue them further here. Once he has recounted the capture of the Yellow Creature, the story shudders to a halt as the *Conger Eel* impales itself on a pointed rock in mid-ocean, another island.

Peake recast this material as a love story in *Captain Slaughterboard Drops Anchor* (which is still marketed as a 'pirate fantasy'). Drawing on his romance with the blonde Maeve Gilmore, whom he married shortly before he started on the book, he makes the Yellow Creature sufficiently human for it to feel lonely, and sufficiently androgynous for us to accept that it might seduce the Captain. This Slaughterboard has no animal body parts and is less cruel. His five remaining crew members are summarily killed off in 'terrible battles' (CSDA 33; not illustrated), which clears the

---

3. All Peake's pirates owe something to *Peter Pan* (published in 1911 as *Peter and Wendy*). The captain's cruelty is like Hook's; Charlie Choke is tattooed all over, just like Bill Jukes; Timothy Twitch is 'most elegant in battle' (8) like Gentleman Starkey, who is 'dainty in his ways of killing'. Smear recalls Smee, who 'more than once on summer evenings had touched the fount of Hook's tears and made it flow' (ch. 14). He is 'the only Non-conformist in Hook's crew' (ch. 5). As John Watney pointed out, Slaughterboard's ship, the *Conger Eel*, bears 'the nickname which Mervyn had heard Congregationalists give to their church' (62).

Captain Slaughterboard
taught the Yellow Creature
some old pirate dances
and they would practice
them together when the
moon was full.

Captain Slaughterboard and the Yellow Creature dancing on deck.

decks for the Yellow Creature. Slaughterboard falls in love, gazing for long hours at the Creature; they dine together and dance in perfect synchrony on the deck. Ultimately they settle down in honeymoon happiness on the Creature's pink island, where the Yellow Creature 'does the cooking' (44) for them both. It's the most satisfactory durable relationship (between humans, or humans and animals) in all Peake's work.

It did not satisfy Peake, who continued his restless exploring. In *Rhymes without Reason* partnerships with animals abound, associated with islands, seascapes and scenes of propitiation. By mimicking human behaviour, Peake's animals question the distinctions between species – and gender roles, as already implied by the Yellow Creature. Abandoned by their respective wives, a Jailor teams up with a Jaguar to seek for 'Warmth and Clothes to Mend' (26–27). In the illustration, the Jailor has his arm protectively round the Jaguar, who wears a skirt. A Greenland whale sneaks into Aunt Mabel's house by night, dresses itself in one of Aunty's nighties, and sits on the mantelpiece, warming its tail at the fire and feeling 'high-and-mighty' (20). Despite that nightie, it is strongly reminiscent of a paterfamilias, warming his back at the living-room fire in the proprietary manner favoured by men. A hostess 'with startled eyes' serves tea to a 'Crocodile in ecstasy' that is sitting on her sofa, dressed in an elegant suit and tie (14–15). Is she hoping to placate his obviously male predatory nature, and is he in ecstasy because he knows that in fact he can gobble her up at any time? There are certainly hints that civilization may only thinly overlie man's animal nature. What is more, these animals suffer from being treated as natural resources: a tearful mother elephant warns her children that, when they grow old and die, pirates will 'swarm ashore / And chop' their ears from their heads, to sew them into sails (24–25; reproduced in MPMA 130). However, the brevity of these pieces and discrepancies between text and illustration make it difficult to draw firm conclusions from them.

In Peake's next work, the ideas are more clear-cut: the Lost Uncle hates society. Rejecting the constraints of civilization – he throws his collar into the sea, vowing 'never to start that sort of nonsense again' (29) – he leaves England on the *SS Em* to go and prove the existence of the White Lion of the Snows. The ship's name corresponds to the initials of the 'School for the Sons of Missionaries' that Peake attended, hinting that the Uncle's search may be an education in itself. Soon he too is tossing cubes of cheese to a grateful shark, but Peake has him witness nature's rule of 'eat or be eaten'. By the light of a strange radiance from below, he sees through the

The Jailor and the Jaguar courageously stepping
out from *Rhymes without Reason*.

ice at his feet 'fish with teeth like tombstones ... a shark with its ghastly white stomach, and an octopus that was gobbling up something' (100). Only a layer of ice, the fragile restraint of civilization, separates him from them.

Life among wild animals is therefore perilous. A polar bear takes the Uncle in its arms 'as though ... to kiss him' (92). Only by tickling it into convulsions of laughter does he escape being hugged to death. He loses a leg to a swordfish, kills it and appropriates its spike as a prosthesis, for it is just the same length as his missing limb. With this exchange of a leg for a life he loses his human aggressiveness, killing only for food and clothing, or in self-defence, wielding the spike like a sword. What he calls his 'weapon' is his box camera (65), which he loses shortly before the climax of the story. So when he ultimately meets the White Lion, he is unarmed.

But first he pressgangs a turtle into his service, drives nails in its shell, hooks on his paraphernalia, and hauls it off around the world, calling it Jackson. (Part of Peake's grotesquerie consists in giving human names to animals and animal names, like 'Steerpike', to humans.) Jackson wears an effeminate headscarf, which makes him as androgynous as the Yellow Creature. Towards him the Uncle behaves abominably, just like an intolerant husband, impatient with his shortcomings (for he is natu-rally slow and clumsy) and showing no sympathy when he catches a cold. This treatment deeply offends Jackson, but the Uncle ignores his feelings. Having acquired his animal partner, he devotes all his efforts to finding the White Lion whose image 'possesses' him and 'fills his brain' (65).

This quest for the 'lord of snow' takes on a noticeably spiritual aura. First the Lost Uncle saves Jackson (by means of his spike) from slipping to his death in a chasm, which they cross by pretending to be dead. As arctic vultures close in, taking them for prey, they leap up and catch hold of the birds' ankles so that they get carried over. Immediately afterwards the Uncle notices that Jackson's footprints in the snow make the shape of a fish, the oldest symbol for Christ. By faking death they seem to have entered the next world: they see 'steeples of ice' in the distance, 'as though [they] were approaching a city of glass churches' (98). In the 'church' that is 'loftier and vaster by far' they see a white hillock (called an *island* in the text) and climb it to 'admire the view' before exploring 'the crystal spires of the shining cathedral that shone above' (102). Jackson does not like this at all, whereas the Uncle is unaccountably filled with all sorts of memories, 'especially of the white lion whose haunting presence in my mind had changed my life and made me one of the greatest explorers the world has never [sic] known' (103). The 'island' is of course the White Lion itself and when it gets to its feet they tumble off, much to the amusement of Jackson, who has 'the same sort of smirk on his face' (109) as when the Uncle nearly got hugged to death by the polar bear.

The Uncle's mistake is understandable, though, for the White Lion's pelt is pure white; 'even the snow looks dirty and grey' (111) in comparison. In fact 'nothing could change his whiteness. He was apart from everything else' (118). Peake's White Lion stands in a similar relation to Christ as C.S. Lewis's Aslan. While 'coloured crosses and circles' (112) appear in the sky, the White Lion, who is 'ready to die' (110), approaches the cathedral, turns to the east, enters and ascends a throne. Before 'a vast and silent congregation' comprising 'all the arctic beasts and polar fowl' and 'every kind of polar creature' (117), it roars its last roar, shakes its mane, and instantly freezes to death.

The Uncle is both proud and humbled to have seen the White Lion face to face. 'Somehow I didn't want to do anything except look and look and look' (122), he says. The ineffable experience leaves him 'all aglow inside' and 'in a kind of trance' (121). Afterwards, he is anxious to report his find to the Natural History Museum, which makes of his book a kind of gospel, bringing the good news back to the land of man, although 'it does not matter what words I use ... for there he was, and there he will be for ever, alone and beautiful in the wild polar waste – alone in his cathedral, my Lion of white ice' (120).

This story marks a new stage in Peake's explorations: when a man has resolved his problem of loneliness on the physical level, he can address his spiritual solitude. But not even a face-to-face encounter with Christ can assuage it, although the seeker may feel fulfilled by witnessing His death. As for humanity's absurd dignity, its self-proclaimed superiority over animals, well, animals would laugh in scorn, were they capable of laughter. From now on, it's the humans who get 'animalized' in his stories, and many of his drawings imply parallels between animals and man. His dogs are always mangy mongrels and his horses mock their riders. The fear of violence from within, symbolized by sharks that need propitiating, has abated, although the daily struggle for survival, Tennyson's 'nature red in tooth and claw', continues as ever. Mr Pye has his own way of putting it: 'the more one knows of nature the more one realizes what a bloody-minded old thing she is' (MP102). A major step forward though this may be, it left Peake's fundamental desire for company on his island unsatisfied.

Before turning to the Titus books, we might note that those two most unsociable men, Mr Slaughterboard and the Lost Uncle, are both misogynists – and compulsive collectors. The former (whose mother was 'hideous' (PP65) and whose father obsessively catalogued Indian flowers and orchids) fears women and collects books. About the time the Lost Uncle marries an appallingly ugly woman, he begins to collect 'different kinds of insects, mushrooms and rats', which he keeps in the lounge – 'the best place for them from the point of view of their health' (26)! Of the two other male characters from Peake's pre-war writing, Captain Slaughterboard might be said to be a collector of islands until he meets his Yellow Creature, and Mr Stewflower, in 'The House of Darkstones', has devoted his life to studying 'the Rong (Wrong) beetle' (PP106). (The name says it all.) For all these men the mascot substitutes for a spouse and their collecting sublimates their sexual energy.

This continues in *Titus Groan*: Lord Sepulchrave is estranged from his wife and devotes all his spare time to his books; after the loss of his library, he starts to believe that he belongs among the owls in the Tower of Flints. With her clowder of white cats and strange communion with birds, the Countess surely ranks as a collector too, with similar motivation. (For all their marital difficulties, Lord and Lady Groan really are birds of a feather.) Sometimes she speaks to her birds as she might to a child – 'Are you hungry, my little love?' she asks a wood warbler (TG307) – or to a spouse. When she chides her favourite albino rook Master Chalk (note his title), she sounds just like a loving wife reprimanding and forgiving her errant husband: 'So it is the truant back again. … What a bunch of wickedness! … Three weeks I've been without him; I wasn't good enough for *him* … and here he is back again, wants to be forgiven!' (TG54; Peake's emphasis). This scene is paralleled in *Titus Alone*, after Titus has been absent from Juno for a while. 'So you thought you'd come back, my wicked one. Where have you been?' she says, echoing the Countess's question. The latter actually asks her rook what clouds he has been flying through and Titus's response to Juno that he 'caught a plane' and 'sliced the sky in half' (TA91–92) could equally well have been the rook's answer to the Countess! Although these men and women relieve their solitude and sublimate their sexual frustration with animal companions, the animals remain animals.

Yet these creatures arouse strong feelings. On Prunesquallor's fantasy travels, his mule is suddenly waylaid by a python.

> Even at that ghastly and critical moment I could see what a beautiful thing
> it was. Far more beautiful than my old brute of a mule. But did it enter my

Horseplay from *Figures of Speech*.

head that I should transfer my allegiance to the reptile? No. After all, there
is such a thing as loyalty as well as beauty.                          (G40)

Beauty may tempt a man to change partner; loyalty – and a touch of
realism – keeps him faithful. Prunesquallor adds, 'Besides, I hate walking,
and the python would have taken some riding, your ladyship: the very
saddling would tax a man's patience' (G40–41). Sex is never far away.

Peake's animals may procreate but their eyes are loveless. The human
capacity to see beauty and feel love raises us above the animal, although
we often fall short of the ideal. Discovering a dead rat in his path one
morning, Peake recognizes that 'Were I a farmer I would call you vermin'.
But he is not a farmer: 'unmanly / Unfarmerly, and most impractically'
he feels that 'rats even have a right to live' (RoB25). The beauty of its
body, 'Dusted with starry marvels of bright frost', and its little paws
crossed upon its breast recall for him the killing of Christ, the supremely
innocent and loving being.

WITH THE TITUS BOOKS, we come to the problematical Thing. Introduced at the end of *Titus Groan* as the human child of Titus's
wet-nurse, Keda, and her lover Rantel, she is cast off by the community
of Bright Carvers and turns 'wild, like an animal, and as untameable'
(G281). She lives on stolen food and small animals, particularly birds,
that she catches in the woods. Comparing her to a whole catalogue of
creatures, 'a faun or a tigress or a moth or a fish or a hawk or a martin'
(G411), Peake consistently makes her more animal than human and thus
a potential companion for Titus. He falls in love with what he imagines
to be her 'arrogance and swallow-like beauty of limb' (G416), only to
discover, when he finally sees her close up in Flay's cave, 'a creature radically at variance with the image that had filled his mind'. Crouched over
a camp fire, with the feathers of a magpie scattered about her, she looks
'like a frog in the dust'. 'Was this the lyric swallow' who 'had floated
through his imagination in arrogant rhythms that spanned the universe?'
(G416). What he had fallen in love with was indeed 'the chimera of a
daydream' (G131), and not the Thing itself.

The status of the Thing raises many questions. First Peake calls an
androgynous yellow humanoid of indefinable species a *Creature*; now
he names a feminine feral child the *Thing*. What distinguishes humans
from animals for him? Mr Slaughterboard has already provided the short
answer: the soul, 'that stuff within which longs for more than material
things' (PP69). It is a traditional one, of course. For Congregationalists

Dead rat.

it is the duty of humans to renounce all selfhood, that God might fill them with Himself, whereas animals, having no soul, can have no self-awareness, and are therefore exempt from any such obligation.[4] Having no conscience either, they cannot be considered good or evil; they stand outside the moral sphere that humans inhabit. For Peake (as for Walt Whitman, quoted in the epigraph to this chapter), this makes them 'enviable' (G316).

Of the Thing we learn that 'she was always alone. It seemed unthinkable that she could be companioned. There was no soft spot in her self-sufficiency' (G281). In this respect she resembles all the animals in Peake's world: they accept their existence, in particular their solitude, without question. The Countess's cats, for instance, 'behaved as though each one were utterly alone, utterly content to be alone, conscious only of its own

---

4. Our thinking about animals has evolved so rapidly since Peake's time – and is accelerating as we come to realize how close we are to them at the genetic level – that some readers may need reminding that until quite recently it was commonly believed that, since animals had no self-awareness, they could not experience pain. This authorized – in fact it still does – all kinds of cruelty to animals, from laboratory experiments to ritual killing.

behaviour, its own leap into the air, its own agility, self-possessed, solitary, enviable and legendary' (G316). The raven that Titus encounters in the hollow halls walks with 'a self-absorbed air' (G182), and in Gormenghast Forest a fox acts 'with extraordinary self-possession' (G135). Having the unselfconsciousness of an animal, the Thing knows nothing of a human institution like Gormenghast – or of any values, human or divine, for that matter. She lives untroubled by any sense of sin or isolation. Consequently she 'explode[s] at the very centre of [Titus's] conventions' (G507).

The other character that Peake qualifies in any comparable way is Tintagieu, the brazen whore in *Mr Pye* who aspires to nothing beyond the satisfaction of her physical needs and desires:

> She was in some strange way both innocent and menacing.
>
>     Innocent in that she had no say in her own personality. She was merely the vehicle through which was poured the very juice of animal existence. She was and could be nothing else. Self-conscious as a monkey, and about as refined … but complete as an acorn.[5]                    (MP69)

Peake qualifies her too as 'self-absorbed' (108) and 'self-contained, childish, amoral, primitive, the mistress of many and the property of none' (124). These terms confirm my reading of the Thing as a creature who, through lack of education (or 'nurture'), has reverted to the level of an animal and could therefore share Titus's island with him as an innocent sexual partner like Tintagieu. Peake plays with this possibility right up to the last moment.

Animals are incapable of speech, which in the past was seen a sign that they have no soul. The Yellow Creature manages a single 'Yo-ho!'; Jackson says nothing; the Thing never learns to speak. The sounds she makes bear 'no relation to human speech' and have 'no concern with communication' (421). Titus realizes this only moments before she makes her abortive leap for freedom and, hampered by his shirt, falls into his waiting arms. That she can be assimilated to an animal liberates Titus's desire. He has a similar response to Cheeta: 'That he abhorred her brain seemed almost to add to his lust for her body' (TA169). At this point, Peake has assembled all his usual motifs that accompany an underwater encounter, with

---

5. The reference to the acorn is noteworthy, for Peake 'perceives in the acorn not only the oak but the whole vegetable universe, and in the whole vegetable universe the vital source of all things, and in this matrix, a god – perhaps of beauty, or sublime indifference – at any rate, a god' (AW4).

the rain 'pounding' and 'roaring' (G422) in the background like the sea. The Thing's head is 'like the head of a sea-blurred marble long drowned beneath innumerable tides' (423). Titus is about to have sex with her, 'his body and his imagination fused in a throbbing lust'. Gripping her 'even more savagely than before' he tears away the shirt from her face. It proves 'so small' that he begins to cry and 'the first wild virgin kiss that trembled on his lips for release died out. ... He knew that there would be no climax' (423). The detumescence is instantaneous.

Peake seems to have suddenly realized that the amoral anthropomorphic animal partner is a male sex fantasy, part of the drive that makes men predators. No wonder he calls this moment 'the death of [Titus's] imagination' (424). Consequently there are no more exploited, anthropomorphic animal companions in his work, nor animalized human partners. As the nature of mankind continued to trouble him, the hybrids that he depicts are either comic, or moral and physical disasters.

What distinguishes humans from animals is the theme of Titus's tenth-birthday masque, a kind of animated painting enacted by 'beings of another realm': 30-foot-high figures of a horse, a wolf, a lion and a lamb. It is one of Peake's 'miracles', as confirmed by his observation that 'the crowds that stared up at them from below [were] not only shrivelled up into midgets, but were also made to appear grey and prosaic' (G328), repeating the idea in *Drawings* that great works make 'the room we stand in like a land of the dead' (D7). Five pages of description end with a memorable comment:

> the grandeur of the spectacle and the god-like rhythms of each sequence were of such a nature that there were few present who were not affected as by some painful memory of childhood. (331)

As to what those 'painful memories' might be, he does not say. Considering that he imagined this masque to be 'a formula as ancient as the walls of the castle itself' (331), we might suppose it to be a 'throw-back to some savage rite of the world's infancy' (382) when man worshipped 'the dim primordial gods of power and blood' (381). Indeed, the giant figures act out basic emotions: the sense of fear mingled with respect (that leads to allegiance) in front of great power; envy or jealousy leading to hate and murderous urges; and delight (sublimated energy) in poetry. Animals share all but man's spiritual aspirations, expressed through love and appreciation of beauty. It's a small difference, and a painful one to realize for someone brought up in the Western tradition of a deep conceptual chasm (dug with the three-pronged fork of ethics, religion and philosophy) between ourselves and animals.

This realization was undoubtedly brought home to Peake by his visit to the newly liberated concentration camp at Bergen-Belsen in 1945. Faced with a horrific example of man's inhumanity to man, of the ease with which humans can cast off moral restraint, he lost faith in the innate goodness of human nature. He returned to England 'a man with a shadow ... damaged' (Gilmore 59). Thereafter he increasingly identified and sympathized with the victim, man or animal.

Early in the 1950s Peake penned a short story in which he adopted, for the first time, a first-person narrator, so that author and reader share the victim's point of view. At the age of 23, the pathetic hero of 'Same Time, Same Place' suddenly tires of life at home with his parents and sets off by bus – Peake is so good at bathos – to find 'adventure' and 'a beautiful woman' (PP144). Having quit his parents because he hates them 'for being human' (143), he is almost tricked into marrying the least human woman that Peake could imagine in the realistic setting of London. As the youth approaches the registry office, he glimpses his bride through the window and realizes that she is a dwarf, so short that at first he takes her for a dressed-up dog standing on its hind legs. Worse,

A dressed-up circus dog.

she has 'a mouth that, taking a single diabolical curve, was more like the mouth of a wild beast than of a woman' (PP150). So this seductress is an animal of the devouring kind, and diabolical at that. Furthermore she is accompanied by a selection of circus freaks: the bearded lady, the man with the longest neck in the world, the man all blue with tattoos and gold teeth, and the man with cloven hoofs for hands. The narrator flees home in horror, vowing never again to venture beyond the door of his parents' suburban house or to entertain thoughts of marriage.

The tale is full of ironies: the young man travels straight from home to Piccadilly *Circus*. 'Here was the jungle all about me and I was lonely. The wild beasts prowled around me. The wolf packs surged and shuffled' (144). Loneliness and fear drive him into a familiar Lyons Corner House, which turns out to be a 'lion house' instead. There he falls into the mantrap laid by a 'beast' from a circus. Thus Peake reverses the roles and makes us feel all the revulsion and terror of a hapless human that an animal wants to mate with. Book IV of *Gulliver's Travels*, in which a female Yahoo lusts after Gulliver, may have contributed to this story.

Peake's one novella, 'Boy in Darkness', develops this reversal more physically, framed within the same pattern of leaving home in search of adventure, encountering animalized humans who threaten lifelong enslavement, responding with horror, narrowly escaping and returning to the comforting routine of home. The first steps of this pattern, expressed in maritime metaphors, can be found in Peake's poem about youths who rebel against their parents and make for the nearest city: 'Snapped is their childhood's anchor-chain, / The helm shakes, and a tide is running.' Having cut themselves loose they discover that they are 'more lonely among pards / Than when [they] cursed [their] parents' love' (Gb31). 'Boy in Darkness' opens with similar images. In his bedroom at Gormenghast Titus looks up at a

> familiar patch of mildew that stretched across the ceiling like an island.
>
> He had stared many times at this same mildew-island with its inlets and its bays; its coves and the long curious isthmus that joined the southern to the northern masses. He knew by heart the tapering peninsula that ended in a narrowing chain of islets like a string of discoloured beads. … He had many a time brought imaginary ships to anchor in hazardous harbours, or … set new courses for yet other lands.
>
> But to-day … the only thing he stared at was a fly that was moving slowly across the island.
>
> 'An explorer, I suppose,' muttered the Boy to himself.          (BiD158)

From this germinates the idea of having an adventure of his own, of leaving the castle to explore 'other lands'.

Once out in unfamiliar terrain, he is 'shepherded' across a river by dogs and finds himself in a desert where he is captured by two chimeras, a Goat-man and a Hyena-man. They take him to their lord, a blind Lamb who has transformed every creature he can lay hands on into a hybrid. This is genetic engineering in reverse, active atavism. Titus is to be 'reshaped' too, the first fresh victim for many years. Only Goat and Hyena have survived, perhaps because the men they used to be were a lecher and a cowardly predator, respectively. The Lamb, 'so agile of brain, so ingenious, was unable to keep [the others] alive'. This bald statement is followed by a comment (in which the narrator slips in and out of the point of view of the Lamb) of chilling callousness:

> In most cases [their death] did not matter, but there were some of his beasts who had become, under his terrible aegis, creatures quite superbly idiotic in their proportions. Not only so but they, having their curious interplay between the beast and human within them, gave him continued sardonic pleasure, as a dwarf provides diversion for a king.      (BiD192)

This evil, blind and bloodless Lamb (a man who has allowed the beast within to triumph) transforms other men into animals and cannot save them; they even serve him for his sport. Contrast with the loving, all-seeing Lamb of Christianity (an incarnation of the god within) whose blood was shed to save men from being beasts, and forgives them when they fall short. Peake builds his story on numerous such reversals and kaleidoscopic remixes of cultural symbols and values. To some, it verges on the blasphemous, as when Goat and Hyena address the Lamb as 'thou by whom we live and breathe and are!' (209), which echoes 'in Him we live and move and have our being' (Acts 17.28). Peake's message is rather that man's innate need for 'something to worship' (notes on *The Cave*) can inspire him with beliefs that lead him to behave worse than animals, as the countless atrocities of religious wars continue to demonstrate.

In travelling to the Lamb's domain, like the fly crawling on his bedroom ceiling, Titus merely crosses to an inverted reflection, or negative counterpart, of the typical Peake island: the depths of an abandoned mine in the midst of a sea of dust. In lieu of a beach sloping up, the ground subsides in a series of terraces; in place of the pinnacles of rock, there are the chimneys and shafts of old workings, surrounded by iron girders and chains rather than palm trees and lianas. A 'shipwreck of metal' (190),

Chimeras.

it recalls the broken metal bridges of failed attempts at communication between lovers. Does this 'shipwreck' also recall *The Tempest*? This 'island-mine' certainly echoes Caliban's 'This island's mine' (I.ii)!

Down in the pit, the Lamb's vaulted chamber with its books and carpets closely resembles the library where Mr Slaughterboard reads Shakespeare with Smear. The Lamb also treats everyone around him like animals, only he *wills* them to *become* 'beasts while they were yet men' (191). He can feel the potential in a person 'and pronounce at once the animal, the prototype that brooded, as it were, behind or within the human shape' (191). Assessing Titus's head, 'the little finger of the Lamb's left hand … like a short, white caterpillar … appeared to suck at [his] temple like the sucker of an octopus, and … left behind it from the hair-line to the chin a track or wake so cold that his brow contracted with pain'. In Titus the Lamb finds 'a thing of quality, a thing of youth and style; … a mortal unbeasted'. The effect is instantaneous – and sexual: 'a kind of covetous and fiery rash spread out beneath the wool, so that the milk-white curls appeared to be curdled, in a blush from head to feet' (213). When Titus hears that apparently 'his very bones cry out for realignment: his flesh to be reshaped; his heart to be shrivelled, and his soul to feed on fear', he is filled with 'a disembodied pain, an illness so penetrating, so horrible, that had he been given the opportunity to die he would have taken it' (212–13). Death is preferable to being turned into an animal.

Peake makes us feel the 'darkest hell of all' (212), the horror of being treated as a soul-less animal, by means of imagery (the sucker of the octopus, the slime of the snail and those curdled milk-white curls) that makes the flesh creep and turns the stomach.[6] To conclude that all this is a far cry from the honeymoon happiness of the Yellow Creature would be to miss Peake's point. Put yourself for a moment into the shell of a turtle pressed into service by a Lost Uncle, or (for that matter) the skin of a sacrificial lamb or laboratory monkey, and you will begin to appreciate his message. His ability to 'slide into another man's soul' (so memorably expressed in his talk on 'Book Illustration') enables him to empathize with the animals we torture. Making the victim human puts his message over all the more powerfully.

The blurb that Peake imagined for *Titus Groan*, reading simply, 'It is, and is not, a dream', would be apposite for this story: just as our dreams

---

6. Amazingly, this novella is currently marketed in Britain as a book for young readers.

Animal heads on human bodies.

evaporate on waking, the experience fades from Titus's mind as he staggers home. Another nightmarish dream of Peake's, a play for children that has so far passed entirely unnoticed, goes back to the biblical roots of man's relationship with animals. In *Noah's Ark* (pronounced 'Noah Sark'?) a nameless Boy falls asleep while playing with his Ark. Outside there's a rainstorm and he dreams that he is back with Noah, adding his own warning to the angel's voice that has advised Noah to build the Ark. He helps drive all the animals on board and then, with Noah's connivance, stows away with them – now that's a new way of sharing someone's island!

Hearing 'Voices' (Peake's capital) plotting 'deep down in the black hold' (PP419), the Boy warns Noah of mutiny on the Ark. The ringleaders – the Wolf, the Vulture and the Hyena – take the Boy hostage and announce their intention of killing all the humans on board so that they can be 'the natural emperors of the world' (434). The slogan 'DEATH to the human race' (435) meets with widespread approval among the animals, but just as Noah is praying for a miracle ('another voice'), the Boy shouts that he has seen the first ray of sunshine and the Dove flies in at the porthole. In the excitement of rediscovering land the animal revolution is forgotten and humanity survives – by divine intervention, or sheer luck?

With this play, Peake takes his thinking about animals to its logical conclusion: given the chance to express themselves, animals would demand equal rights on our little island in space. Aboard the Ark, they outnumber Noah and his family, who have saved them from the Flood. This gives the cowardly Vulture the courage to express his feelings about humans: 'I hate them for ruling the world. Hate them for their power' (438). The collapse of the animal revolution as the Ark beaches on Mount Ararat does not signify peace and equality on earth, despite the rainbow glimpsed through a porthole, but the return of man's domination. Now that God is so distant, what can hold man in check? Can his animal nature be muzzled?

*Titus Alone* dramatizes these questions. Early in the book, Titus looks down through a skylight at people attending a cocktail party, shortly before inadvertently dropping in on them (a vertical variation on gatecrashing). For a moment he sees nothing but animals and vegetation:

> They were all there. The giraffe-men and the hippopotamus-men. The serpent-ladies and the heron-ladies. The aspens and the oaks: the thistles and the ferns – the beetles and the moths – the crocodiles and the parrots:

the tigers and the lambs: vultures with pearls around their necks and bison
in tails.                                                                    (TA38)

Then he realizes that he is 'among his own species' after all – but some
of the men are nearly animals. One is called Kestrel, another is wearing a
lion skin, and a third, 'a narrow-chested creature with reddish hair above
his ears, a very sharp nose and a brain far too large for him to manage
with comfort' (45–46), looks like a fox. The gap between human and
animal is narrow.

The laughing of a distant hyena is heard at various moments in the
novel. Does this scavenger's bone cracking symbolize man's number-
crunching ability and propensity to tackle knotty problems with his
brain? At any rate Peake mocks the ingenious devices invented by over-
large brains to dominate and exploit the natural world – and other people.
When Titus wanders onto an airfield a pilotless 'dart' begins to circle him.
'This exquisite beast of the air; this wingless swallow; this aerial leopard;
this fish of the water-sky' has some of the characteristics of the Thing, but
it is man-made and mechanical, the 'god-like child of a diseased brain'. It
spies on people,

> sucking information as a bat sucks blood; amoral; mindless; … and having
> no heart it becomes fatuous – a fatuous reflection of a fatuous concept – so
> that it … gobbles incongruity to such an outlandish degree that laughter is
> the only way out.                                                    (TA35)

Man's desire to dominate others through information finds negative
expression in these machines, produced by brains like that of the brilliant Mr Zed, who 'turns his eyes to his wife and sees nothing but Tx¼
p¾ = ½-prx¼ (inverted)'. This is disembodied intellect at work. 'Why
don't he laugh and play?' asks Crack-Bell (123). Laughter restores our
humanity. It also celebrates the body – as when Titus and Juno fall in love
and satisfy their desire for each other, shouting with joyous laughter – but
in the world of this novel, where there is 'more darkness than light' (166),
the laughter tends to be, like Veil's, 'intolerably cold and cruel' (129).
Man's condition is no joke. Gradually, Titus finds himself 'laughing in
a different kind of way and at different things. He no longer yelled his
laughter. He no longer shouted his joy. Something had left him' (166).
Only Cheeta's attempts to use her power over him can cause 'a gale of
uncontrollable laughter' (230) once again.

Throughout this novel, Peake juxtaposes and contrasts animals, men

A late drawing of a pathetic group of waifs, human and animal.

Footfruit's dog laughs at him as he takes a rest.

and machines. One day, the three vagrants from the Under-River, Crabcalf, Slingshott and Crack-Bell, who are following Titus for the crumbs that they hope will fall their way, picnic on a stolen turkey. Just over the hill, 'the belly-brained … jackals and foxes' are similarly at work on a carcass. Overhead passes a flight of planes in search of Titus, 'like coloured gnats emerging from the night'. At once, 'the jackals lift their vile muzzles. Slingshott, Crabcalf, and Crack-Bell lift theirs' (178). They are all scavengers: foxes, jackals, parasites and information-sucking drones alike. Then come the dreaded helmeteers in whose gaze is 'such a world of scorn that Crabcalf and his two trembling pards felt an icy blast against their bodies' (179). They hear 'a growl as the teeth of one of the jackals met in the centre of some dead brute's intestines, and at that sound the tall pair turned upon their heels, and moved away' (178). The jackals leave too, 'for nothing was left on the bones of the poor dead beast. Like a canopy the countless flies hung over the skeleton as though to form a veil or shawl of mourning' (179). Only the natural world shows respect; the heartless gnat-like planes cannot form a 'shawl of mourning' as insects do.

Like Mr Slaughterboard, Muzzlehatch behaves brutishly towards other men, so Titus sees 'no reason why he should obey, like a dog to the whistle' (TA26), as Smear does. Like the Lost Uncle, Muzzlehatch has turned from human society to live with animals, becoming a 'lord of the fauna' (157). Under his benevolent care, his private zoo seems ideal, another miracle of creation, the sunlight falling on it 'like a gold gauze':

> the bars of the cages were like rods of gold, and the animals and birds were flattened by the bright slanting rays, so that they seemed cut out of coloured cardboard or from the pages of some book of beasts. (24)

Gold or no gold, the bars are real. It is no fairy tale to live in a cage, as Peake shows by bringing in other cages. Inspector Acreblade, for instance, thinks of Titus as 'some kind of caged animal' (63). Black Rose was literally caged in a prison camp. 'One night they took her naked from her bed' (125) and tortured her with 'whips and burning stubs' (126) to the point where 'sometimes she did not know whether it was herself or someone else who screamed' (125). Veil, a guard, exploits her there, feeding her extra bread through the bars. 'And how you barked for more,' he sneers (127). He lords it over her, revealing the abyss of inhumanity that separates him from Muzzlehatch.

Humans are at their worst when they lord it over each other. Like Swift in his 'Modest Proposal', Peake uses cannibalism to express his disgust at man's exploitation of man – and women. Looking at Cheeta's legs, an old man observes, 'They'd go down very nice, with onion sauce' (206–07). In Swift, it's 'with a little pepper or salt' (NAEL 1: 2745). To ensure that we sympathize with the victim, rather than dismissing such comments as jest or even expressions of love, Peake has Tintagieu respond to Thorpe, 'Very nice for me, I suppose' when he says, 'Oh, Tanty, I could eat you!' (MP71). Blood-sucking predators serve a similar purpose in Peake's ironical evocation of London businessmen:

> It's not their fault if, in the heat
> Of their transactions, I repeat
> It's not their fault if vampires meet
> And gurgle in their spats.
>                           (BN65)

So it may be that Muzzlehatch's name implies that in him at least this animal appetite is kept in check: his mouth (as in phrases like 'down the hatch') is muzzled.

Muzzlehatch's humanity makes him vulnerable. After the scientists have vaporized his animals with their death ray, he is 'lord of nothing', 'no longer balanced or entire' (157). He decides to destroy their head-quarters, which turns out to be situated in Cheeta's father's factory. This is another vast cage, a 'ghastly hive of horror' (199), where the scientists 'lived or partly lived in cells, sealed from the light of day' (157),[7] doing unmentionable things to pitiful creatures who can only whimper, 'No, no, no! I want to *live*. I want to *live*. Give me a little longer' (204; Peake's emphasis; the phrasing echoes Marlowe's *Edward II*). The hive metaphor links the factory with the masquerade at the Black House, which was

> a thing like a honeycomb which Cheeta alone apprehended in its entirety, for she was no drone; but author and soul of the hive. The insects, though they worked themselves to death, saw nothing but their own particular cells.
>                                                                            (200)

As the masquerade collapses, Muzzlehatch's time bomb destroys the factory, killing hundreds of prisoners for whom it means an end to pain and torture. For Peake this is euthanasia, an act of compassion, it being

---

7. The chorus in T.S. Eliot's play, *Murder in the Cathedral*, repeats 'living and partly living'.

better to die than to be reduced to a barking animal. 'That would be the last roar of the golden fauna' (247), says Muzzlehatch as the bomb goes off, linking the destruction of his storybook zoo with the death of the Lost Uncle's White Lion. Although he is introduced as 'a man of small compassion, hurtful, brazen and loveless' (TA17), Muzzlehatch remains a man of heart, for all his imbalance of mind. Dangling the hated scientist at arm's length like a malodorous object, he declares, 'It's beastly and it's alive' (250), and tosses him to Cheeta. He cannot kill in cold blood.

Muzzlehatch is an idealist, treating his animals as 'the natural emperors of the world' (PP434). He hopes that by feeding them a suitable diet (such as giving 'fruit and onions' to the camel and the mule), by cleaning out their cages 'with pearl-handled spades' and protecting them from 'the carnivores and the bow-legged eagle' (24), he can make the lion lie down with the lamb. But keeping them in cages annuls all his hopes. They continue to nourish 'the evil of jealousy' (PP407) that the Boy warns Noah of aboard the Ark and that leads to hate and murderous rage, as demonstrated by the Wolf at Titus's tenth birthday masque. One day a mule and a camel escape from their cages and fight. 'Stark naked except for a fireman's helmet' (23) – that is, reduced to man as arbiter among animals – Muzzlehatch separates them with a fire hose, and sends them steaming with animal heat back to their cages. As they go, the narrator wonders 'What was going on in those two skulls?' and speculates that perhaps they felt 'some kind of pleasure that after so many years of incarceration they had at last been able to vent their ancient malice, and plunge their teeth into the enemy' (24). As we saw earlier, imprisonment may reinforce faults rather than reform them. 'Anything but embarrassed' the camel and the mule swagger with 'indescribable arrogance' (25), making the other animals madly jealous:

> If hatred could have killed them they would have expired a hundred times on the way to their cages. The silence was like breath held at the ribs.
> And then it broke, for a shrill scream pierced the air like a splinter, and the monkey, whose voice it was, shook the bars of its cage with hands and feet in an access of jealousy so that the iron rattled as the scream went on and on and on, while other voices joined it and reverberated through the prisons so that every kind of animal became a part of bedlam.          (25)

Caging brings out the worst in living creatures, and Peake's use of 'prisons' and 'bedlam' show that he had man in mind, quite as much as animals. Although the fault lies with Muzzlehatch's method and not his 'inordinate friends', he reproaches the camel and the mule for their atavism.

'Oh, the ingratitude!' he exclaims. 'Unregenerate and vile! So you broke loose on me, did you – and *reverted*' (24; Peake's emphasis).

Nevertheless, Peake does show animals behaving better than humans. During the construction of the scenery for Cheeta's parody of Gormenghast at the Black House, 'scores of small forest animals' forget 'their tribal feuds' and follow everything with their eyes and ears, 'forming a scattered circle of flesh and blood' (TA215), a phrase generally reserved for human family relationships. Conversely, the party guests – 'glittering beauties' and 'glittering horrors' – are 'arrayed like humming birds' and have tongues that 'flicker' (217). As the masquerade degenerates, they turn upon each other, the women 'striking out at their husbands or their lovers' (249) and among the men 'chivalry … lost itself in a swarm of knees and elbows' (256) – the *swarm* recalling bees and gnats. Meanwhile, among the assembled animals who are still looking on in astonishment, there was 'an understanding that they left one another alone, until dawn, so that the birds of prey sat side by side with doves and owls, the foxes with the mice' (244). The wild animals naturally achieve what Muzzlehatch could not and set an example of 'civilization' to the glitterati (who are too busy fighting to notice).

Throughout this novel, Peake uses 'beastly' to qualify human behaviour, particularly in the context of sexual relations. He starts with comedy: at the cocktail party, Mrs Grass, who does not recognize her ex-husband in a lion skin, addresses him as the 'King of Beasts' (46). Then Black Rose calls Veil (her ex-jailor, lover and tormentor) a beast – 'Kill the beast,' she whispers (130). Finally Cheeta, who loses all human dignity in this novel, screams at Titus, 'You *beast*. … You ungrateful *beast*' (173; Peake's emphasis). When she realizes that he does not love her, she wants 'absolute revenge'. 'Beast, beast, beast!' she repeats. 'Go back to your filthy den. Go back to your Gormenghast!' (184). At the climax, she reiterates, 'You beast! Bloody beast!' (252). The irony is heavy here, for she has clawed Titus with her nails and made his neck bleed; reproaching him for what she has done, she acts worse than the beast whose name she bears.

Depicting characters who deny their animal nature at the same time as wanting an animal partner on their island brought Peake face to face with man's animal nature. Then the reality principle led him to throw off Paley's chain. As the Vulture tells the Boy on Noah's Ark, 'Deep down inside you are one of us' (PP411). So long as we neglect our self-awareness and prey on other people, he is right. Only when we strive for 'more than material things' (PP69) and allow our souls to love, and appreciate beauty, do we rise above our animality.

# Love

I must begin to classify
My loves, because of my
Disorganized desire to live
Before it's time to die. (BN82)

A planet lit a cheekbone and revealed a tear.
(TA258)

A tear … the loveliest emblem of the heart's
condition. (G337)

Lord Sepulchrave 'mourns through each languid
gesture, each fine-boned feature, as though his
body were glass and at its centre his inverted
heart like a pendant tear.' (G8)

P EAKE WAS UNTIRING IN his search for a cure to man's essential isolation. Islands are by definition separate, and animal companions no
solution. So he hoped that rather as God's love used to hold the universe
together, so human love might soothe the lonely soul and join the
sundered islands. Beside solitude, love is the main theme of his work.
The end of *Titus Groan* proclaims that 'love itself will cry for insurrection!' (506); the end of *Gormenghast* sees Titus fulfil the prediction by
rejecting his inheritance and leaving the castle. The third volume recounts
his fruitless quest for love.

In English we make the word *love* work pretty hard. It is what we call
our feeling for our place of birth, our home and our country, our favourite

foods, colours, sensations and perceptions, books, music, pictures and other cultural artefacts, what we feel for animals, children, parents and siblings, for close friends and a potential life partner, for a spouse, for God and, so we are told, what He feels for us. Peake writes about almost all of them, in one way or another.

Let us begin at the beginning. In 'Grottoed beneath Your Ribs Our Babe Lay Thriving', Peake offers his newborn son comforting reassurance:

> O little island, sleep or wake,
> What though the darkening gusts divide your mother's
> Rich continent
> From all you are, yet there's a sacrament
> Of more than marl shall make you one another's.
>
> (Gb4–5)

That more than material sacrament is love. Following the irreparable separation of birth, he would reassure his child that love can unite him with his mother.

However, in the 'economics' of Peake's world, the demand for love always exceeds supply; his characters, like Juno in *Titus Alone*, regularly 'run out of love' (TA67). When the Countess *empties* a look of love at one of her birds (TG113), the dead metaphor might pass unnoticed, but it recurs in Nannie Slagg's mouth: having lavished her love on Fuchsia and Titus, she complains that she has 'poured it all away until [she is] hollowed out' (TG486). The paucity of human love underlines the emptiness caused by God's absence. Moreover, the equation of love is for ever unbalanced. Those who hand out much love expect to receive equal quantities in return; they are invariably disappointed, for people have no more love to give than they have received in the past. That is, those who get but little love as children prove to have little to give when they grow up.

Even maternal love is in short supply; Peake's mothers are shadowy figures, often absent or dead. Mr Slaughterboard's mother died when he was three, for instance. Peake's most developed mother figure, the Countess of Groan, seems utterly heartless, almost like a wicked stepmother out of a fairy tale, for her 'maternal instincts' are 'shockingly absent' (G44), but she is not actively cruel. She merely loves animals more than humans. In this she is like many other Peake characters who love objects that cannot reciprocate. One thinks of Titus and the Thing, of course, but also of

'"Were you happy in prison, dear child?" said Haigha. Hatta looked round once more, and this time a tear or two trickled down his cheek.' Haigha and Hatta from Peake's *Through the Looking-Glass*.

Pentecost, the gardener, with his apple trees, Lord Sepulchrave with his library, Rottcodd with his Hall of Bright Carvings, and Fuchsia with her attic. The Countess's heart is 'awakened to tenderness only by her birds and her white cats' (TG415), which she treats like people, reading fairy tales to the cats as she would to a child (TG297–98). Being ordinary animals (and not anthropomorphosized creatures), the birds and cats do not love her in return. Appropriately then (and scandalously by all conventional expectations), her eyes take on a 'concentrated, loveless, cat-like look' at the moment when Nannie Slagg brings her newborn son to her (TG57).

She is equally indifferent to her daughter Fuchsia, having lost patience with her even before she was five years old because she 'used to ram the flowers into the vases and bruise the stalks' (TG399). As a metaphor, this applies equally to the Countess's treatment of other people, for she leaves them feeling bruised. After Fuchsia's life is cut off in the bloom of youth, the Countess seems concerned only for the physical comfort of her corpse.

> The face of the Countess showed nothing, but once she drew the corner of the sheet up a little further over Fuchsia's shoulder, with an infinite gentle-ness, as though she feared her child might feel the cold and so must take the risk of waking her.          (G462)

This tenderness contrasts with her insensitivity to the feelings of the living. Titus also is paying his last respects to Fuchsia: 'mother and son stood side by side in worlds of their own. ... Neither knew nor cared what was going on in the breast of the other' (462). Like mother, like son. As love engenders love, so indifference breeds indifference.

To the infant Titus the Countess herself might as well be dead for all the mothering she does. At his birth she declares, 'I would like to see the boy when he is six' (TG61), and indeed she sees him only 'seven times in seven years' (G12). She has but two projects for the role she intends to play in his life, and she fulfils neither of them. She plans to tell Titus, when he is old enough to understand her instructions, 'how to keep his head quite clear of the duties he is to perform' (TG399). She even promises her birds that she will take Titus under her wing: 'Within four days the Earling – and then I'll take him, babe and boy' (TG477). But she doesn't. She proposes to 'teach him how to whistle birds out of the sky' (TG398) when he is 12 years old. On the chosen day, she orders him to take a walk with her. 'Yes, mother', he answers, at which 'a shadow settled for a moment on her brow' for 'the word *mother* had perplexed her'. She is so completely detached that she does not think of herself as his mother – but she has to admit that 'the boy was quite right, of course' (G315). In the event, the lesson is interrupted by the whistling of the Thing, and never taken up again. Only once does the ice melt in her eyes: after Titus, aged 16, has killed Steerpike, 'a kind of beauty' comes over her face and she casts – not upon Titus but upon the whole scene below her window – 'that look which she reserved, unknowingly, for a bird with a broken wing, or a thirsty animal' (G500).

Lord Sepulchrave and the Countess are unable to relate to each other with pleasure; she has 'never loved' him (TG413); their union has been 'passionless' and 'embarrassing yet fertile' (TG204–05). In Peake's work marriage typically ends in indifference, and often in death. Barquentine coldly recalls having been married at one time; 'he assumed that [his wife] had died' (G267). Not even Nannie Slagg escapes the blight. Revealing that her husband died on the very night of their wedding, she adds, 'and no wonder' (TG465), as though accepting that death were the natural consequence of marriage. In 'Danse Macabre', an estranged couple are brought back together by supernatural forces, but they are truly united only on the last page, together in their marital bed, dead. After years of indifference, the marriage of Lord and Lady Groan ends with his suicide.

As unloving parents, they are much alike. Lord Sepulchrave's estrangement from his wife never grieves him (TG205) and he has no idea how to show his children his affection for them. The birth of an heir stirs the need to express love, but he is too out of practice to know how to go about it. When he reflects on what he is going to teach Titus, he wants to 'instil in his veins … a love of his birthplace and his heritage, and a respect for all the written and unwritten laws' (TG228). He says nothing of loving other people, not even of the old injunction to 'honour thy father and thy mother'.

It takes the destruction of Lord Sepulchrave's beloved library to jolt him into speaking tenderly to Fuchsia, causing 'a warm jet of love' to flow within her for 'she had never before heard that tone of love in his voice' (TG345). For the first time she feels that she has a father (347). But he cannot sustain the impulse and wonders pathetically, in Peake's most Shakespearean phraseology, 'Why break the heart that never beat from love? We do not know, sweet girl' (427). As he sinks into madness and 'the last tides are mounting' (402) around his island, her 'frozen love' for him 'that was beginning to thaw' congeals again. Even when their mutual love is most needed, they cannot reach out to each other (366). Like an undersea creature, their love surfaces, breathes once and then returns to the depths. In his madness, Lord Sepulchrave takes the Gormenghast owls for his natural companions and joins them in the Tower of Flints, hoping to find it 'lined with love' (427), but he is clawed and pecked to death, the victim of his own misdirected love.

Peake knows how we all need parental figures and that, in the absence of attentive parents, children seek surrogates. As Lord Sepulchrave plays no paternal role in Fuchsia's life, Dr Prunesquallor and Mr Flay replace him in her affections. The doctor loves her 'as though she were his own daughter' but he generally leaves the initiative to her and makes few attempts to seek her out (G335). Understanding her feelings of rejection and jealousy on the occasion of her brother's birth, he gives her a large ruby pendant and helps her 'with words well chosen and thoughts simple and direct that touched deftly on the areas of her sorrow' (TG483). During the Dark Breakfast, he and Fuchsia have their little fingers 'interlocked under the table' (TG389). He even dreams of her and in a nightmare anticipates her drowning, floundering after her and stretching out his hand as she sinks (G196). He loves to put her at her ease – as when he pulls down a curtain and drapes it around himself (G189–90) – and she appreciates this, knowing too how he loves his clowning. For all his facetiousness, though, Dr Prunesquallor both feels and communicates his love. Paying his last respects to Fuchsia, he briefly touches the arm of 'the brother of his favourite child' and then he wipes his eyes and peers at his glasses 'with that kind of concentration that is grief' (G462). By contrasting his behaviour at this moment with the Countess's, Peake ensures that we realize how he loved Fuchsia – and cared – far more than her mother ever did.

As Lord Sepulchrave's personal servant, Flay was the closest man to Fuchsia's father and in many ways most like him, solitary and taciturn. In fact, with his dry body and insect-like movements, he must have been something of an animal companion, like a cricket in the hearth. He too loves Fuchsia. Handicapped by his uncommunicative nature as well as by his status as a servant, he never quite manages to show his affection for her, which yet 'was something quite alone in his sour life' (G358). After he has been banished from the castle, he misses Fuchsia 'more than he had imagined possible' (TG442). Only then, when he is rarely to be glimpsed, does she acknowledge his affection and love him for it (G191). His warning to her, murmured from the lintel over the door to Steerpike's secret lair (G452), echoes the Doctor's words: 'Be careful!' (TG483). Having played a paternal role in protecting her, Flay fails to look after himself and dies impaled by Steerpike's deadly throwing knife.

Because Fuchsia's parents take no active part in her upbringing (not even giving negative attention, like the Lost Uncle's parents strapping him down in his cradle), her old nurse Nannie Slagg substitutes for her mother. In her, Peake jokingly evokes the devouring mother: '"Babies?" said Mrs Slagg. … "I could eat the little darlings, sir, I could eat them up!"' (TG74). Fuchsia loves her dearly, for all her petulance and childishness, and the naturalistic expressions of both tenderness and rejection in their relationship are signs that Peake took it seriously. The most eloquent scene comes when Fuchsia notices that Mrs Slagg has a piteous expression on her face and gives her a hug but inadvertently squeezes too hard, hurting 'the wrinkled midget'; so she allows her nannie the petty triumph of a slap on her hand by way of punishment (TG293–94). But as in all Peake's relationships, communicating love is problematic: Fuchsia leaves a loving message for Mrs Slagg on her bedroom wall, but the old woman never looks at it (TG291). Similarly, public demonstration of love seems impossible. When she sees Mrs Slagg lying like a discarded doll on her deathbed, she is as awkward as her mother: 'it was in Fuchsia to take the beloved relic in her arms in a passion of love, but she could not' (G185).

Titus finds himself similarly placed: he is a year old when his father dies; his wet-nurse commits suicide at about the same time, and he is neglected by his mother. Of course Nannie Slagg's heart goes out to him and as his surrogate mother she protests, 'How could they, how *could* they!' (G13 and 185; Peake's emphasis). Unlike Fuchsia, he finds no father substitute, although both Bellgrove and Dr Prunesquallor pity him, for his life is destined to be a round of ritual and duty. Peake writes a whole page, characteristic of his dual response of hope and disappointment, about how boys can love their schoolmasters, trusting their lovable weakness – 'for what is more lovable than failure?' – and he deplores that it is not in Titus to love Bellgrove, despite his 'fondness and inexplicable respect' for him (G152–53).

Flay plays a briefly significant role in Titus's life. They meet when Titus discovers him fishing on the opposite bank of the river. To join him he has to walk half a mile upstream to the 'perfect ford' (G138) that Flay has made. Had we not already seen crossing water as a metaphor for the difficulty of making loving contact with another person, the significance of this scene for Peake might have been lost upon us. Thanks to Flay's constructive effort, Titus crosses easily and falls into his arms. Thereafter, although they meet rarely, Flay serves as a role model for him. Their relationship climaxes with the unmasking of Steerpike, which ends with Flay's death. So Titus grows up 'virtually an orphan' (G413), much like a classic nineteenth-century hero or heroine. Readers accustomed to such novels will expect his solitude to be cured by love, and to some extent his feeling for the Thing fulfils this purpose, but not for long. Peake's fictional world offers no superficial consolations.

Growing up in Gormenghast owes more to Calvin's Christianity than to Margaret Mead's New Guinea, for 'it was the pride of the Groans that their childhood was no time of cotton wool' (G306). In fact, none of the inhabitants of the castle seems to have had a happy childhood that they might wish to replicate for the next generation. Barquentine's youth is typical in having been 'dark and loveless' (G265). Only Flay has a bright childhood memory to cherish: one sunshine-filled morning 'a giant in gold' (presumably the then Lord Groan) gave him an apple. It has remained for him 'a vignette of crimson, gold and grey' in a life that had otherwise been 'hard, grinding and monotonous'; all his other memories are associated with 'fears and troubles and hardships'. He seems to have no memory even of having had parents; in his sole happy vignette he is accompanied by an anonymous 'guardian' (TG415). Understandably, then, 'it was not often that Flay approved of happiness in others. He saw in happiness the seeds of independence' (TG26). And in the ritual-bound castle, independence is tantamount to revolt.

As Titus grows up, he gradually discovers his sister's love. It's a long time coming because no one thought to prepare Fuchsia for the birth of a sibling. Peake writes perceptively of her sense of being supplanted as the sole offspring of her parents (TG95) and her difficulty in accepting her little brother. 'Why do you love him?' she asks of Mrs Slagg, who naturally cannot offer a rational answer (TG272). It takes years for her feelings of rivalry to give way to love, although she sometimes plays with Titus for half an hour or so at a time when he is a little baby. Only after his first escapade, when he is aged seven or eight, do they finally share their hunger for affection, declare their love for each other and celebrate by spitting into the morning sun (G145). Thereafter, they support each other faithfully, although Fuchsia's relationship with Steerpike comes between them. Then Flay is killed and she realizes what kind of man has been wooing her. This numbs her emotions:

'I love you, Titus, but I can't feel anything. I've gone dead. Even you are
dead in me. I know I love you. You're the only one I love, but I can't feel
anything and I don't want to. I've felt too much, I'm sick of feelings … I'm
frightened of them.'                                                    (G397)

Of all the characters in Gormenghast, Fuchsia is the most loving and
the most needful of love, but her life is blighted by lack of fulfilment on
both counts. At first, as she 'never had either positive cruelty or kindness
shown to her by her parents … she was not conscious of what it was
she missed' (TG271). When she realizes, her yearning for love becomes
as urgent as Titus's desire for freedom (G397). Peake compares her to 'a
dusky orchard [that] had never been discovered. … No travellers came
and rested in [its] shade nor tasted the sweet fruit' (G452), which delicately suggests both the spiritual and the physical aspects of the love relationship that she is deprived of. (Steerpike greedily consumes a pear that
she has nibbled and left in her attic, just as he would have raided her
orchard, if given the chance.) After she has learned the truth about Steerpike and most needs comfort, she has no one to turn to, for the flood
disrupts their lives. Her mother, to whom she would never have turned
anyway, is masterminding the retreat from floor to floor, and Dr Prunesquallor, 'who would have left the world bleeding to help her' (G452), is
too busy to see her. Then the melancholia that racked her father comes
to the fore and her thoughts turn to suicide. In the event, her death is
accidental; she falls from her bedroom window, 'striking her dark head
on the sill as she passed, and [so she] was already unconscious before the
water received her, and drowned her at its ease' (G454). This moment,
if no other, brings it home to the reader how much the Titus books are
about love, the need both to give and to receive love, and the terrible
consequences of leaving those needs unsatisfied. Although love may not
enable us to share our respective islands, without it we are likely to drown
in a sea of indifference.

The intensity of Fuchsia's frustrated love may be gauged by her first
words in *Titus Groan*: 'Oh how I hate! hate! hate! How I *hate* people!
Oh how I *hate* people' (TG52; Peake's emphases). As Mr Pye observes,
'Hatred is very close to love' (MP161). For Peake, hatred is born when
natural love is withheld or thwarted, and sustained by the absence of
love. In *Mr Pye*, Miss Dredger's ungenerous refusal to allow the lame Miss
George take a short cut across the corner of her property is the source of
their mutual hatred. It takes all Mr Pye's skill to persuade the two women
to live under the same roof, for sometimes Miss Dredger's 'heart would

fail her and she would stiffen with resentment' (MP52). In the end, he himself fails: at the sight of his wings Miss George dies falling down the stairs. In Peake's work, human love is no more powerful than hate.

The crippled dwarf Barquentine, who has all that's bad and frightening in Long John Silver and none of the attractive or good, loves the castle's law 'with a love as hot as his hate' (G266). As a child he was the 'target for jibes and scorn' (268) and bullying, his crutch kicked from beneath him. Once he becomes Master of Ritual, he behaves in a similar manner towards others, making himself 'feared and hated' (268), especially by Steerpike and Titus (G169). In all Gormenghast no sound 'could strike so chill against the heart' as the crash of his crutch on the flagstones 'like a whip-crack, an oath, a slash across the face of mercy' (158). He has a son, unseen for 40 years. 'All he remembered was that a birthmark took up most of the face and that the eyes were crossed' (268). Barquentine bullies Steerpike instead, who as his assistant and successor usurps a role that rightfully belongs to the neglected son (whom Peake seems to have forgotten about too!). Steerpike is jibed, scorned, 'spat upon and reviled by the withered cripple' (269), just as Barquentine was as a boy. We even start to sympathize with Steerpike at this point, so that when he is about to kill Barquentine we know full well why hatred should sweep across his face 'as though a frozen sea were whipped of a sudden into a living riot of tameless water' (270). After Fuchsia's 'frozen love' for her father, the image of ice confirms that Steerpike has lived unloved. (Peake tells nothing of his first 16 years.) Swelter's scornful jibes are the springboard for his career.

Fire and ice regularly serve Peake as metaphorical extremes in the need for balance. As a symbol of civilized restraint, ice separates the Lost Uncle from the sea creatures that prey on one another. But as we have just seen, too much icy restraint leads to heartless indifference. Fire has a similar dual significance, being the expression of both love and hatred. Peake evokes love in images of fire and burning, as in

> The vastest things are those we may not learn.
> We are not taught to die, nor to be born,
> Nor how to burn
> With love.
>
> (Gb14)

The image is there again, mixed with snow this time, when he evokes a chance encounter with a girl carrying 'An Armful of Roses':

> I turned to look again, and as I turned
> She turned a little also, so that something burned,
> Something of fire that mixed itself with snow
> In a great whorl of exquisite heat and cold.
>
> (P&D)

In love-making the 'qualms of love' lead to conception and 'set fire the nine-month burden' (Gb4). Typically, Peake reverses tenor and vehicle at the end of *The Rhyme of the Flying Bomb*, making the fire literal (with a hint of the orgasmic) and the love spiritual and symbolic: the sailor and the babe decide to make the flying bomb fall on themselves, that they might 'explode in one flash of love' (PP460) and prevent the suffering of others.

Throughout Peake's work, fire is also the primary expression of hatred. In his earliest known poem, 'The Touch o' the Ash', a sea captain throws a sailor into the ship's furnace, only to be killed by the wraith that rises from the ashes. Arson plays a major role in the Titus books. An anonymous young man's 'thwarted passions [find] vent after thirty years of indecision' (G75) in setting the old philosopher's beard ablaze. His inability to express his need in a loving way is revealed by his eyes which (ironically) 'made a tremendous effort to flash; but either the tinder was wet or the updraught insufficient, for they remained peculiarly sparkless' (74). This youth disappears at once and is never heard of again. Steerpike, on the other hand, starts two fires and stays around to reap the benefits. First he burns the library, which results in the death of Sourdust. Then he tries to kill Barquentine by setting fire to his beard, but the old cripple is too quick for him; with his own clothes ablaze, Steerpike has to leap into the moat to save himself. Fire expresses both love and the consequence of lack of love, hatred.

F OR A CHAPTER ON love, we are seeing a great deal of hatred and death – for that is Peake's world. In his heart he knows that love cannot move an island back to the bay created by its separation from the mother continent, and this leaves him feeling 'gulfed in a failure of love' (Gb37). So he depicts it as eminently fragile, soon ended by death or disappointment, and associates tears, salty like the surrounding sea, with the heart. Love cannot overcome strong negative feelings: the rivalry between Keda's lovers, Braigon and Rantel; the long-standing feud, born of resentment, between Flay and Swelter; and the conflict between Titus and Veil in the Under-River – each ends with a duel in which four of these characters are killed. The 'sacrament' of love that 'shall' make us one another's is highly to be desired, essentially fallible and ultimately unobtainable.

However, Peake would not be human if he did not hope against all hope that romantic love might bring an end to isolation. For him it is a moment of light and colour in a life that is otherwise dull and drab. This is epitomized by the Bright Carvers who love with great intensity, but their passion is as ephemeral as their beauty; after the age of 20 or so their lives are devoted to sculpture in a climate of bitterness and jealousy (TG15, G430). In the castle, only Irma seems to have enjoyed any kind of romance, and that was singularly short-lived: a man named Spog-frawne (a spoonerism of 'frogspawn' – what *did* Peake have in mind?) sent her passionate letters on tissue paper. Such was the power of his feelings that his pen went straight through the paper, and she could not read the purple passages. (Perhaps he was related to Lord Sepulchrave's favourite poet, 'Andrema, the lyricist – the lover – he whose quill would pulse as he wrote and fill with a blush of blue, like a bruised nail' (TG347).) When she asked him to repeat his effusions on ordinary paper, he stopped writing. End of romance.

It's no better for Fuchsia: early in *Titus Groan*, before she has met Steerpike, she dreams of a man with a long black cloak, 'strong like a lion and with yellow hair like a lion's', who will fall in love with her at first sight and (ominously) 'he'll enjoy having me because of my pride' (TG146). Such innocent romanticism, and her deep need for love, make her a perfect victim for Steerpike. At Sourdust's funeral, she quite unconsciously makes 'a motion of recognition, of friendliness' to him, for in a castle singularly devoid of young people 'she only knew that the figure across the grave was young' (TG339). In her eyes he is brave, having rescued her and her family from the library fire. Little does she realize that from the moment of their first meeting in her attic, he is coldly assessing her needs and feeding back to her a precise simulacrum of what she wants – the black cloak, the rosebud on the dressing table (G25), and the secret trysts. It's like adding up accounts – with her death as the bottom line.

Steerpike's self-serving imitation of love is particularly revolting; 'his every sentence, every thought, every action was ulterior', whereas she 'lived in the moment of excitement. ... She had no instinct of self-preservation' (G344). His behaviour towards her is pure hypocrisy, for he detests love (G350). He counterfeits 'that complete companionship, that harmony of mind and spirit – that sense of confidence, of which she had been so starved'. Worse, he knows that 'she was starved of more than this.

He knew her life had been loveless' (G343) and so he says things like, 'I love you Fuchsia. You are all I ever longed for' (G355). He claims to love her 'as the shadows love the castle' (G356) and the image is apt: shadows have no identity of their own; they vary with the angle of the light and the shape of the objects illumined. Fortunately, Peake ends their relationship before Steerpike can execute his plan to seduce or rape her and then blackmail her, for 'with so dark a secret … she would be at his mercy'. By having him think that this is 'no time for mercy' (G357), Peake leaves little doubt in our minds that Steerpike would indeed have enjoyed 'having her' if he had not caused Flay to intervene so opportunely.

The only romance that Peake depicts without irony is between Titus and Juno. Centred in the body, 'a game of the fantastic senses; febrile; tender, tip-tilted' that 'set their pulses racing' (TA88), it evolves in a typically Peakean cosmic context. His lovers experience each other not just as a new world to be discovered and explored (as in John Donne), but a whole 'universe over whose boundaries … they had not [yet] dared to venture' (88). Thus, 'when they said "Hullo!" new stars appeared in the sky; when they laughed, this wild world split its sides' (88). Predictably, sound plays quite as important a part as touch and sight: they are 'sometimes happy to talk – sometimes basking in a miraculous silence' (88), and ever 'trembling at the sound of each other's footsteps' (89). It is a fragile, ephemeral experience, 'something that will always melt away' (89).

As we might expect, the one love affair in the Titus books that leads to marriage opens with pure slapstick and ends in pathos. The initial situation between Irma Prunesquallor and Bellgrove is classic comedy material: at relatively late stages in life each is looking for a partner. Neither realizes – or is willing to face the possibility – that their heart has already been singled out as 'the ultimate quarry' (to borrow a phrase from MP49), so that they are primed to fall in love on first meeting. Peake narrates their brief courtship with bitter relish, pointing to the self-deception required by romantic love, the rationalizing of purely emotional motives, and the manoeuvres to entrap the other. With his tongue in his cheek he celebrates the glorious moment when 'the clocks of the world stand still, or should have done' (G224) and the cosmic exaltation of falling in love, 'the glory of standing with one's love, naked, as it were, on a spinning marble, while the spheres [run] flaming through the universe!' (243). (For all its irony, this statement places Peake's 'vastation', expressed in 'Walking along the

Open Road' (SP36), in a new and positive frame.) The tone makes their relationship one of the humorous highlights of *Gormenghast*.

As neither Bellgrove nor Irma has any practice in the art of seduction, their beliefs about the opposite sex are purely theoretical and highly generalized. According to Irma, 'every woman knows' that a man is 'a mere tag-end of a thing until the distaff side has stitched him together' (222), and their notions of courtship are sometimes nightmarishly funny and thoroughly unromantic. Irma's body language, for instance, has no word for 'subtle'. As Bellgrove tastes 'love's rare aperitif, the ageless language of the eyes', he discovers in Irma's eyes 'so hot and wet a succubus of love as threatened to undermine her marble temple and send its structure toppling' (232–33). Nor does Peake depart from his belief that the most intimate of meetings take place in the depths of the sea: hearing a gurgle from Irma's hot-water-bottle-bosom, Bellgrove assumes that it 'must have been a sign of love, of some strange and aqueous love that was beyond his sounding' (253). Indeed, with Irma he is quite out of his depth.

Sometimes Peake's irony and comic distance suggest that he borrowed an idea or two from Byron, particularly in the use of bathos. Irma's smile, for instance: 'She played with it for a moment or two, like an angler with a fish, and then she let it set like concrete' (223). And here's Bellgrove imagining the comforts of married life:

> He thought of cushions and of bedroom slippers. He thought of socks of long ago with heels to their name. He even thought of flowers in a vase.
>     Then he thought of Irma again.                                        (G200)

The subjective selection of referents, the reiterated verbal structure with just a hint of rhyme (name/again), and the unexpected shift in the fresh paragraph all recall the techniques that make the first canto of *Don Juan* so comic:

> And then he thought of earthquakes, and of wars,
> How many miles the moon might have in girth,
>     Of air balloons, of the many bars
> To perfect knowledge of the boundless skies;
> And then he thought of Donna Julia's eyes.
>                         (Canto 1, st. 92; NAEL 2: 634)

Those slippers, like the shoes that betray Don Juan's presence in Donna Julia's bedroom, may also remind us that although Peake abstains from explicit reference to sex in *Gormenghast* (excepting that moment when

Titus wants to *kiss* the Thing, of course), his descriptions are suffused with awareness of it. Irma's garden, for instance, is thoroughly eroticized, 'a place of mosses and ferns and little flowers that opened at odd hours during the night. Little miniature grottos had been made for them to twinkle in' (202). Her brother cannot bear it, of course; he crosses the garden with his eyes shut. It is a perfect venue for Irma's first tryst with Bellgrove and also – by way of contrast, but no less comic – the scene of poor Professor Throd's naked flight, which recalls Don Juan's nocturnal flight, in the same state of undress, from his tryst with Donna Julia (Canto 1, st. 186–88). Peake's scene, however, caps Byron's, for 'the last that was ever seen of Mr Throd … was a lunar flash of buttocks where the high wall propped the sky' (255), making this probably the first instance in English literature (and possibly the sole instance, for all I know) of streaking followed by mooning. Byron would have envied that.

As we might expect, Bellgrove and Irma come down to earth with bitter disappointment when they face the drear reality of married life together. Underlying Peake's portrayal of them is pity rather than cruelty, and the final scenes are full of pathos. At the last he leaves them staring at a small grey pattern in the shape of a heart on the plaster of their old attic; their love 'is no longer green' (451); it has gone grey, cold, and rigid like a corpse. Romance has failed them.

Peake has ambiguous feelings about that dreaded f-word, *failure*. In love

> The bitter
> Knowledge of failure damns us where we stand
> Withdrawn, lonely, powerless, and
> Hand in hand.
>
> (Gb10)

but it will be noticed that although it makes the lovers feel lonely, it does create a sense of community: they stand 'hand in hand'. This aspect of failure is most evident in the 'conclave of the displaced' (TA132) in the Under-River – Peake's only instance of social solidarity. The inhabitants of 'two great cities that faced one another across the river' do their best to ignore or forget that below their feet there exists a counterpart to their society, peopled by all

> the failures of earth. The beggars, the harlots, the cheats, the refugees, the scatterlings, the wasters, the loafers, the bohemians, the black sheep, the chaff, the poets, the riff-raff, the small fry, the misfits, the conversationalists,

the human oysters, the vermin, the innocent, the snobs and the men of straw, the pariahs, the outcasts, rag-pickers, the rascals, the rake-hells, the fallen angels, the sad-dogs, the castaways, the prodigals, the defaulters, the dreamers and the scum of the earth.                                                   (TA132)

In other words, something like half the human race, all who reject a life of moderation and fall from 'the tightrope of success and failure' (LF57):

To those ignorant of extreme poverty and of its degradations; of pursuit and the attendant horrors; of the crazed extremes of love and hate; for those ignorant of such, there was no cause to suffer such a place.  (TA112)

The city is characterized by light, noise and movement, the bustle of life; the Under-River is dark, 'as though from a failure of the candle's nerve' (111), motionless and silent, save for the 'muffled reverberations' (112) of the river overhead. Water drips incessantly from the cavern roofs, forming shallow pools on the floor. Like figures in limbo, the outcasts of the Under-River sit at tables with their belongings or lean against pit-props and pillars, gathered in 'ragged groups so that it seemed that the dark scene was seismic and had thrown up islands of wood and iron' (111). These poor wrecks are not only negative images of the society above, but are themselves reflected in the pools at their feet, the clear water 'revealing a world in so profound and so meticulous an inversion as to swallow up the eye that gazed upon it and drag it down, out-fathoming invention' (111). This recalls Peake's comparison of artistic failure to 'the lethal still-ness of … that landlocked harbour where the craft of an artist can gaze at its own image in the water' (D8). Whereas successful art is conceived to the sound of the throbbing of the heart, of 'hope's bubble, bobbing in the breast' (TA110), failure is characterized by stillness and silence. But failure can only be achieved by those who have tried; it is the necessary counterpart to success.

Consequently, Peake is inclined to celebrate failure – not the failure of the 'mimic' artist who ceases to invent, like Thorpe in *Mr Pye*. He rightly calls himself a fake and a failure because he chooses the kind of painting that he finds easy, 'Atmosphere. … The Coupée at dawn! Melting distances and all that racket' (MP69). The failure Peake admires is ambi-tious, as when Thorpe conceives of a painting 'unlike any other painting – yet in the tremendous tradition of the masters' (93) – but the image slips from his mind before he can preserve it on canvas. In this case, Mr Pye reassures him, 'failure is glory':

It is success that looks so tarnished and jaded the next morning. It is failure that keeps its freshness. Failure is the thing. Success is finite, but failure is infinite.                                                                                  (MP235)

Peake would have concurred with Dorothea's judgment in *Middlemarch*: 'Failure after long perseverance is much grander than never to have a striving good enough to be called a failure' (ch. 22). So failure is also lovable, because it is essentially human, as in a character like Bellgrove. For all its bitterness then, failure of love is equally infinite.

The one character in the Titus books whose love is a failure by human standards, yet approaches the infinite on the scale of spiritual values, is the one whom Peake failed to make convincing: Keda. To my knowledge, no one has dared challenge Batchelor's dismissal of the Keda–Braigon–Rantel sub-plot on the grounds that it is 'loosely written': 'the language becomes unfocused and emotive' (Batchelor 80–81). It is true that brief summary turns Keda's story into pure cliché: it begins with her marriage, 'forced upon her by the iron laws' (TG190) of the Bright Carvers to an older man who dies just as she realizes that she is pregnant by him, followed by the death of her child, soon after birth. Immediately two men vie for her love; she distances herself from them by going to suckle Titus in the castle. On her return she sleeps with one man and then tells the other that she loves *him* best; the rival suitors fight and kill each other. She wanders off, comes back heavily pregnant again and is cared for by a hermit. After giving birth to a daughter among the Bright Carvers, she abandons the child to them and commits suicide by throwing herself off the local cliff. It does indeed sound like soppy stuff from a station bookstall.

More careful reading, however, suggests that in the story of Keda Peake is describing a state that is barely expressible in words, a state which once experienced remains in the memory like a jewel, of great spiritual value and importance, but which resists communication. It may be called 'a mystical state' (William James), 'ecstasy' (Marghanita Laski) or (a term with ironic echoes here) a 'peak experience' (Abraham Maslow). Freud described it as 'a feeling of an indissoluble bond, of being one with the external universe as a whole' (*Civilization and its Discontents*, quoted by Storr 187). For Keda, it begins as a feeling of universal love.

After three months in Gormenghast as Titus's wet-nurse she determines to return to the Mud Huts. 'I must have love,' she sighs (TG195), as though the lack of love in the castle has awoken her need. As she reaches the outskirts of the village, she is expecting all the problems that she left there to return and 'lower themselves over her like an impenetrable fog'

(233). Instead, 'the fear that had swept her died and her heart leapt with inexplicable joy and … left her with an earthless elation and a courage that she could not understand' (231). She sees a dwarf dog on mangy legs:

> Since childhood she had been taught to despise these scavenging and stunted curs … but in the sudden gladness that had filled her heart she knew of it only as a part of her own being, her all-embracing love and harmony. … She felt her heart was breaking with a love so universal that it drew into its atmosphere all things because they *were*; the evil, the good, the rich, the poor, the ugly, the beautiful, and the scratching of this little yellowish hound.           (TG232; Peake's emphasis)

The unexpected, inexplicable and wholly unlooked-for experience that Peake describes here is more profound than one of Joyce's epiphanies; it has all the characteristics of *ecstasy* as defined by Marghanita Laski, including the 'generalized love towards everything and everybody, and notably to what is normally repulsive' to the ecstatic (Laski 271). A state of this kind is barely expressible 'because language cannot form the thought, because it is wordless and unimaginable and pictureless' (Margiad Evans, *Autobiography*, quoted by Laski 402). Consequently such experiences rarely feature in novels; they are more frequent in autobiographies, in mystical writings (not only Christian, of course) and in poetry; we think of Wordsworth, for instance, whose heart leapt up when he beheld a rainbow in the sky. It is therefore understandable that less fortunate readers should dismiss Peake's attempt to express the ineffable as 'overwritten' (Manlove 236, echoing a review by Henry Tube). Only when – and if – they have a similar experience will they recognize it for what it is. 'When I was young I used to sneer at the mystics who have described the experience of being at One with God and part of the Unity of things' says the hero of C.P. Snow's novel, *The Search*. 'After that afternoon, I did not want to laugh again, for … I think I know what they meant' (quoted by both Laski 421–22 and Storr 189).

At this point Keda feels that she can express her 'exultation', her striving for 'the whole of the life of which she was capable' (TG236), only through love for a man. So she spends the night with the first suitor to meet her. 'She was not in love with Rantel: she was in love with what he meant to her as someone she *could* love' (236; Peake's emphasis). In his arms she realizes that it is not a man that she wants to hold on to but the present moment, 'the NOW that fills us' (239) – a truth regularly experienced by ecstatics. This puts a fresh slant on the lines I have already quoted:

> Is there no love can link us – I and they?
> Only this hectic moment? This fierce instant
> Striking now
> Its universal, its uneven blow?
>
> There is no other link. Only this sliding
> Second we share: this desperate edge of now.
>                                     (S&S20)

The fruit of ecstasy is the realization that to live 'the whole of the life' we are capable of is to live entirely in the present.

The following morning, Keda's perspective on her life, on all life, on the world itself, has changed entirely; she stands outside everyday experience, having entered the 'desperate edge of now'. The change is so evident that her other suitor, Braigon, sees it at once. 'You have broken free,' he observes. Indeed, with her ecstatic experience she has kicked herself free of this island earth. 'I am clear – clear,' she proclaims (242).

In this state and the concomitant 'mood of invulnerability before the world' Keda thoughtlessly tells Braigon that she loves him too, for 'I am in love with all things – pain and all things, because I can now watch them from above' (242). Her lovers, however, are earth-bound mortals; they decide to fight for the right to her love. In her state of elation, with her 'consciousness detached from the world' (Jung, *Alchemical Studies*, quoted by Storr 193), Keda is unable to prevent Rantel and Braigon from killing each other. She can but recognize that 'this is tragedy' (243).

In common with other ecstatics, Keda experiences great difficulty in climbing down from such a height and coping with everyday life. The loss of sense of self associated with ecstasy can easily lead to depression and suicide. Her situation is exacerbated by the confiscation of her house, for the Bright Carvers consider that by going to the castle she has betrayed her people. So she spends the following months wandering. On her return she has another ecstatic experience at the hermit's; then, seeing the crag like a finger pointing at heaven, she knows where and how she will commit suicide.

Peake devotes several pages to describing the place – the ledge on the edge of the crag – and the sunset. Keda's crag overlooks a 'heart-shaped' gulch (444): unlike Irma and Bellgrove who are left staring at an empty space in the shape of a heart, she plans to throw herself into a vast heart that is open to the sky, recalling Peake's image of love as 'A heart-shaped kite / on the winds of the world' (Gb7). As she stands on the brink, the ledge 'lay behind her like a carpet of dark roses. The roses were stones' (446) – and Peake made this last statement the title of the whole chapter. It implies that in her exultation, Keda perceives even stones as roses – and she turns her back upon them. In so doing she rejects romance and the classic image of pastoral love, as immortalized by Christopher Marlowe, Peake's favourite Elizabethan poet and dramatist, in the invitation of the shepherd to his sweetheart: 'Come live with me and be my love / ... / And we will sit upon the rocks / ... / And I will make thee beds of roses' (NAEL 1: 989).[1] Keda's love is of a higher order altogether.

Through his depiction of the sunset Peake suggests Keda's sense of being one with the universe, 'for this was no callow experiment in zoneless splendour – this impalpable sundown was consummate and the child of all the globe's archaic sundowns since first the red eye winked' (444). He has already prepared us for it; during Keda's fever, 'The sun and the moon had forced themselves behind her eyes and filled her head' (356). From the ledge Keda steps out into space, not to fall but to unite with the cosmos: she has 'her head among far stars' and the 'moon that climbed suddenly above the eastern skyline, chilling the rose, waned *through* her as it waxed' (446; my emphasis). Finally, 'as a smile began to grow' upon her face, 'she stepped outwards into the dim atmosphere and, falling, was most fabulously lit by the moon and the sun' (447–48). Keda is no longer a part; she has merged with the whole.

This brings us back to where we began, to Peake's yearning to reconnect the detached island with its continent, the part with the whole. It recalls Plato's *Symposium*, where love is simply the name for the desire and pursuit of the whole. But as the words 'desire' and 'pursuit' suggest, that 'whole' is unattainable on earth. The search is doomed to be a quest without end.

Peake offers us two direct comparisons with Keda's disincarnate love. The first is a brief glimpse of *caritas*, pure love that is focused on the needs of others and expects no return, in the person of the hermit who ministers to Keda in her late pregnancy. He is entirely accepting of her and her single-minded determination to put an end to her life. Nor is he affected by pity, which Peake recognizes as the emotion that 'punctures

---

1. According to John Watney, Peake 'was particularly fond of declaiming long passages from Marlowe's *Tamburlaine*' (42).

love' (TA91). Keda is slightly puzzled by this and perceives his behaviour as 'a strange kind of selflessness' (TG352). The difference between the hermit's love and hers is epitomized by their differing reactions to Keda's crag: for him it is 'the steeple of all love' (359), symbolizing the descent of love from heaven to earth through the institution of the church. His spirituality is also implied by phrases referring to religious practices: their relationship, for instance, is 'baptized with silence'; since they speak few words to each other, Peake calls it a 'communion of silence' (357).[2] For Keda the finger of rock points upward to her destination, simultaneously a symbol of her aspiration to universal love and the instrument by which she hopes to fuse with that love in death (358–59). Her desire, understandable though it be after her ecstatic experiences, is a selfish one, in contrast to the hermit's altruism.

The other comparison is with Mr Pye, whose apotheosis distinctly resembles Keda's. However, his love and his aspirations are of a completely different order. While her experience is entirely unlooked for and spontaneous, his career as an evangelist is meticulously planned, revealing that his love originates in the head rather than the heart. We will deal with Mr Pye in due course.

---

2. Calling the hermit 'the brown father' suggests that Peake may be thinking of a Franciscan monk. From his missionary childhood, and possibly through his wife being a Catholic, Peake would know that Franciscans wear a brown habit, and are well known for their mission work and dedication to service in the field.

# Birds

Love, I Had Thought it Rock-like

### I

I had thought it rock-like,
Rooted, and foursquare,
But it was a bird of the air,
Restless, winged for flying,
Delicate and perilously rare.

### IV

But it was slight,
Airborne and exquisite,
Half tethered, half running –
A heart-shaped kite
On the winds of the world.

### V

It was a leaf of the aspen,
It was not the aspen.
A ripple of ocean,
It was not the ocean.
It was a bird on a rooted rock
And birds are rootless.

### VI

And in some other climate of the heart
It stands upon a cold, illusory shore,
Or floats, O feckless,
Now and for ever
Over weird water.

(Gb6–7)

O F THE MANY LOVES in Peake's work, we have yet to consider the feeling that Titus has for the Thing. At the age of seven or so he glimpses her in the forest, 'phantom or human, he knew not which … floating … like a leaf, in the shape of a girl' (G187). It takes a few days for this momentous experience to sink in and then he suddenly realizes that 'the slight and floating enigma of the glade had taken on a sex, had become particularized, had woken in him a sensation of excitement that was new to him' (188). Discovering prepubescent love, Titus finds himself 'plunged … into a cloudland of symbols to which he had no key' (188). To better understand his relationship with the Thing, we need to explore this 'cloudland', particularly the symbolism of the bird. And this will lead us to a fresh view of Peake's relationship with his works.

In the arms of her foster-mother at the Earling, the newborn Thing reaches out towards Titus and gives a cry 'like the single note of a bird' (TG497). A year before, Steerpike heard one of the first cries of the infant Titus and mistook it for 'that of some bird, perhaps of a seagull', at which he shivered, 'for if there was anything that worried him it was the super- natural' (TG226). In this indirect manner Peake establishes an uncanny association between Titus and the Thing, at the same time as giving the bird a symbolic function.

Throughout his work, he uses the bird as a symbol of love, often in opposition to rocks, stones or boulders. In a poem composed in the 1940s, while he was writing *Titus Groan* and *Gormenghast*, he says of love that he 'had thought it rock-like, / Rooted, and foursquare, / But it was a bird of the air' (Gb6). It's a fairly classic topos, the gravity-defying flight of the bird having long been used to represent love as the expression of the human soul, liberated from the body. Likewise, God's love for man, symbolized by the dove, wings its way from heaven to earth. For Peake, though, the bird serves a more poignant purpose as well, for when people are islands it might serve as an aerial messenger or bridge to link them. Thus it provides him with a perfect metaphor for love, 'Airborne and exquisite, / Half tethered, half running' (Gb7), separate from the body and yet tied to it, not entirely under conscious control.

His symbolic birds are generally figurative, but may also be literal. When Steerpike first visits the Prunesquallors at the beginning of *Titus Groan*, he flatters Irma and her heart is touched. At once 'somewhere in the vaults of her bosom a tiny imprisoned bird [begins] to sing' (TG188). Mr Pye's attention to Miss Dredger causes a similar sensation in her, 'as though the wing of a bird had flapped beneath her ribs' (MP37). Here

Sita with bird and beast from *Quest for Sita*.

Peake emphasizes the bird's wing because of the importance of wings in the rest of that story. He quite often exploits the attributes of birds. Titus and Juno, for instance, experience the first stirrings of their love as 'an apprehension sweet as far bird-song' (TA88). In these cases, the birds express love, as experienced by the heart.

Context supplies literal birds with their symbolic charge. At the moment when Keda says, 'I must have love,' she moves to the window and 'in the straggling ivy beneath her a bird rustled' (TG195). A similar 'scuffling sound of a bird in the ivy outside the tall window' (TA98) is heard as Juno attempts to regain Titus's affection. This association of the movement of a bird with the fluttering sensation of a heart moved by love is not unique to Peake. In James Joyce's short story, 'The Dead', the sound of birds 'twittering in the ivy' is heard by Gabriel Conroy when he receives the memorable love letter from Gretta, shortly before the closing epiphany (NAEL 2: 2262). According to John Watney, Peake 'was a great admirer of Joyce' (Watney 160), who also believed in the 'soul's incurable loneliness' ('A Painful Case', another story in *Dubliners*). However, there may be no direct influence here, for the same association can be found in writers from Wordsworth to D.H. Lawrence.

Peake names a surprising number of different birds, and of course not all of them are symbolic. At the Earling, at least 20 different species dispute the honour of sitting on whichever parts of the Countess provide a suitable perch (TG491). On the other hand, Muzzlehatch, wanting to know if Juno has developed a fancy for Titus, asks, 'Has he set a sparrow twittering in your breast?' Now the sparrow has long been associated with women's sexual desires, particularly after Catullus celebrated Lesbia's pet sparrow in his erotic verses, and Peake will have been familiar with it as motif in Western art. (He himself depicted both male and female figures with small birds perched on their hands.) Changing bird, Muzzlehatch then wonders if Titus has rather 'woken up a predatory condor' in Juno (TA66). As a rule, birds of prey do not evoke love for Peake. On the contrary, he finds them particularly loveless; there is no love 'in a condor's eye' (G339) or in 'the eyes of a monkey-eating eagle' (TA191). For Dr Prunesquallor 'to attempt to reason with [his sister] would be about as fruitful as to try to christianize a vulture' (TG312). So the condor suggests a loveless appetite for sex, in which the other is but prey to be consumed. In Gormenghast birds are served up as food: Swelter prepares toasted larks as one of the delicacies at Titus's christening (TG123), and for the soirée at which she hopes to catch a husband Irma Prunesquallor has peacock hearts as a side

Boy with bird.

dish (G229). In my view the larks serve primarily for exotic effect, chinoi-series, underlining the castle's heartless indifference towards creatures that (in the Anglo-Saxon world at any rate) we no longer consider as food. On the other hand, the side dish, in the context of Irma's pursuit of a male heart, may well be read symbolically. Each instance of Peake's bird imagery has to be judged on its own merits, and in context.

In one case, he certainly exploits the conventional associations of a specific bird for comic effect. At her soirée, Irma, who during the library fire screamed in panic 'with an effect calculated to freeze the blood of a macaw' (TG311), chooses to advertise her desire for love by wearing a 'corsage of hand-painted parrots' (G94). Not content with outscreaming the bird whose natural cry is universally abhorred, she proclaims her avail-ability with the very bird – the love bird – that loves to imitate humans. To ensure that we get the point on the occasion of that momentous soirée, Peake reminds us of Irma's propensity for screaming: as soon as she feels sure that she has made the desired impact on Bellgrove, she hastens upstairs to her bedroom, a civilized 'silken spinster'. Then 'slamming the door behind her she gave vent to the primeval jungle in her veins and screamed like a macaw' (G225). There is a comic counterpart to this in Bellgrove's behaviour: when he feels triumphant about their relationship he wants to 'crow like a barncock' (249). Peake seems to be implying that Irma and Bellgrove are likely to merely mimic human love and, indeed, once they are alone they parrot trite phrases at each other, while ardently willing themselves to believe in their mutual sincerity. Rather as people are fooled into thinking that a parrot is talking sense when it mimics human speech, so they take each other's words, for better or for worse, as true coin. The avian imagery does not stop here; as their relationship develops, Irma feels 'as young as a fledgling' (251). Finally, as Bellgrove discovers once they are married, Irma's parrot side causes her to spend her days observing him minutely: she becomes a hen-pecking critic of his bachelor habits. What a pair of lovebirds! (Ironically, Steerpike calls the Twins lovebirds (G47).)

We find the simplest and most obvious link between love and birds in the behaviour of the Countess. Only to her birds does she verbalize her love, much to the dismay of those around her who hanker for signs of affection. While she and Mrs Slagg are preparing for Titus's christening, she suddenly says 'Now then, darling, now then' and Mrs Slagg's 'old body thrills, for she has never known the Countess to speak to her in such a way before'. She is 'desolate' therefore (TG373) to realize that the remark is not addressed to her but to a bedraggled finch. The Countess frequently 'nurses' injured birds by placing them between her breasts, 'that nest of nests, softer than moss, inviolate and warm with drowsy blood' (TG317). Lucky birds; they receive from her the 'milk of human kindness' (MP26) of which Titus gets none.

A bird singing in the heart features throughout the story of Keda in *Titus Groan*. Her head is already 'tilted like a sparrow's' (TG194) when she begins to tell her story to Mrs Slagg, just as her daughter's is in the final scene with Titus (G418). The bird that rustles in the ivy beneath the window becomes internalized; its insistent voice cries to her, 'I am with you, I am *life*' (TG237; Peake's emphasis) – but as we have just seen the life it celebrates is not of this world. After her lovers have agreed upon their fatal duel and she has exclaimed 'this is tragedy' to herself, 'the bright bird that had filled her breast was still singing' (243), as though in celebration. It is still singing when she arrives at the hermit's hut some eight months later, and as she rests it sings 'with joy, for me. It is happy for me, for soon [the birth] will be over … and I can do it' – that is, commit suicide – 'with a rope, or with deep water, or a blade' (356). It falls silent only at the last, multiplied into a plurality of birds, as she stands on the brink of her crag: 'the wild birds in her breast climbed to her throat and gathered songless, hovering, all tumult, wing to wing, so ardent for those climes where all things end' (445). For Keda, the bird and its singing lead her to the perfect harmony of uniting in death with universal, eternal love.

This simultaneous association of birds with both love and death is the central motif in the demise of Lord Sepulchrave, who loves the Castle as though it were part of his own body:

> How could he *love* this place? He was a part of it. … To have asked him of his feelings for his hereditary home would be like asking a man what his feelings were towards his own hand or his own throat.
>
> (TG62; Peake's emphasis)

Unhinged by the burning of his library, he takes himself for one of the owls that 'sail out on their courses' from the Tower of Flints (TG196). They appear on the very first page of *Titus Groan*, making 'an echoing throat' of the Tower, and when they kill Lord Sepulchrave his 'inhuman cry of pain … leapt from the Tower's throat' (440). In death his body and his voice merge with the eternal castle, just as he anticipated in his rambling monologue:

> in my annihilation there shall be a consummation … and there shall be no ending and the grey stones will stand for always and the high towers for

always … while among my great dusk haunters in the tower my ghost will
hover and my bloodstream ebb for ever …                    (TG402)

The account of Lord Sepulchrave's suicide immediately precedes Keda's in
the book, establishing a parallel between the drug addict and the mystic.
Each discards the body, seeking to transcend it and fuse eternally with the
object of their love. And in both cases the bird simultaneously links love
with sound and sensation, voice in the throat and the feel of the loving
heart in the breast. As this shows, Peake's bird symbolism encompasses
the whole range of love in Gormenghast.

Sometimes love and birds are associated through physical resemblance.
In *Gormenghast* Peake devotes two-and-a-half pages to describing a
colony of herons who make their nests and breed and tend their young
in an abandoned ballroom, high on the roof of the castle, 'half in and
half out of the clouds'. Paradoxically (but logically for Peake) the light
up there has 'something of an underwater feeling about it' (70), recalling
his ideal undersea meetings. This ballroom is indeed the place 'where
once the lovers of a bygone time paced and paused and turned about
one another' (70–71). The stately movement of the ballroom dancers is
now parodied by herons whose plumage mimics the lovers' clothing and
jewellery: 'The late sunbeams … picked out the long, lustrous feathers
that hung from the throat of a heron that stood by a rotten mantelpiece;
and then … the forehead of an adjacent bird flamed in the shadows.' In
the spring, 'a pale blue-green egg shone like a precious stone, or a nest of
young, their thin bodies covered with powder-down, seemed stage-lit in
the beams of the westering sun' (71). As the traditional hour for ballroom
dances approaches, the birds fly off to fish in the shallows of Gormenghast river and the extended description ends with 'the fatal stroke of the
dagger-like beak' as they skewer their prey. As surely as Irma's parrots,
these herons mirror human love in a world of decay, decline – and isolation, for 'each bird appeared as a solitary figure' (72) on its own. In them
Peake combines his main themes, loneliness and love, with his favourite
motifs: birds and death by the blade in shallow water. What is more,
the chiaroscuro effects of the 'late sunbeams' of the 'westering sun' repeat
his feeling that man has been 'Swung out of sunlight into cosmic shade'
(Gb3), far from the presence of God.

This passage is immediately followed by the Thing's first 'visit' to
Gormenghast and the uncanny 'zephyr' that from the roof dives down
through the castle and clasps Titus 'in a noose of air' (G73). The sequence
of motifs, particularly the lover–heron pair followed by 'fatal stroke' and

then 'noose', give the reader an indefinable sense of portentous and tragic things to come.

With the nests in which they raise their families, birds traditionally offer a metaphor of the human home. Peake comically exploits this association by accompanying Irma and Bellgrove's marital plans with allusions to nest-building. At one point Bellgrove even imagines himself as an eagle returning to the nest on which sits Irma, wearing a nightdress. In his mind, Bellgrove has a reserve of strength for his relationship with her that he thinks of as his nest egg (G339). Along with the nest come the duties of maintaining it. On several occasions the Countess uses this image to qualify life at Gormenghast; in particular she describes Lord Sepulchrave's destiny as 'like a rook's nest with every twig a duty' (TG398). It seems logical then that in his madness Lord Sepulchrave should ask Flay to bring him sticks: he wants to start a new life of love among the owls by making his nest beside theirs, although in fact he is but exchanging one set of loveless twigs for another.

The bird in Keda's breast comes to life in her daughter. Rejected by the Bright Carvers because of her illegitimate birth, the Thing lives alone in the woods, free as a bird, returning from time to time to the Mud Huts, where she leaps derisively from roof to roof. Among the profusion of metaphors and similes that Peake applies to her, the bird is the most consistent. She even hops like a bird on the roof of Gormenghast while Peake is calling her an 'elf' and 'phantom child' (G73). Her ability to leap great distances between trees, as though flying, is an obvious bird-like attribute. Among the Bright Carvers it is rumoured that she can 'float for a score of yards at a time on the wings of a high wind' (281). When Titus first catches sight of her, in Gormenghast forest, he perceives 'a thing of the air, a flying thing' that 'would no more think of bowing' to him 'than would a bird' (134). His first impression is that she floats 'like a feather' (133), and at the last, when she falls into his arms in the cave, he finds that 'he had caught at a feather and it had struck him down' (422).

Months after her death, the Thing is also linked, in a passage that has puzzled readers, with the canoe that Titus is given during the flood (and which Steerpike steals from him almost at once). As soon as he receives it he associates the canoe with the Thing, particularly with his first glimpse of her, in those days when 'he hardly knew himself to be an earl' and he had not yet felt the 'divided loyalties' that she awakens in him. We can understand of course that the canoe affords Titus freedom of movement, for the flood has erased all barriers to forbidden excursions; it is a means to leave his island. Moreover, after a few paddle strokes he will be able to look back and see his home from a distance, just as he did on his escapade. For Peake, though, there is a more compelling, metaphorical reason for this association. Whenever he describes the Thing's flying, he uses images of floating, as though she were on water. When he describes the movement of the canoe, which is as 'swift and light and tameless' (G438) as the Thing, it is in terms of flying: it *skims* the flood and *flies* over the water (G439). So we have a chiasmus of metaphors: the canoe *flies* just as the Thing *floats*. Finally, the surface of the flood is at the height at which birds normally fly; once Titus is out on the water he experiences what he imagines the Thing must have felt as she floated among the treetops, a sense of almost weightless, effortless, forward movement. So there are many reasons why he should associate his canoe with her.

Peake repeatedly attributes bird-like qualities to the Thing, in particular a face 'freckled like a bird's egg' (G277); often it's a robin's egg (178, 417 *et passim*). It may be that the egg-shape recalls the soul, but generally Peake seems to be thinking rather of her complete lack of expression. He stresses that her face is as expressionless as a bird's, hiding rather than revealing her mind, which gives her a 'detached and unearthly quality' (278). With this and something universal that she exudes, Peake links her with her mother Keda: 'she might have been a giant phantom, something too earthless to be held in by the worldly dimensions of this cave, something beyond measurement' (421). At the same time, he links the Thing with the Countess, who looks at Titus quite blankly, making 'no effort to communicate anything' (315) by putting expression into her face. Its 'almost mask-like character', he writes, is 'no index to her state of mind' (317), any more than the Thing's face reveals hers.

The most symbolic scene involving Titus, the Thing and birds occurs on the day when the Countess remembers her intention to teach Titus how to 'whistle birds out of the sky' (TG398). As they approach the woods, she begins to imitate bird calls and birds fly to her in response. Suddenly the Thing starts to whistle back from among the trees, insolently imitating the Countess's calls with echo-like precision. This makes the Countess so angry that she returns to the castle and the lesson is abandoned for good.

With this simple episode, Peake achieves a great deal: first of all, the Countess has waited until Titus is 12 and about to enter his teens before giving him her equivalent to the traditional lesson about the birds and the bees. She is unaware of having already lost Titus to the Thing, and he is still too young to understand what is going on. He does not even know that it is the Thing who is whistling back from the forest, or why this should make his mother so angry. To him it seems as though his mother 'were holding him back from something, as though the wood was hiding something that might hurt him – or draw him away from her' (G318). This echoes the feeling that Titus had just before he first caught sight of the Thing in the forest: 'it was as though he were being drawn towards some dangerous place or person, and that he had no power to hold himself back' (132). Here Peake is writing of what happens to every heterosexual adolescent boy: sooner or later he finds a girl who supplants his mother as the primary love of his life. And the mother's initial reaction is ambivalent: she wants her son to be initiated into the world of adult love at the same time as wishing to protect him from possible heartbreak and keep his love for herself. This is summed up in the single word, 'Beware!' (318) which the Countess flings out as a challenge to the Thing and which the Thing echoes back to her uncomprehendingly. The mother defies her prospective rival and the rival responds in kind. So the Thing, a literal feral child, is also a symbol of the love that challenges the mother of every boy. She frees Titus from his mother's apron strings and in so doing from the castle too.

This exchange is as significant a moment as any in the book, for it is the one and only time that the Countess (who, unlike Titus, has realized that only a human could respond to her whistling like this) is obliged to acknowledge that there is anyone outside the community of Gormenghast. In the Thing Titus 'had seen something which lived a life of its own: which had no respect for the ancient lords of Gormenghast, for ritual among the foot-worn flagstones: for the sacredness of the immemorial House' (G134). In short, 'Gormenghast meant nothing to this elastic switch of a girl' (411) who is unique in standing outside the closed system of the house of Groan. As such she represents the fault, the chink in the walls of the castle, through which Titus can ultimately escape. The single word that she exchanges with the Countess sums up this role: she challenges not just motherhood but also everything else that Gormenghast stands for: unchanging continuity, and fidelity to the ritual, to the stones themselves. Thus she represents all that Titus is not and has not, with the result that in his mind 'the physical *she* and what she symbolize[s] become fused into one thing' (411; Peake's emphasis). This is an important notion: what Titus perceives is as much symbol as physical reality. (It has also been a standard romantic one, ever since Wordsworth's observation in 'Tintern Abbey' about what we 'half create' and half perceive.) By seeing Gormenghast through her eyes, he can imagine an elsewhere, and a life separate from Gormenghast. And this is achieved through what Titus calls 'love'.

Brought up with such a mother and in such an unloving environment as the castle, Titus has little idea about love at this point. 'He had heard of love; he had guessed of love; he had no knowledge of love but he knew all about it' (G410), or so he thinks. It is notable that Peake generally uses rhetorical questions when it comes to the love that Titus feels for the Thing. On his first escapade, at the age of seven, either he or the narrator asks, 'What was this shock of love?' (G104); in the cave, there is again doubt as to who asks, 'What, if not love, was the cause of all this?' (G410). Since Titus knows almost nothing of the Thing, his image of her is formed by his own projections. Her expressionless face indicates that she cannot reciprocate his feelings in any way, as he discovers in the cave. She is even less capable of love than the Countess; having reverted to the level of an animal, she has no love to offer, not even to birds, for they are her food. But love is what he feels, and it feeds his imagination. Because love, 'like an earthquake or some natural and sinless force, is incompatible with a neat and formal world' (G351), his love 'will cry for insurrection' (TG507) and cause him ultimately to revolt against the destiny that his ancient heritage holds in store for him.

The bird-like 'volitation' (G133) of the Thing contrasts with all that is earth-bound and fixed. In the poem quoted at the head of this chapter, Peake writes that he had thought that love was 'rock-like, / Rooted, and foursquare'; he had believed that it was 'founded / Like a city of stone'. Then he realized that, on the contrary, it is 'a bird of the air, / Restless, winged for flying / … / slight, / Airborne and exquisite / … / a bird on a rooted rock' (Gb6–7). The rootless, unearthly Thing is opposed to the immobile rootedness of 'a city of stone' like Gormenghast, or an island in the sea.

Another contrast that Peake makes in the same poem is between the tree and its leaf: love 'was a leaf of the aspen, / It was not the aspen'. Interestingly, among his original names for the Thing were 'Leaf' and 'Branch', and the numerous comparisons of her to a sapling, for instance, that remain in the text confirm his initial intention to echo her name in the imagery he applied to her. She was to be, like Titus, 'a leaf from the forest of man's passion' (TG115). In the cave her hand is 'like a beech leaf' (G416) and the lightning burns her up 'as though she had been a dead leaf in its path' (424). One of the reasons why he abandoned this association is no doubt a question of *roots*. If anything is rooted it is the tree, and the Thing of course is rootless; so out went 'Branch' and 'Leaf' as inappropriate to his purposes. In fact the reason may be (like roots) deeper than this.

In the Titus books roots appear in unexpected places. The most memorable one belongs to the Twins. It is actually a whole roomful of roots, 'a thousand branching, writhing, coiling, intertwining, diverging, converging, interlacing limbs' (TG251) that form such an inextricable maze that even the coldly cerebral Steerpike cannot find his way through and has to be helped out by Clarice. The Twins have painted the tangled 'limbs' in many colours, hoping that birds will come and nest there. Predictably, no birds have come and their hopes (like Fuchsia's love) have 'frozen' (TG252). The Twins suspect the Countess of 'stealing' their birds, which Steerpike intuits as an expression of their need for love and attention, and he exploits it accordingly. So when we learn that, up in her attic, Fuchsia also has 'a great writhing root, long since dragged from the woods' which she has 'polished to a rare gloss, its every wrinkle gleaming' (TG83), we may guess that it stands for her need for love and attention too. She has after all, brought it in from the woods to the heart of her most private sanctum. And the root is indeed Peake's recurrent symbol for the woman's capacity for love, and more particularly the rootedness of a stable sexual relationship. Polished and preserved in her most secret attic, Fuchsia's root is her virgin sexuality. That Steerpike finds it 'horrible' (TG160) tells us how fundamentally ill-suited to each other they are.

Peake's association of the root with female sexuality is illustrated in his long 'nonsense' poem about a 'Hideous Root' (BN59–64) which a plumber's wife keeps beside her at all times. (I will abstain from reading his profession as symbolic.) On one occasion she mislays her root and only then does her husband realize that 'without it her beauty is never no more' (62). He quickly finds it, though, and restores it to her, and 'a vision of all that her beauty had been / Return[s] to enchant the connubial scene'. In his eyes she is 'once more / An ornament made for his praise' (63). Thus the root quite literally casts a spell over the plumber and ensures that he continues to love his wife and find her beautiful. It is her means for gaining and retaining her husband's love. No wonder, then, that the most stinging insult that Titus flings at Cheeta, the frigid virgin in *Titus Alone*, is: 'I told them you were frozen at the very tap-root' (TA190). She has not made contact with her sexuality, and has not that means to retain a man – none of the sensual 'writhing, coiling, inter-twining, diverging, converging, [and] interlacing' of limbs that Peake seems to associate with sexual congress. We might recall here that the Bright Carvers, whose daughters are so beautiful and who experience such passionate (albeit brief) love lives, subsist on a diet of roots. We might also consider that roots belong in the earth, and a woman with *earthiness* is 'direct and uninhibited, especially about sexual subjects or bodily func-tions' (NODE), like Tintagieu (MP218). In 'The Hideous Root' the narrator asks, 'what can more furnish a bride / With tranquillity, faith and a pride in her lot / Than a foil of the kind that the lady has got' (63). The answer, of course, is that love is not limited to physical passion but expresses something more spiritual. This is why Peake's symbolic birds are rootless, while unloved women like the Twins have roots that are birdless.

Although the Thing does arouse sexual feelings in Titus, Peake did not want her to be too closely associated with roots and earthiness, which exclude the spiritual. He went for something more idealized and aesthetic by likening her to a piece of sculpture produced by the Bright Carvers. Right from the first she has 'flesh like alabaster' (TG489), a traditional material for statues. Peake even suggests that she may be less substan-tial than this: at the Earling Fuchsia thinks for a moment that she can see the falling rain *through* the Thing's limbs (TG492). In movement she is sculpturesque, with 'slender arms along the sides of the gracile body, the head turned slightly away and inclined as though on a pillow of air' (G132). In this she resembles the dryad that Keda's first husband, the old master sculptor, was carving at the moment when he died (TG194). What is more, her ability to float from tree to tree makes her a living embodiment of the symbol of love that her father Rantel promises, on the day of her conception, to carve for Keda: 'It will leap,' he says, 'and have hands as tender as flowers.' And its eyes shall be 'violet like the edge of the spring lightning' (TG238). There are two uncanny things here: violet is the colour of Titus's eyes, not the Thing's, and the Thing is killed by a flash of lightning. Peake associates her with sculpture in yet another way: she defaces or steals the works of the Bright Carvers (G281). She secretly watches 'the evolution of [a] wooden raven' (G395) in the hands of a great carver, and she makes away with it in that dramatic scene, observed through Titus's eyes, at the annual ceremony of the Bright Carvings:[1]

---

1. Is the raven itself symbolic for Peake? It is the bird with a silver bracelet in its beak that guides Titus out into the woods from the hollow halls beneath the castle (G182). Is Peake thinking of Noah's raven (Gen. 8.7) or perhaps the folk belief repeated by Shakespeare: 'Some say that ravens foster forlorn children' (*Titus Andronicus* II.iii.154)? It is doubly linked with the Thing, since Peake writes that for the Bright Carvers, she was 'a raven, a snake, [a] witch, all the same' (G280). Maybe it is simply the bird that flaps its wings in the heart.

A coal-black raven, its head cocked, its every feather exquisitely chiselled, its claws gripping a wrinkled branch, was about to be thrown into the flames when, as Titus watched, in a half-dream, ... as unforeseen and rapid as the course of a dream, there leapt from the body of the fire-lit crowds something that, with a mixture of grace and savagery quite indescribable, snatched at the height of its leap the raven from the air, and holding it above its head continued without a pause or break in the superb rhythm of its flight and, apparently floating over an ivy-covered wall, disappeared into the night.                                                            (G402)

This sculpturesque highjacking of a carving fills Titus 'with a joy too huge for him to contain, which took him and shook him out of his indecisions, and swept him' – in terms that are literalized within a few pages – 'into a land of hectic and cruel brilliance, of black glades, and of a magic insupportable' (G402). He leaves at once to seek out the Thing. After their brief encounter in the cave, she runs out into the storm-dark clearing where she is cruelly burned up like just another bright carving by the 'searing flash of flame' that breaks loose from 'the heart of the storm' (424). In this dramatic demise she proves to be a true product of the Bright Carvers. Years before Peake wrote of her death, he had characterized them as being

> bright with a kind of *unnatural* brightness. It was not the wholesome lustre of a free flame, but of the hectic radiance that sheet-lightning gives suddenly to limbs of trees at midnight; of sudden flares in the darkness, of a fragment that is lit by torchlight into a spectre.
>
> (TG92; Peake's emphasis)

The repeated images link these passages: this 'child of clay, like alabaster, the earthless daughter who had startled all' (TG446) and who is Titus's 'dream girl', becomes a unique piece of living sculpture, 'an original' (G416). She meets a fate that corresponds to both the destiny and indeed the very nature of the Bright Carvings.

I have already shown how Titus's discovery of the Thing mirrors Peake's own process of creation; what Titus sees in her is an embodied figment of his own imagining. She becomes a living work of art. Moreover, she is exactly what he needs, 'something for which he had unconsciously pined' (G133), the fulfilment of his unspoken wishes. Consequently, when she dies, it is part of him that dies too, 'burned away even as she had been burned away' (424). In falling in love with this 'statue' that is largely of his own creating, Titus is like Pygmalion faced with Galatea. Indeed, at the moment when finally he clasps her in his arms and tries to kiss her, she is more like a statue than ever, for her face, 'closely shrouded in wet linen … was like the head of sea-blurred marble' (423). (The shift from *alabaster* to *marble* may relate to Peake's evocation of 'the glory of standing with one's love, naked, as it were, on a spinning marble, while the spheres [run] flaming through the universe!' (243).) In his world, however, despite the magic, the uncanny parallels and the unnatural qualities of light, the gods do not turn statues into living beings. Titus loses his Galatea the very moment he takes her in his arms.

At one point in *Titus Alone* it seems that Peake is going to let the miracle take place. With the statuesque Juno, who is the next object of Titus's love, he unites the same motifs, right down to the 'watery light' that fills the sky (90). It begins with Juno in her elegant room, where there's a small marble statue on a pedestal. Through the window she sees Titus, 'a creature far from marble, waving to her from the statue'd garden, and the sight of him swept cogitation from her face as though a web were snatched from her features'. Titus notices the change and the accompanying 'movement of her marvellous bosom' (90); they trigger his desire for her and by the next page they are making love. Unlike the scene in *Gormenghast*, then, there is 'a climax' – but Titus leaves Juno nonetheless.

Later in the book, Peake varies the pattern by showing Titus's face from Cheeta's point of view:

> It was, taken all in all, a young face, even a boyish face, but there had been something else about it not easy to understand. … It was as though the gauze of youth had been plucked away to discover something rougher, something nearer the bone. It seemed that a sort of shade passed to and fro over his face; an emanation of all he had been. In short, his face had the substance out of which his life was composed. It was nothing to do with the shadowy hollow beneath his cheekbones or the minute hieroglyphics that surrounded his eyes; it was to her as though his face was his life.
>
> (TA161)

In these scenes where characters turn into carved marble, their heads partially veiled, or faces reveal the bone beneath the flesh, the meaning is always just beyond grasp, 'something else' that is 'not easy to understand', like the hieroglyphics around Titus's eyes.

In a poem he wrote during WWII, Peake describes digging up a heart-shaped stone and holding it in his hand,

> As though it were a wounded bird whose breast
> Throbbed delicately against my finger-tips.
>
> And it grew heavier and heavier
> Until it had become your heart and mine
> Fused in a fierce embrace of solid stone.
>
> (Gb8)

Here he expresses his ultimate hope that two people might become one in the same way that the Coupée makes one of the two halves of the granite island of Sark. His characters come together in hope of fusion, of finding a fellow 'creature far from marble', but they always elude each other in the end. The bird-like Thing that has become a statue escapes Titus's embrace, slipping away from him 'like a stream in his arms' (G423), as though the marble has turned to water. He is left holding his shirt in the cave while with what proves to be her last breath she screams her derision from outside under the falling rain.

More than once Peake depicts this change of state at moments of emotional climax, points of no return, and each time all that is left is 'so much dead rock' (G425). The Lost Uncle's White Lion of the Snows turns to an ice statue the moment he discovers it, for instance. Keda steps into space from her crag, leaving cold stone behind her. After Mr Pye has taken flight from the Coupée, 'the island was suddenly empty – and was nothing but a long wasp-waisted rock' (MP254). At such moments, Peake pulls back from the intense subjective experience of the acting character to bring us instead the response of the witnesses present: Fuchsia outside the cave, the Lost Uncle, Mr Flay, or Miss Dredger and Tintagieu respectively. They are left feeling desolate and powerless, yet strangely uplifted at the same time. It is a moment that affects Peake profoundly, for it not only reflects his belief in the impossibility of sharing islands but also his experience as a creator.

His feelings at such a moment are best expressed in the poem, 'On Fishing up a Marble Head', which opens, 'What is it then that has so swathed your face? / Have time and water blurred you to a boulder?' As he holds the carving in his hands, he exclaims

> Now is your hour to draw your breath, but oh,
> How can I let you go
> Yet hold you so.
>
> (P&D)

This is the predicament of the artist-creator: having fished up a work of art from the depths of his subconscious, he holds it in his hands and knows that once it is finished he cannot keep it, however much he may love it. The moment it draws its first breath, like a newborn infant, it is separate and he must let it go – or destroy it. The ambivalence of Peake's feelings is neatly expressed in these lines by the question that ends without a question mark, turning it simultaneously into a statement. In life he managed both to preserve and to destroy: he allowed the works he created, all these novels and stories, poems and paintings, to go out into the world and live their independent lives. Simultaneously, he destroyed works such as the Bright Carvings created *within* his fiction, thus annulling the pain of separation as though they had never existed.[2] This is the response that he attributes to Titus on the death of the Thing: 'Something had died as though it had never been' (G424).

The Thing becomes an enigma for the reader because of the enormous weight of symbolism that she has to bear. Peake makes her a work of art of both kinds, to be preserved as well as destroyed, just as she herself preserves the carved raven from destruction by fire, yet destroys other pieces of sculpture. Preserver and destroyer, bird and statue, she is also poetry in motion, a 'lyric swallow' (G416) without a voice. (In this she is like Philomela, in Ovid's *Metamorphoses*, who turns into a swallow after her tongue has been cut out.) The complex association of birds, rocks, poetry and death can be found in the epigraph to this chapter. There Peake declares love to be

> The last of a species;
> Or a last duet
> Of lovers, of birds –
> The last of all lyrics,
> Its blue ink drying
> On a poet's words.
> (Gb6)

The moment when lovers sing their last duet (dare I say 'swan song'?)

---

2. The fate of the Bright Carvings in Gormenghast – the creations of artists in Peake's creation – parallels the threat that supposedly hangs over God's creatures on earth: the most worthy are rewarded with eternal preservation in the Hall of Bright Carvings, or heaven (although no one but the curator ever sees them); the rest are consigned to a fire, i.e. hell.

resembles the moment when the poet lays down his pen: creator and creation, lover and loved one are about to be separated for ever. Once on paper, the poem acquires independent life, yet for the poet it is at the same time dying, undergoing *rigor mortis* as its lifeblood dries. As a lyric bird and frozen statue, the Thing unites all these motifs.

The bitter sweetness of this separation leaves Peake desolate, but it is an act of love indissociable from the process of creation. So of course he returns to it, and to its paradoxical nature, time and again. In *Gormenghast* he imagines a cruel winter during which thousands of birds die, their bodies littering the snow, so that

> it seemed that upon the vast funeral linen of the snowscape, each bird of all these hosts had signed, with an exquisite and tragic artistry, the proof of its own death, had signed it in a language at once undecipherable and eloquent – a hieroglyphic of fantastic beauty.          (G294)

To appreciate this thought, the reader needs to see Peake's words not as printer's ink on white paper but as dead birds on a white coffin cloth. There's a comparable nexus of motifs in *Letters from a Lost Uncle*: in a region 'even more desolate than usual', where the snow lies 'in great soft deathly silent mountains', 'swarms of little creatures' suddenly stream past the Uncle, 'wringing their hands as they run' and leaving 'little footmarks in the snow, like smallpox'. Then a 'tremor' runs down his spine, 'for suddenly the silence had come again and it was as white and empty as the snowy hills before the footmarks came' (LLU62–63). These wide expanses of white space correspond to the 'speckless' page or virgin canvas on which Peake creates his works 'of fantastic beauty' in solitude and silence, leaving the marks of his passage on its surface. The moment of separation leaves him feeling that 'in some other climate of the heart' (as he puts it in the last stanza of 'Love, I Had Thought it Rock-like') love

> stands upon a cold, illusory shore,
> Or floats, O feckless,
> Now and for ever
> Over weird water.
>                                         (Gb7)

The writer's pen makes hieroglyphics on the page, 'in a language at once undecipherable and eloquent' like dead birds on snow. Then the work that was part of himself, his companion in solitude, must go off and live its independent life, leaving him alone again on his island. It feels like giving up a loved one, for creation is an act of loving separation. It feels like death for the artist, yet it is an opportunity to start again, and therefore a potential rebirth. These are the feelings of Titus on the death of the Thing: 'with the beauty and the ugliness, the ice and the fire of it on his tongue and in his blood he could begin again' (G424).

The emotion that Peake expresses here is familiar to us from the Romantic poets. While the attentive reader may have noticed an echo from Shelley a couple of paragraphs back, it is Keats that I am thinking of at this point – and I suspect that Peake was too. The lines quoted just above remind me of the closing words of 'When I have Fears …':

> then on the shore
> Of the wide world I stand alone and think
> Till love and fame to nothingness do sink.

The connection is based on feeling quite as much as the words employed. I mention it here because Peake makes other, more direct allusions to the famous ballad by Keats in which 'La Belle Dame Sans Merci' bewitches a knight-at-arms and abandons him beside a lake where 'The sedge has withered … / And no birds sing' (ll. 2–3). Her other victims, 'pale warriors' all, confirm that 'La Belle Dame Sans Merci / Thee hath in thrall' (ll. 39–40). In Peake's stage play, *The Wit to Woo*, the protagonist, Percy, is several times compared to or treated as a knight (PP277 and 369, for instance). Shortly before literalizing the image by hiding inside a suit of armour, he exclaims,

> Oh give me strength to take the nymph by storm!
> Without her, what is there …? Oh what is there?
> Nothing but space, gray space. A world of sedge
> Without a feature save from time to time
> When there emerges from the coiling mists
> A sodden spectre, obviously me –
> A failure …
>
> (PP301)

Percy has been captivated by Sally, here called a nymph (as is the Thing), so the language, setting, and sentiment all point back to 'La Belle Dame Sans Merci'. With the 'world of sedge' Peake alludes to the condition of Keats's spectral warriors – and then extricates his character from the rut the knight-at-arms is stuck in. By pretending to be an artist and therefore viewing his predicament through artist's eyes, Percy gets Sally to return his love.

In the story of Titus and the Thing we find the same motifs as in 'La Belle Dame Sans Merci'. A not quite human female figure casts a spell, symbolized by a garland in Keats and a 'noose of air' in Peake, upon a young aristocratic male. Keats has the 'faery's child' (l. 14) lead the knight to 'her elfin grot' (l. 29) where he falls asleep. Pursuing the Thing, Titus finds himself at Flay's cave, falls asleep inside it and discovers the Thing there with him when he wakes. Then comes the abrupt reversal, in which the female figure disappears, leaving the male 'alone and palely loitering' (l. 2). Now it is quite probable that Peake was unaware of this parallel at the time when he wrote *Gormenghast*, otherwise he would have introduced a verbal echo as he did some ten years later in his play. Describing the wasteland of 'Boy in Darkness', which also dates from the 1950s, he uses the phrase 'and no birds sang' (187), which suggests that by the time he wrote these works, he was aware of a community of emotion with Keats. The crucial difference lies in Peake's treatment of his male protagonist: in both cases, his character breaks out of the enchantment by adopting the viewpoint of the artist.

From start to finish, Titus's relationship with the Thing mirrors Peake's own relationship with the works of art he produces. Just as the Thing comes to Titus, so inspiration comes to the artist like a gift that he has always pined for. With love he shapes it; he would willingly keep it for himself, but ultimately he has to let it go if he is to share it with the world – or else destroy it. Out of love, the artist grants independence to his work, and suffers the pang of separation. In so doing, he transcends the enchantment that the work has cast upon him.

Here we can draw a parallel with modern man. Previous generations inhabited a universe in which they could read God's Word in everything. Nature was the book in which His presence was writ large. The very rocks were not only the foundation of His church but tangible proof of His love. And man was a character in that book too. By Peake's time, God had withdrawn, granting independence to His work, and with Him the meaning went too, leaving man to grope through a 'cloudland' of symbols, a world of hieroglyphics. As a twentieth-century artist, Peake responds by adopting the god-like stance of the creator and, repeating the act of love in which God let His creation go, leaves his readers to decipher for themselves the hieroglyphics on his page.

# Identity

If only people would stop trying to be things! What
*can* they be, after all, beyond what they already are?
(G75; Peake's emphasis)

Their past, which made them what they were and
nothing else, moved with them, adding at each
footfall a new accretion. Two figures: two creatures:
two humans: two worlds of loneliness. Their lives up
to this moment contrasted, and what was amorphous
became like a heavy boulder in their breasts. (TA189)

Let us possess one world; each hath one and is one.
(John Donne, 'The Good-Morrow'; NAEL 1: 1237)

FOR PEAKE, THE ACT of making a drawing or painting is an existential statement of identity, an expression of his self. While great artists
may, metaphorically, 'paint, draw, write, or compose with their own
blood' (D10), the work is in fact separate from the body of its creator;
it merely takes the colour of 'the globe it flew from'. Looking at his own
work, Peake writes 'This is not me' (D11), which immediately raises the
question, who is he? To answer 'that one's name is Brown or Robinson is
nothing to the point'. Peake is in search of his 'elemental name – [his] root
name as an artist' (D10). This core activity of seeking to establish, affirm
and maintain a sense of identity runs throughout his work, especially the
Titus books. However, as he did not manage to take his hero into adulthood, his main emphasis falls on the adolescent stage of this quest. This
accounts for part of the attraction of his fiction for teenagers who, like
Fuchsia and Titus, are at just this stage of defining their identity.

Identity is a problematic notion, raising more questions than answers, as Tristram Shandy so memorably reminded us. Subjectively, we experience it as an abiding quality that makes each of us different from all other people; at the same time it makes us certain that we are the same person today as we were yesterday. Objectively we are defined by factors that were fixed before we were aware of *being* at all: our gender, the family we were born into, and its socio-cultural context. Moreover society continues to label us throughout our lives, so that we are liable to confuse our social roles with our personal identity and come to believe that we *are* what we *do*. Yet we can change job, partner, place of residence, nationality, name, even gender, and continue to feel that we are the same person inside. In fact, we generally make just such changes the better to express who we feel ourselves to be. So our identity is a subtle combination of sameness and difference.

The word *identity* is itself paradoxical since we use it to express absolute sameness, as in 'identical twins'. What a wonderful solution to solitude it would be to share one's island with a twin, a clone of oneself! It's even better than the two-islands-in-one that make Sark. The identical twin offers indefectible companionship, perfect continuity between self and other, fusion at the same time as separateness. 'I am For Ever With Me' writes Peake in one of his poems. 'I am always / Companion to the ghost-man whom I nurture.' 'Bound together', he and his inner other drift 'through starlight on a bruise-blue harbour' (S&S11). This 'great yearning one for the other' crops up at unexpected moments in the Titus books. Irma Prunesquallor complains of a gap in the curtains. 'Are you speaking of a brace of spirits? ha ha ha! – twin souls searching for consummation, each in the other?' asks her brother (TG214).

Peake plays with twinning in his various doubles, producing comedy with Cora and Clarice, and horror with the helmeteers in *Titus Alone*. Because the Twins are identical, they need only to look at each other to see themselves as others see them:

> 'When I'm looked at at the Breakfast I want to know how they see me from the side and what exactly they are looking at; so turn your head for me and I will for you afterwards.'
>     Cora twists her white neck to the left … her head a fraction more …
>     'That's right, Cora. Stay like that. Just like that. Oh, Cora!' (the voice is still as flat) 'I am perfect.'                    (TG385–86)

They look alike, and think alike. In the chapter of Reveries, Peake does not give us Clarice's thoughts because they are 'identical with those of her sister in every way'. We just have to substitute Cora's name for Clarice's 'wherever it appears in the reverie' (TG398). Having the same thoughts, they form a single identity, only their imbecility prevents them from realizing it. Their lives are the same, all the way down to their simultaneous deaths. The Twins are parodies of people. Loss of all difference spells the death of identity. Horror and comedy in one.

One of the memorable characteristics of Gormenghast is its determination to deny difference and remain the same for ever. When the Black House in *Titus Alone* is turned into a parody of the castle, Peake underlines how 'everything' has to be changed

> and yet nothing had changed. ... The change was entire. Nothing was as it was before. ... There was no end to the change.
>     And yet it was the same in so far as the mood ... of unutterable desolation that no amount of change could alter.                                  (TA216)

Incredibly, the Groan dynasty has retained the same title and the same home for 77 generations; not even the Vatican can rival that. Its codified ritual preserves it, making the earls subservient to their function. A few have managed to express themselves by designing and decorating additions to the castle, but this activity has ceased, for Gormenghast has grown too big to cope with its sprawling structure; some buildings have been abandoned and are falling into ruin. Expression of individuality is tolerated among the Bright Carvers who live just outside the castle, but each year their works are burned, except for one or two, preserved in a gallery that no one ever visits. This is the circumscribed, preordained existence that the castle holds in store for Titus, whose birth is seen by Flay as confirmation that there is to be 'no *Change*' (TG23; Peake's capital and emphasis).

After Steerpike has become an outlaw, the castle-dwellers wonder if they should carry on as usual with the Ceremony of the Bright Carvings, or whether it should be curtailed, as a security measure, until he has been hunted down. For the Countess there is no question: tradition should be observed, and Dr Prunesquallor concurs: 'You are right,' he tells her. 'There must be no difference.' And the Countess repeats grimly, 'There is never any difference' (G390). She resists change more than anyone; for her husband, 'it would be a grim and evil thing were she to change' (TG311).

Peake knows, and shows, that nothing is unchanging, except death itself. Change is synonymous with life. Take a character like Deadyawn, the erstwhile headmaster who, toppling from his high chair, falls on his head and is instantaneously transfixed by *rigor mortis*. Balanced upside down upon his crushed skull, he appeared to have 'more life in him than he had ever had before' (G113). He owes his name to the utter boredom of his existence, for he had always believed that 'the only difference between one day and the next lies in the pages of a calendar' (G57). In this he is like Opus Fluke, for whom 'every evening was an identical yawn' (G125). Deadyawn's *rigor mortis* set in long before his fatal fall. (In the BBC adaptation Deadyawn was appropriately renamed De'ath, played by the immortal Spike Milligan.) In death he seems more alive than in life because he has shown a sign of change, and his demise triggers off several changes, the first of which is the immediate suicide of the usher, known as The Fly, who throws himself out of the nearest window and crashes to the courtyard a hundred feet below. And then Bellgrove gets promoted to headmaster. This, Peake seems to say, is the spice of life, for at this point he suddenly names four of the schoolboys who witness Dead-yawn's demise: there's Parsley, Chives, Sage Minor and Mint (G114). The missing herb is Thyme.

Time is of course the agent of change. Time is the enemy of Gormen-ghast. The birth of Titus at the beginning of the first book is like the beginning of time, as though the clocks begin to tick at that moment. For Peake, life is that moment that 'links the dark domains of the womb and the tomb' (MP249); life is difference between two featureless same-nesses. To live is to be different, and therefore to make a difference. The first thing that we learn about Titus is that he has violet-coloured eyes, which in itself makes him different. Peake spelled the colour 'violate' in the MS: Titus is born to *violate* the rules by rejecting his inheritance. His birth means change, irrespective of what the castle may wish.

Stone is Peake's metonym for the castle's resistance to change. Gormen-ghast is nearly all stone: it has stone lanes, stone halls, stone floors and stone walls. Bricks may be used to pave a courtyard for their decorative effect (e.g. G127 and 173) but only the apartment in which Steerpike starves the Twins to death has walls and floor of brick. (Is it coincidence that the first bricks we encounter in the Titus books are in the mouth of Steerpike himself? He identifies Lord Sepulchrave as the owner of 'the whole caboodle, bricks, guns and glory' (TG49). This associates Steer-pike with difference.) In the castle 'where lived, where died, and where was born again the lit line of the Groans' (TG443), it is each earl's duty to 'instill into the first male of his loins reverence for its every stone' (TG493). So, being of 'the bloodstock of the stones' (TG116), Titus is enjoined at his christening to 'remain faithful to the stones' and Sourdust intones the command that is metaphorically 'carved in stone' in the books of ritual: 'I do adjure you hold each cold stone sacred' (TG123). For every act of disobedience, Titus is incarcerated in the Stone Fort, to force his body, at least, to submit to the 'immemorial stone' (TG443). His spirit resists.

As a symbol of the centrality of stone to the house of Groan, he has to wear a stone strapped to his forehead throughout the Day of the Bright Carvings. Rather appositely Peake has Steerpike express his revolt against the castle by lodging stones from his catapult in that self-same spot, 'in the bone above the eyes' (G397) of his hapless victims. The Thing flings a stone at Titus when they meet in Flay's cave, and 'what was she doing but defying, through him, the very core of Gormenghast?' (G420), just as Steerpike is. Titus demonstrates his friendly intentions by picking up a stone (not a pebble, mind you) and tossing it 'over his shoulder where it clanged on the solid rock of the wall behind him' (G421). He would willingly have tossed all Gormenghast over his shoulder to join her in her elemental freedom. But Gormenghast is rock solid. To over-throw it requires imagination, not stone, and the Thing inspires Titus to envisage a different way of life in which to gain his freedom and express his identity.

The obstacles to doing this are enormous. To start with, like his father, Titus associates his self with his body – and his body with his home. The first is quite natural: he became a separate island at birth, with the cutting of the umbilical cord. 'Stretch your small wrinkled limbs in shrill delight!' Peake tells the newborn infant. 'Gulp at the white tides of the globe, and scream / "I am!"'(Gb5). We are coterminous with our bodies: where it is, we are too. Directing attention to the body – in Peake it's generally the hands and the fingers – can remind us that we *exist*. When Titus gets lost in the 'hollow halls' (or 'stone halls'; Peake uses both names) beneath Gormenghast, 'all the sounds of the Castle's life – the clanging of bells; the footsteps striking on the hollow stones; the voices and the echoes of voices; all were gone' (G179). The only familiar thing left is his own body; bringing his fist to his mouth he bites his knuckles and the pain gives him 'a sense of his own reality' (180). And what should he take with him when he leaves Gormenghast to explore the world but a 'small knuckle of flint, … as though to prove to himself that his boyhood was real, and that the Tower of Flints still stood' (TA11). This chip of flint is egg-shaped (TA21), like the traditional image of the self (and wholeness); whenever his identity is questioned or threatened (e.g. TA52), he feels for it in his pocket. It serves as a literal touchstone; it confirms *who* he *is* by affirming *where* he is *from*: identity, existence and home, at a stroke.

Other characters in Gormenghast also associate their bodies with their home. For Peake, as for all English-speakers, the notion of *home* carries a rich emotional charge (that is impossible to render fully in other languages, as translators of the film *E.T.* discovered). Our first home is our body. Soon the term applies to the physical structure (be it bedsit or palace) that houses our immediate family. As Carrow puts it in *Titus Alone*, which is all about relationships to home, home is 'a room dappled with firelight [where] there are pictures and books' (116). Then, with our widening awareness, it extends to the town, county (only England could possibly have 'home counties'), country and, these days, the planet we live on. Clichés embrace the range of associations: the Englishman's home is his castle, and at the other extreme is God, who is our home.

We love this expanding home in a manner not unlike the way we love our own body. For just as we appropriate our body, so we appropriate our home; it belongs to us because we belong to it. (Was it not an ancient Greek who said that a man loves his city not because it is *great* but because it is *his*?) It is typically human to feel that what we discover belongs to us, even though it may have been there long before we were born and belonged to many other people before us. When Titus discovers a mouse-riddled, painted landing and exclaims, 'This is mine, mine, I found it!' (G50), he illustrates this process. For the reader there is of course the irony here that 'the whole caboodle' belongs to him anyway. Gormenghast, which is the size of a small town, is his home, and *all* his. Fuchsia feels this equation of body and home most strongly when Steerpike comes between herself and 'the long, notched outline of her home'. Behind him she sees

> something which by contrast with the alien, incalculable figure before her was close and real. It was something which she understood, something which she could never do without, or be without, for it seemed as though it were her own self, her own body, at which she gazed and which lay so intimately upon the skyline. Gormenghast.          (TG273)

Because its inhabitants fail to distinguish between the castle and their bodies, they can no more imagine leaving it than leaving their bodies.

Rising at the centre of Gormenghast 'like a mutilated finger from among the fists of knuckled masonry' (TG15), the Tower of Flints stands for the castle itself. Lord Sepulchrave, for whom body and home are one, dies by affirming his identity (in both senses) with the Tower. Titus manages to leave, but clings to his flint from the Tower and continues to define himself by the castle. Questioned in court as to what Gormenghast is and what it means, he tells the judge, 'You might as well ask me what is this hand of mine? What does it mean?' (TA76). Moreover, the Tower has a voice, to which Lord Sepulchrave adds his dying cry. Logically, then, when Titus loses his flint, he finds that he has 'nothing to prove [his] hands. Nothing to prove [his] voice' (TA105). The voice is important not only because the earl is, metaphorically, the voice of his castle, but also because it is with the voice in the throat that we audibly affirm our exist-ence at the same time as our identity. The infant's first cry says, 'I am!' In Peake's work, one must speak up, or remain anonymous. 'Does he know who I am?' Titus asks Juno. 'How can we know about you, dear, if you won't tell us?' she replies (TA61). In court he vigorously states who he is. 'So passionate was his outcry that the Court fell silent. That was not the voice of a hoaxer. It was the voice of someone quite convinced of his own truth – the truth in his head' (86); in other words, he might be mad. It's hard for Titus to find his own voice, for in his castle home 'stones have their voices. ... Voices that grind at night from lungs of granite. ... The voice of stones heaped up into grey towers' (TG112–13). Only after losing his knuckle of flint does he truly separate from the castle and find his self.

While still in Gormenghast, Titus's first concern is to keep his body and his home separate, no easy thing when the characters around him do not. Lost in those hollow halls where no sound breaks the silence of the stone, Titus sinks to the floor in despair – 'but a sense of terror jerked him to his feet again. It seemed that he had begun to be absorbed into the stone' (G181). In what he refuses, characters like Lord Sepulchrave and Flay find fulfilment. Peake consistently describes Flay in terms of rock and stone; he imagines that instead of words 'something perhaps more in the nature of a splinter or a fragment of stone' might issue from his mouth. What does come out is, 'It's me' (TG20), a stony affirmation of identity. Flay has a gift for merging with the fabric of the castle: 'knowing every bay, inlet and headland of the great stone island of the Groans, ... he had ... only to lean against the cliff face and he was absorbed' (TG414). In his exile, Flay recreates the great stone island in the form of 'a flat, sun-baked rock the size of a table' (G136) in the middle of Gormenghast river; that's where Titus discovers him fishing.

Having 'something tenacious and hard in his centre' (TG327), Flay makes himself a new home in the woods, with 'stone ovens and rock tables' (TG441). To his surprise he discovers that he has 'a woodland instinct which must have been latent in his blood' (TG442) and takes pride in his new-found skills, catching rabbits, fishing and preparing his food. Yet he cannot quite reconcile himself to seeing his hand produce something for himself alone, not in selfless service of the castle. 'Was this rebellion?' (TG443) he wonders. Eventually, his skills do serve the castle. When he returns to unmask Steerpike, his experience of navigating the pathless woods helps him chart the labyrinth beneath the castle, for 'his sense of orientation has become uncanny' (G336). What is more, he can merge with new backgrounds: 'He had only to stand still and he was absorbed into a wall, into a shadow or into rotten woodwork' (G296). Like his master, he happily identifies with Gormenghast, and consequently merges with it.

Peake implicitly contrasts Titus's situation with that of the Grey Scrubbers whose hereditary duty is to clean the stone walls of the castle kitchen. Through this daily proximity, they have become like the walls themselves, their faces expressionless slabs, their mouths mere cracks (TG27–28). They have been assimilated and lost all individuality:

> It had been their privilege on reaching adolescence to discover that, being the sons of their fathers, their careers had been arranged for them and that stretching ahead of them lay their identical lives consisting of an unimaginative if praiseworthy duty.        (TG27)

This is exactly how Titus views his future and the prospect fills him with dread. Simply because he is the son of his father there stretches before him a life that is 'no more than a round of preordained ritual' (G342), identical to the lives of generations of forebears, a career of unimaginative duty to sameness. For much of his youth he cannot bring himself to speak of this dread, even to Dr Prunesquallor. In itself this means repressing his sense of identity. Down in the stone halls, he reasons aloud with himself and finds his own secret passage to the world beyond the walls. This neatly underscores the difference between him and the Grey Scrubbers, who rarely speak and are traditionally deaf (TG28): they unthinkingly accept their condition and become like the flagstones that the rest of the castle walk upon.

The Grey Scrubbers may have their role to play in the society of Gormenghast, as 'any sociologist searching … for … a gamut of the lower human values' (TG27) would confirm, but Peake is interested in earls rather than urchins, and aesthetics rather than political science. He compares the great artist to 'a prince who with a line of kings for lineage can make no gesture that does not recall some royal ancestor', and goes on with a telling metaphor:

> Tradition is the line that joins together the giant crests of a mountain range – that links the great rebels, while in the morasses of the valleys in between, the countless apes stare backwards as they squat like tired armies in the shade.                                                                    (D8)

Peake's sympathy is with artists like Rembrandt and El Greco who create a new tradition in art by revolting against the old. And he feels pity, a withering pity that verges on scorn, for those who, like Crust, misuse their imagination by inventing a colourful social identity:

> Everyone knew that Crust had no wife in exile, ill or otherwise. … To have a wife in exile who was dying in unthinkable pain appeared to Crust to give him a kind of romantic status. … Without an exiled and guttering mate what was he? Just Crust. That was all. Crust to his colleagues and Crust to himself.                                                          (G64–65)

Not even Crust's pale romance is available to the Grey Scrubbers, in whom 'there was more than an echo of the simian' (TG27); they clearly belong among 'the countless apes' of Peake's world.

He considers that a person of high social class, like Titus, suffers a conflict between fidelity to their personal identity and absorption by the fabric of society that the countless apes do not. It's a matter of education, of self-image and – most important of all – imagination. Thanks to the Thing, Titus imagines another world for himself:

> The world that he pictured beyond the secret skyline – the world of nowhere and everywhere – was necessarily based upon Gormenghast. But he knew that there would be a difference; and that there could be no other place exactly like his home. It was this difference that he longed for.
>                                                                             (G506)

Breaking with tradition and imagining something so unknown puts Titus on a par with the rebel artist. He looks forwards to construct a future for himself, rather than backwards like the apes. Thanks to the imagination he has *vision*.

The Countess has found a way to resolve this conflict between self and society. As she walks surrounded by the 'white tide' of her cats, Peake sees her as 'a rock that moved with them, crowned with red seaweed' (G27): rock-like in remaining faithful to herself, as evinced by the flinty flash of her eyes, yet mobile in performing all her ritual duties, while remaining aloof from them. Responding to a critic who found his characters neurotic, Peake maintained that 'if she hadn't allowed herself to have all those cats, she would have become neurotic' (RTO12). She has found a balance that maintains her sanity. She even swears by the stones of the castle (G482 and 485) and when the flood comes and Steerpike has to be hunted down she takes command as though she were herself of Groan blood, turning over her thoughts 'like boulders' (TG413). This is the way of life that she intends to impart to Titus, teaching him

> how to live his own life as far as it is possible for one who will find the grey stones across his heart from day to day and the secret is to be able to freeze the outsider off completely and then he will be able to live within himself. … how he can keep his head quite clear of the duties he must perform day after day until he dies here as his fathers have done.          (TG398–99)

But she fails to do so, because she treats him, like everyone else, as an 'outsider' and completely freezes him off. In fact, with the 'snake-like coils' of her hair that 'all but hissed' (G38), she is very much a Medusa figure, wanting to petrify Titus in his role as earl.

So the 'grey stones' do indeed lie heavy on his heart, and by himself Titus cannot imagine how he can possibly live his own life – until he learns from the Thing. Like identity itself this happens through a combination of sameness and difference. There is similarity between Titus and the Thing beyond the fact that she 'breathed the same air and trod the same ground' (G411). From birth she is ostracized by the Bright Carvers, who consider that her illegitimacy makes her (as Fuchsia puts it, somewhat clumsily) 'not really like other babies' and 'different apart from that as well' (G192) because her mother Keda committed suicide. She is rejected by her people as though these differences were faults of her own. Titus is suckled by Keda, on milk that the Thing never gets to taste. He too is unlike other babies, being both 'hideous' (TG51) and, as an earl, intrinsically *different* (italicized in the text, G306). At an impossibly early age he is considered to be responsible for actions such as tearing the pages of the book at his christening, or dropping the symbols of his title into the lake at his earling. Just as the Thing challenges the castle by her way of life and flouts tradition by stealing carvings, so does he by desiring his own life, and by leaving the Ceremony of the Bright Carvings. They both defy the conventions of their culture.

However, what attracts Titus to her is not 'closeness or a sameness. … It was the difference, the *difference* that mattered; the *difference* that cried aloud' (G411; Peake's emphasis). At first the reader may take this in the sense that every young man has in mind when he looks at a girl and cries '*Vive la différence!*'[1] A hundred pages later, Peake shows that he means something else by it: 'She had shown him by her independence how it was only fear that held people together. The fear of being alone and the fear of being different' (G506–07). From her Titus learns to accept his solitude and to assert his right to be different, to be *himself*.

It takes belief in the possibility of action to effect change, and until almost the end of *Gormenghast* Titus feels helpless. Although he is treated, even as a baby, with the deference due to his rank, he feels he has no power or authority. At school, the other boys see 'no difference between themselves and Titus' (G306), but he has duties to perform; the ritual hobbles him 'ankle-deep in stone' (G7). Titus finds this ambiguity hateful. 'Was he a lord or an urchin? He resented a world in which he was neither one thing nor another' (G306). Despite being 'lord of a tower'd tract' he is nonetheless 'at the beck and call of those officials whose duty it was to advise and guide him' (BiD157). Worse, Titus feels subsumed beneath 'that other child, that symbol, that phantom, the seventy-seventh Earl of Gormenghast who hovered at his elbow' (G332–33). He fears his head may become 'an emblem', a 'mere token' like his father's, and his heart 'a cypher' (TA231) like the plaster heart of Bellgrove and Irma. Only after he has killed Steerpike and finds himself treated as the 'dragon-slayer' (G505) does he realize that the power of symbolism is his to take. As heir to the castle and the tracts of land about it, not to mention a whole population beneath him, and as the young earl who has triumphed over

---

1. Peake explores the evolution of difference in a love relationship through Irma Prunesquallor and Bellgrove: first she favours him with a 'devastatingly winsome' smile for being 'something different' (G222); then his solicitude makes her feel different from her guests (G238); only when married do they discover that their 'different spirits, different needs and different lives' (G392) no longer attract, but separate them.

Steerpike, he has enormous power. At the moment of realization, he feels its corrupting potential and rejects it:

> The heady wine of autocracy tasted sweet upon his tongue – sweet and dangerous – for he was only now learning that he had power over others, not only through the influence of his birthright but through a native authority that was being wielded for the first time – and all this he knew to be dangerous, for, as it grew, this bullying would taste ever sweeter and fiercer and the naked cry of freedom would become faint and the Thing who had taught him freedom would become no more than a memory.
>
> (G469)

He uses his power to liberate himself; he determines that 'with a single jerk' he must 'wrench himself free of his responsibility to the home of his fathers' (G467). Although it means turning 'traitor in his mother's eyes and in the eyes of the castle' (G505), he must bid farewell to Gormenghast. As Cheeta puts it ironically in the following book,

> a farewell from his old self to his new. How splendid! To tear one's throne up by the roots, and fling it to the floor. What was it after all but a symbol? We have too many symbols. We wade in symbols. We are sick of them.
>
> (TA231)

So Titus takes his stand: 'I want to be myself, and become what I make myself, a person, a real live person and not a symbol any more' (G459). And with these words he rides away from home.

BECAUSE WE EASILY LINK identity, body and home, living for a long time in the same place may dull our awareness of our own evolution. This happens to Steerpike: 'Whatever he now believed about himself was based on the assumption that he was the same Steerpike as his former self of a few years earlier. But he was no longer that youth' (G383). Conversely, changing place of abode questions identity and calls upon memory. Who has never felt a moment of puzzlement (edged with panic) on waking in an unfamiliar room? It's not just a matter of 'Where am I?' but also, by implication, 'Who am I?' Our sense of identity depends on memory – hence the fascination of stories about people suffering from amnesia. And memory may play false. It does with the professors at Gormenghast: they have only to desire a romantic youth for themselves and 'false memories flower within them' (G228). In his exile Flay sometimes fears that there may be no Gormenghast, and that his memory is playing tricks on him.

So he runs to check and sees it 'as real as the hand which shielded his eyes' (TG443) – notice the familiar pattern of the hand as the link with reality and the castle as extension of the body. Leaving Gormenghast, Titus takes his knuckle of flint, which is, 'in microcosm, his home' (TA21), to guarantee his memory and thereby his identity.

To defend his right to go where he will without being spied upon, he throws his flint at a remote surveillance device, the spy globe that follows him about. Without it he is

> even more lost than before. For I have nothing else to prove where I come from, or that I ever had a native land. And the proof of it is only proof for me. It is no proof of anything to anyone but me. I have nothing to hold in my hand. Nothing to convince myself that it is not a dream. Nothing to prove my actuality. (TA105)

Without the touchstone in his pocket he questions his identity and his sanity over the following 150 pages, and is almost unseated by Cheeta's attempt to drive him mad with her parody of Gormenghast.

He recovers on the last page of the book: after months of wandering he comes across a boulder that he recognizes from his childhood, and knows that the castle is just over the hill. This releases 'a flood of memories' (TA261) – exactly as when the Lost Uncle climbs onto the hillock that is in fact the White Lion. For Titus this boulder – another stone – confirms the reality of his past. He recovers 'all he had lost; all he had searched for. … The proof of his own sanity and love' (TA262). Like cutting the umbilical cord, severing the link between body and home confirms that home no longer contains us. Instead, we carry our home within us. We leave home to find out who we are; having found out, we cannot return, for we are no longer the same. As Peake puts it in *Mr Pye* (at one of those moments when he seems to be rather lamely echoing T.S. Eliot), 'one can never return' (MP208). So 'in a flash of retrospect' and with 'a sense of maturity, almost of fulfilment' Titus realizes that he 'carrie[s] his Gormenghast within him'. Peake expresses this new-found sense of identity quite simply: 'There he stood: Titus Groan'. He has fulfilled his desire 'to travel, not as an earl but as a stranger, with no more shelter than his naked name' (G506). He no longer defines himself by the castle or his title. The novel ends with him leaving by a track 'that he had never known before. With every pace he drew away … from everything that belonged to his home' (TA283).

The boulder that enables Titus to situate himself, geographically

and psychologically, is another touchstone. First of all, it was a boulder
– or 'what appeared to be a great boulder' – that enabled him to get
his bearings at the beginning of the book (10). That the touchstone
should be a boulder first and last is consistent with Peake's perception
of boulders as rocks that have withstood the test of time and tide. On
fishing up a marble head, he asks of it, 'Have time and water blurred you
to a boulder?' (P&D). At the masquerade at the Black House, Cheeta
gives the Countess a face 'like a great, flat boulder that had been washed
and worn smooth by a thousand tides' (TA235). Perhaps she got the idea
from the shape of Titus's skull: it too looks like a boulder, 'blunted by
the wash of many tides' (G413). In it Peake perceives 'youth and time
… indissolubly fused' (TA99). For him the boulder links the distant past
with the present, as when he writes of Titus that 'there was the history
of man in his face. A fragment from the enormous rock of mankind.
… That was the ancientness of Titus' (TG115). The boulder acts as a
reminder that man's solitude is as old as time. Like Madagascar, that 'the
seas encircle with chill ancientry' (Gb4), he is an island long detached
from his Africa.

Here we find the pattern that underlies all Peake's work. Whether it is
man's separation from God, the Earth flung out from the sun, or Titus
as a fragment from the rock of mankind, the relationship is always that
of a part to a whole. On leaving Juno Titus realizes that 'he was a part
of something bigger than himself. He was a chip of stone, but where
was the mountain from which it had broken away? He was the leaf but
where was the tree?' (TA102). (This echoes his father's feeling that 'the
long dead branch of the Groans has broken into the bright leaf of Titus'
(TG402).) As long as the part has not separated from the whole, it yearns
for independence. The moment it detaches and becomes aware of itself
as separate, it aspires to regain the whole but cannot, for it has become
a whole itself. What the part wants most is to reunite with the whole
without loss of separate identity: sameness with difference. What it fears
most is sameness without difference. As we have seen, the word *identity*
contains both.

Loss of difference is to be dissolved in or absorbed by the whole. In
*Titus Alone*, Peake uses the term 'zoneless nullity' (98) for the state in
which the boundaries of the self have been lost. This is what Titus fears
when he feels threatened with absorption by the stones of his home. Flay,
banished by the Countess, feels a sense of dissolution: his world – 'his
security, his love, his faith in the House, his devotion – is all crumbling

into fragments' (TG377). He experiences the silence of the hollow halls, whose boundaries he cannot find, as 'a kind of death' (G298). The limits of life itself, birth and death, are like the outline of an island. Peake's typical island is either a monolith rising directly from the sea, or a single block of stone set in sand. That rock stands for identity. The difference between it and the surrounding sea is evident. Rock may be eroded to a boulder but remains durably separate. To lose that sharp separation and be dissolved in the ocean is to die, to return to the state of unconscious fusion with whole that characterized the part before birth. Surrounding the island, then, lies an ocean of oblivion.

This is why leaving home is fraught with such conflictual feelings in Peake. It's like setting out on the sea, with the risk of being carried away by wind, wave or current. In 1932, as the time approached for him to leave home, he wrote a poem about Vikings 'Exploring the wonderful world' and 'Questing an unknown sea' (PS 8 (April 2003), ii: 7). His young 'Rebels' who run away from home discover that 'Snapped is their childhood's anchor-chain, / The helm shakes, and a tide is running' (Gb31). Titus's knuckle of flint is 'his only anchor' (TA21). When Juno leaves home with a new partner, she decides to call him 'Anchor' (196). She thought that 'the past is over. My home is a memory. I will never see it again.' She soon realizes that she needs her past. 'Without it I am nothing. I bob like a cork on deep water' (212).

Peake's metaphor of the island as the prototype of this homomorphic pattern of parts to wholes is a severely limiting belief: an island cannot return to the continent from which it detached and still remain an island. The idea of home, as a whole from which teenagers must part and to which they yearn to return, suffers from the same aporia. Going back home threatens the sense of identity gained by leaving it. This is why many of Peake's characters are displaced persons, uprooted wanderers who cannot go home, although they are forever in search of it. 'Whatever they eat, whatever they drink, is never the bread of home or the corn of their own valleys. It is never the wine of their own vineyards. It is a foreign brew' (TA69). Home starts as a haven and ends a prison. 'Home is where I was safe,' says Carrow, and then, 'Home is what I fled from' (TA116). Home is the paradoxical place that Titus wants to be free of (G506) but he spends the third book 'aching to be once again in the land from which he grew' (69), only to reject it when he's almost back there, in the name of his new-found identity.

Leaving home features in most of Peake's stories; on one occasion he made a horror story of it. The nameless protagonist of 'Same Time, Same Place' (an ironical title) is exceptional in still having both parents and a home at the age of 23. Like Titus he is expected to take over his father's business. One evening however he suddenly decides to 'forgo [his] birthright' and 'shake off the smug mortality' of his home (PP143). Looking at his mother's down-at-heel slippers and his father's nicotine yellow moustache, he feels he will suffocate if he does not leave at once. The words 'mortality' and 'suffocate' conjure up the threat of death by surfeit of sameness.

So out into the jungle of London he goes, to fall victim to the mesmerizing eyes of a 'glorious creature' (145). They hardly exchange a single word, for the young man believes 'she knew everything that was going on in my breast and in my brain. The look of love which flooded from her eyes all but unhinged me' (145).[2] Thereafter he acts as though he has indeed lost his mind; the scales fall from his eyes only moments before the wedding ceremony. So shocked is he by this encounter that he renounces differentiation and falls back into the morass of the safe sameness of home. Images of what he has just escaped fill his brain. In fact 'they fill it still' (150). Now he approves of the things that originally drove him out: 'I stared at it all and I loved it all' (150). No wonder he has no name; he has become as faceless and undifferentiated as a Grey Scrubber. The horror (and the irony) lies not so much in his close escape from animals – for he becomes one of the 'countless apes' himself – but in the life of oblivion, of 'zoneless nullity' that he embraces.

This young man is no true rebel. He lacks the voice of the heart, the imagination and the self-awareness required to succeed. In fact, so little is there in his breast or brain that he thinks the 'glorious creature' can know it all at a glance. What he lacks most of all, though, is *a world of his own*. This is a crucial concept for Peake. (Maeve Gilmore divined its importance and titled her memoir about him, *A World Away*.) Becoming a part that can unite with the larger whole without loss of identity requires that one create, or already possess, a world of one's own. As we saw earlier, to affirm his identity 'the artist must fling out into space, complete from pole

---

2. An unfortunate misprint in the first edition of *Peake's Progress* caused 'unhinged' to be repeated in front of 'brain' in this passage. I had Penguin correct it, along with more than 150 other errors, in the first (large-size) paperback edition of 1981. Stupidly they reverted to the faulty Allen Lane text when they reissued the book as a Penguin Classic in 2000. *Cave lector.*

to pole, his own world' (D11), a fragment detached from a larger whole from whom (or from which) it takes its colour. Within Peake's created world, we find the same pattern: Titus is always 'haunted by the thought of this other kind of world which was able to exist without Gormenghast' (G507). Finally he sets out to find it: the last words of *Gormenghast* are, 'Titus rode out of his world' (G511). That Titus has one of his own, in addition to his home, suggests that ultimately he will find resolution of a kind – if not a home in the sense that we have been using the word so far.

Within Peake's created world, there is then the inner world of his characters, 'a reality, a world apart, a secret place to which they alone [have] access' (G150). These worlds vary in richness, depending on the extent to which Peake develops the character. Some are superficial and ephemeral: on hearing that he has been invited to Irma's soirée, Opus Fluke yells with laughter until he is breathless. 'As he panted hoarsely to a standstill, he did not even look about him: he was still in his own world of amusement' (G123). Some are profound, like Bellgrove's inner world where he has 'a kind of golden fund, a reserve of strength' (G339) that he has never drawn upon. Some lead to a breakdown of all communication: in front of the stretcher bearing Fuchsia's drowned body, Titus and his mother stand side by side, 'in worlds of their own' (G462). A rich private world can be an object of envy: for Juno, part of the attraction of Titus is the inner world that he wears 'like a cloak' (TA89). It can also be a place of retreat from the everyday world, a solace. Less positively, it can involve flight from 'reality': in *Titus Alone*, Old Crime invites Titus to join him in his world within the world of the prison, 'away from the filthy thing called Life' (73; Peake's capital).

For Peake, fulfilment comes when a person manages to make the 'real' world they live in reflect or participate in their inner world, so that there is a sense of continuity or flow between the two, as in Peake's creative process. In this world of one's own, a person feels free to express themselves most fully (though not necessarily with ease), so that there is a sense of wholeness, of plenitude: self, activity and place become one. This state is another of the loves that Peake describes and is clearly akin to Keda's. 'It is the love of a man or of a woman for their world. For the world of their centre, where their lives burn genuinely and with a free flame' (TG77). Although the phrase 'the world of their centre' might seem to suggest a place within the body, perhaps we should understand it as 'the (place in the) world where they feel centred' as they express themselves in action. Certainly, this is something of what Crabcalf means when he points to the pile of unsold copies of his lifework and says, 'They are my centre' (TA186). Acting in accordance with their centre, Peake's characters express loving acceptance of who they are, like Fuchsia drawing hearts on the wall of her room, repeating 'I am Fuchsia. I must always be. I am me' (TG147) to herself.

Peake's description of this state comes at the moment in *Titus Groan* when Fuchsia is climbing the spiral stairs to her attic. Her experience is memorably (and poetically) compared with that of a pearl diver 'in his world of wavering light' (77), of a painter, in his world of 'a rented room, and turpentine' (78), and of a farmer letting the 'rich soil' of his land crumble through his fingers. Each of these men is expressing himself fully through an activity that leaves him feeling in complete harmony with his surroundings. We might call it a state of 'everyday ecstasy',[3] in contrast to the more intense experience such as Keda has, although it falls not far short of hers. After all, the diver is fishing for pearls, the traditional metaphor for the precious self (or soul) within us. Seeking it he feels 'complete and infinite. Pulse, power and universe sway in his body' (77).

There are many parallels with Keda's ecstasy: the pearl fisherman feels 'at one with every swarm of lime-green fish' (77) and the painter notices such things as 'the dust beneath the easel' and 'the paint that has edged along the brushes' handles' (78) in a manner that recalls Keda's experience of loving the mangy dog. In this state, the very ordinariness of humble things becomes lovable, suffused with significance. Thus Fuchsia, passing under 'the vague rafters' that loom above her in her attic, 'unconsciously' loves them (79), rather as the Ancient Mariner looking down at the watersnakes 'blessed them unaware' (NAEL 2: 430). This contrasts with the defeated young man's undifferentiated 'love' for 'it all' on his return home (PP150).

Each of these persons is 'in love', experiencing 'a love that equals in its power the love of man for woman and reaches inwards as deeply' (TG77). We are so used to assuming that to be 'in love' requires a romantic relationship between two persons that it may come as a shock to realize that Peake means something rather different. He is expressing a notion that has been largely forgotten in the past hundred years or so, ousted by the Freudian belief that meaningful love is exclusively centred in our

---

3. I coined this term before realizing that Marghanita Laski wrote a book with this title. My use of it here owes nothing to hers.

interpersonal, and especially romantic, relationships. Peake is talking of love for things like one's job and one's home that can eloquently reflect a person's sense of their own unique worth, and be a primary source of self-esteem and personal fulfilment.

This experience 'reaches inwards' quite as deeply as romantic love, as is clear from Peake's choice of examples. The pearl fisherman works down on 'the ocean's faery floor', the place where Peake situates our most intimate encounters.[4] With one hand 'clasped to a bedded whale's rib' (77) he anchors himself down there (and we have already noticed how anchors secure identity). This undersea love, that does not involve another person, is a counterpart to the love that Peake compares to a bird of the air: it is like a rooted rock, anchored deep in the earth.

Twenty pages later, Peake expands on the figure of the yeoman who crumbles 'the rich soil' between his fingers. He devotes a full page to Pentecost, the gardener, whose walk has 'something ridiculous about it', his legs being 'too short in proportion to his body' but his head is 'nobly formed and majestic'. Peake loves grotesques like this in much the way that Pentecost loves his flowers, particularly his apple trees: 'the mother would not love the child the less were its face to be mutilated' (99). That he is in his own world of 'everyday ecstasy' is clear from how he walks (just after turning his back on the castle):

> it seemed that he was moving into the earth. Each stride was a gesture, a probing. It was a kind of downward, inward search, as though he knew that what was important for him, what he really understood and cared for, was below him, beneath his slowly moving feet. It was in the earth – it was the earth.                                                    (99)

It is also confirmed by a passage that Peake deleted from the manuscript in which he compared Pentecost with 'the mystic [who] is fulfilled among his clouds and stars and made consummate by the soil' (MS 1: i). This sudden shift from the earth as planet to the earth as soil suggests that, like Keda's ecstasy, this state involves the whole universe in a moment of being.

In each of these vignettes, the characters affirm their unique identity as they occupy an inner world that is co-extensive with the outer world, extending from the stars, down through clouds, dust and earth to the ocean floor, with equal heights and depths within the body. They

---

4. Keats spells 'faery' like this in 'La Belle Dame Sans Merci'.

participate in the universe, from the macro- to the micro-cosmos. At the same time, they declare this fusion of worlds that they love to be their *home*:

> As the pearl diver murmurs, 'I am home' as he moves dimly in strange water-lights, and as the painter mutters, 'I am me' on his lone raft of floor-boards, so the slow landsman on his acre'd marl says with dark Fuchsia on her twisting staircase, 'I am home.' (TG78)

In this state of being in love with being, a person's island ('his lone raft'), identity, body, world and home all become one. The part affirms itself and fulfils its separate identity, at the same time as enjoying an ecstatic sense of unity with the universe. Sameness and difference fuse into wholeness. We may guess that this five-in-one integration is the ideal towards which Titus was to tend.

# Evil

Mary  How do we know what is evil? What is evil to
      you is not evil to me.
Miles Listen to her. 'How do we know what is evil?'
      she says. It is all written down. There are the
      ten commandments, heretic!
Mary  Not everything is written down.
                                            (*Cave*, Act III)


Crocodiles … cannot recognize fear any more than
they can recognize evil. If they did recognize evil I
doubt whether it would change their habits. But man
is not like that.                                (MP118)


O foul descent! that I …
               … am now constrained
Into a beast, and mixed with bestial slime.
               (*Paradise Lost*, IX: 163; NAEL I: 1965)


THE NOTION OF EVIL came to preoccupy Peake with increasing acuity.
In early works like 'The Touch of the Ash' and his Slaughterboard
tales, he amused himself with the cardboard characters of boys' stories.
In *Titus Groan*, he depicted a character who consciously and deliberately
chooses to do evil in pursuit of power. This led to his most developed
– and literary – examination of human evil in *Gormenghast*, as Steerpike's
choices reduce his options until he is cornered, literally and figuratively,
and killed. Having done this, Peake began to reflect on the relationship
between evil and art.

Between writing *Titus Groan* and *Gormenghast*, he visited the newly
liberated concentration camp at Bergen-Belsen, and the experience no

doubt contributed to his depiction of Steerpike's villainy. It also made him question the nature of man and wonder if some people might have no ability to choose the good, or even awareness of having choice, and be therefore incapable of anything but evil. In the immediate postwar years, he wrote a poem about such a man, whose very head and hands, eyes and mouth 'Leave him no option but to harm / His fellows and be harmed by them' because he was 'built for sin, / As though predestined from the womb' (Gb1). In 'Boy in Darkness', written in the early 1950s, Peake explored these new anxieties (as hinted at by the title itself). For *Titus Alone* he created a character called Veil, 'born with a skull so shaped that only evil could inhabit it' (136). (The word *veil* is an anagram of *evil* as well as both *vile* and *live*. The reader may like to observe how often *veil* and *vile* appear in the quotations in this chapter: Peake associates them with evil right from the beginning of *Titus Groan*.) However, a character who can do only evil may be philosophically interesting but having no human complexity does not involve the reader. We cannot project into Veil as we can with Steerpike.

Peake was also worried by the accidental evil that characterizes all creation. 'Bad' things happen all the time, to animals as to man. During the Dark Breakfast in *Titus Groan*, rainwater leaking through the roof of the castle causes a puddle to form on the floor of the refectory. 'Near the margin of this inner rain-fed darkness an ant is swimming for its life, its strength failing momently for there are a merciless two inches of water beneath it' (TG406). The natural world can be 'merciless' because it is quite unaware of the consequences of its working. In *Mr Pye*, a drifting dead whale disrupts a missionary meeting. Such things are bound to happen in a world that enjoys freedom of action; they are caused, in nature as in man, by lack of awareness. (Peake never states what he seems to imply, that the ultimate cause is the absence of God.)

As we saw in the chapter on animals, creatures like the cat (TG57), the lynx, the hawk and the vulture (TG136), or the lilac jellyfish floating in the depths of the sea in *Mr Pye* (15), are conscious only of their own behaviour. The self-possession and self-sufficiency that distinguish them from man make them innocent. Conversely, when humans act without awareness and cause harm, they are to blame. Even the need to relieve simple urges like an itch or a full bladder provides Peake with examples. To scratch himself, Barquentine rubs his back against a wall,

> disturbing in the process a colony of ants which (having just received news
> from its scouts that the rival colony near the ceiling was on the march

and was even now constructing bridges across the plaster crack) was busily
preparing its defences.

Barquentine had no notion that in easing the itch between his shoulderblades he was incapacitating an army.                                    (G161)

By behaving with the unselfconsciousness of an animal, he causes a
disaster in the world of the ants, just as nature's unthinking actions wreak
havoc in ours. For Peake no thoughtless action can be called entirely
innocent.

In *Titus Alone* a naked baby in the Under-River piddles on the ground.
Within moments,

> in all innocence, and in all ignorance, it has saturated a phalanx of warrior
> ants who, little guessing that a cloudburst was imminent, were making
> their way across difficult country.                                    (TA122)

In that infant Peake would have liked to see 'an innocence quite moving
to behold. A final innocence that has survived in spite of a world of evil.'
But that would presuppose a total absence of self-awareness in the child,
reducing it to the level of an animal, like the Thing or Tintagieu. So Peake
was left with a paradox: 'would it be too cynical to believe that the little
child was without a thought in its head and without a flicker of light in
its soul?' he asks (TA122). He never resolved the problem of accidental
evil.

On the other hand, he knew that self-absorption and private purpose
in man make him behave with the unselfconsciousness of an animal.
Peake regularly calls Veil the 'mantis man' for this reason, as much as
for his physical appearance. (It also suggests a praying/preying pun.)
Unlike the two women glimpsed smiling at each other 'with unhealthy
concentration' in *Titus Alone* (27), Veil cannot be blamed for his behaviour. 'His body, limbs and organs and even his head could hardly be
said to be any fault of his, for this was the way in which he had been
made' (TA129). Steerpike, on the other hand, is fully human, able to
experience and express a range of values such as Peake observes in the
face of the newborn Titus: 'Sin was there and goodness, love, pity and
horror' (TG96). But Steerpike decides on his own separate purposes and
independent action: he inflates his self with ambition. Although he is
represented at the last as 'the skewbald beast' of Gormenghast (G406 and
427), he is no animal, and not blameless. To Peake's missionary ancestors the evil of his purposes would have been obvious; today, when self-
development and self-sufficiency are viewed as virtues, Steerpike seems

far less reprehensible to readers who admire his initiative and courage. He is a fine example of the attractiveness of evil depicted in art.

When he wrote *Titus Groan*, Peake believed in man's ability to choose, to discern 'the gap between evil and innocence' (G169). His characters may err out of ignorance or lack of self-awareness, but like Bellgrove they hope that 'ultimate innocence, like a nest egg, awaits its moment in the breasts of sinners' (G339). On the other hand, when they do things that they *know* to be bad, and abuse their freedom by *deliberately* choosing evil, a point of no return is soon reached. Steerpike's career is an exemplum of just such a journey to hell.

In writing as in drawing, Peake had the 'poetical character' defined by Keats: he took 'as much delight in conceiving an Iago as an Imogen'; he made no attempt to censor the 'light and shade' of the imagination and its products 'foul or fair' (as Keats put it in his letter to Richard Woodhouse, 27 October 1818; NAEL 2: 894). Peake's terms for it are more Blakean: his pencil could evoke both 'heaven and hell' (CLP2). He depicted pure innocence and also created a horrific portfolio purporting to be 'by Adolf Hitler'. Likewise Fuchsia imagines on her attic stage 'fierce figures' that 'brooded like monsters or flew through the air like seraphs' (TG80). Having no preconception of the plot of *Titus Groan*, and acting as an 'Authorjehovah', Peake granted independence to his characters, allowing them to evolve as they would. Created with this attitude, uncensored works of art inevitably depict good and evil alike. Thus the foul Steerpike rose from the shadow regions of Peake's imagination.

With eyes that, for all his 17 years, 'were dark and hot with a mature hatred' (TG45), Steerpike represents 'the dark side' right from the start. Exploiting one of the oldest symbolic polarities that associates light with good and dark with evil, Peake depicts him leaning against 'the shadowy side' of a pillar (TG32) in the foetid castle kitchen. Later, Steerpike tells Fuchsia that he loves her 'as the shadows love the castle' (G356). In the final pages of Gormenghast, as the flood waters rise and the hunt drags on, Titus recalls 'the days when there was no Steerpike at large like a foul shadow' (438). Once cornered, Steerpike takes refuge on a ledge 'where the shadows were at their deepest' (472). From first to last, Peake associates him with shadow; neither his motives nor his actions will bear the light of day.

To establish Steerpike as 'a shape still darker than the darkness' (G357) chapter 19 of *Titus Groan*, 'Over the Roofscape', opens with a passage in the anaphoric style of Dickens's evocation of fog in *Bleak House*:

> The darkness came down over the castle and the twisted Woods and over
> Gormenghast Mountain. … Darkness over the four wings of Gormen-
> ghast. Darkness lying against the glass doors of the Christening Room
> and pressing its impalpable body through the ivy leaves of Lady Groan's
> choked window. … Darkness over the stone sky-field where clouds moved
> through it invisibly. Darkness over Steerpike, who slept, woke and slept
> fitfully and then woke again.                                  (TG131)

Darkness ushers in the night. A year later, as Steerpike looks down into
the burning library from the top of his improvised ladder, Fuchsia,
preparing to break the window from the inside, finds herself staring
into 'a face framed with darkness' with eyes like 'narrow tunnels through
which the Night was pouring' (TG319). With these dramatic words the
chapter ends. There is no explanation for the capitalized 'Night' and
no further reference to it in the book. Yet its terminal position suggests
that it meant much to Peake.[1] He knew the physiological reason for the
look of Steerpike's eyes: their pupils have dilated the better to see in the
dark. He shows the same thing in the Twins: as they gaze at Barquentine,
their pupils are 'so wide open as to cause these caverns to monopolize
their faces to the extent of giving to their countenances an appearance
of darkness' (TG405–06). Symbolically, night stands for the primordial
darkness before God declared 'Let there be light!' – what Milton calls 'the
wide womb of uncreated Night' (*Paradise Lost* II: 150; capitalized in most
editions but not in NAEL 1: 1839). He in turn would have known that
for Spenser, Night is the mother of Falsehood. Whatever its origin, that
capital letter in Peake signals that, as Steerpike discovers the pleasure of
inflicting fear and pain on the Groan family, he stands for evil itself.

His first evil trait is his propensity to manipulate other people, treating
them as disposable objects. Escaping from the kitchen, Steerpike divines
the enmity between Flay and Swelter and attempts to play them off against
each other. Flay locks him in the octagonal room while he thinks about
what to do about him. Sent back to Swelter, Steerpike might 'put it to the
chef that he had been lured away from his province and incarcerated for
some sinister reason of his own invention' (TG125). Steerpike solves his
dilemma by escaping them both. With its combination of exploitation,
manipulation and incarceration, this little episode contains a pattern that

---

1. At the climax of the Black House masquerade, Cheeta calls, 'Let in the night!'
(TA227).

is repeated and amplified throughout *Titus Groan* and *Gormenghast* until it ends with Flay's death at the hands of Steerpike.

By allowing Steerpike to peep through the spyhole, Flay unwittingly provides him with a new aim in life: 'an occupation among those apartments where he might pry into the affairs of those above him' (TG53). This phrase not only reveals Steerpike's acquisitive mind but also contains a metaphor that Peake instantly literalizes (or should we say *materializes*, here?). *Up* is the direction of status and power. Steerpike becomes a social climber, up the wall from the octagonal room, and up through the ivy to the window of Fuchsia's attic, just for starters. He advances rapidly up the social ladder of Gormenghast: from the kitchen to the Prunesquallors' and the Twins'; then he becomes amanuensis to Barquentine, who through the ritual wields the true power in the castle. Steerpike wants power and the more he has, the more he wants. Eliminating Barquentine, he becomes Master of Ritual himself. With Titus still a minor, he is effectively the ruler of Gormenghast. As we know from Lord Acton, power corrupts, and it corrupts Steerpike absolutely.

Peake's spatialization of power along a vertical axis takes up a dead metaphor that permeates our language; a politician *rises* to power, or *falls* from it, for instance, just as we *look up* to someone we admire (which puts us in their power) and *look down* on those we scorn (and therefore feel we have power over). Steerpike does not have exclusive rights to this metaphor; even Fuchsia succumbs to it as she looks down from her attic window on the morning of her brother's birth. Seeing little knots of people congregating in the squares and alleys of the 'poor quarter' far below, she asks, 'What are they all doing like a lot of ants down there? Why aren't they working like they should be?' (TG82). Looking down upon the rest of the world has always aroused feelings of superiority.

Steerpike's aims crystallize in the episode of the stone skyfield. After escaping from the locked room, he decides to climb to the highest vantage point, 'an area the size of a field' overlooking 'the heavy, rotting structures of adjacent roofs and towers'. By the time he reaches it, there is just enough light for his 'greedy eyes' to 'devour the arena' (TG130). Then 'the sun withdrew' (TG131). Unable to sleep, he undertakes to grope his way round this high terrace in the darkness. As he does so, the weather changes; 'a kind of weight seemed to lift from the air, and … he stopped as though his eyes had been partially relieved of a bandage'. Steerpike is going to receive some kind of revelation:

he felt, rather than saw, above him a movement of volumes. … That there
were forces that travelled across the darkness he could not doubt; and then
suddenly, as though another layer of stifling cloth had been dragged from
before his eyes, Steerpike made out above him the enormous, indistinct
shapes of clouds following one another in grave order as though bound on
some portentous mission. …

   Then came the crumbling away of a grey veil from the face of the night,
and … there burst of a sudden a swarm of burning crystals, and, afloat in
their centre, a splinter of curved fire.                          (TG133–34)

The moon that lights his darkness is the third motif associated with
Steerpike.

   There are two ways in which Peake associates the moon with evil. The
first harks back to the artist and his created world that takes 'the colour of
the globe it flew from, as the world itself is coloured by the sun' (D11).
By appearing to shine with its own light, when in fact it only reflects the
sun's, the moon comes to be associated with dishonesty and falsehood.
Moreover, 'it's a coward anyway. Only comes out at night!' (TA176).
When the wandering Titus sees the moon, he 'hated its vile hypocrisy of
light; hated its fatuous face; hated it with so real a revulsion that he spat
at it and shouted, "Liar!"' (TA11). The second link is equally traditional.
In a poem, Peake writes how, 'When God had pared his fingernails /
He found that only nine' slivers lay on his tray. '"Rebellion!" cried the
Angels. "Where / Has flown the Nail of Sin?"' (RoB20). It is there in the
sky, the moon. As in Crabcalf's lifework, the moon 'figures quite a lot'
(TA176) in Peake's writing.

   While Peake does not specify whether Steerpike receives his 'portentous mission' directly from the moon and the 'forces that travelled across
the darkness' or conceives for himself his 'purpose most immediate', of
the effect there is no doubt. By the light of the stars and this 'splinter' of
moonlight, 'it was possible for Steerpike to continue his walk without
fear' (TG134). The next morning,

   it was as though he found himself transplanted into a new day, almost
   a new life in a new world. Only his hunger prevented him from leaning
   contentedly over the warming parapet and, with a hundred towers below
   him, planning for himself an incredible future.               (TG135)

Overnight Steerpike coalesces into a man of ambition. I write 'man' advis-
edly, for so far the narrator has referred to Steerpike as a boy; from now on,
only the other characters call him 'boy'. What is more, until this moment

Steerpike's name was 'Smuggerly' in Peake's manuscript; the change of name reflects his new identity. Under the pen of an 'Authorjehovah', he begins to lead his own existence, characterized by independent affirmation of self, and a quest for power conducted through guile, hypocrisy and lies. He becomes a Machiavel, exploiting every object and person that he encounters. His conscience he flings 'so far away that were he ever to need it again he could never find it' (G14).

More than four years after writing this passage, Peake saw his own creative process enacted by glassblowers at work. He was much impressed by the idea that sand, 'once … perhaps, the sea-doomed castle of some long-dead child', can be turned into a hollow glass vessel at the end of a blowpipe:

> Far from gull-wailing strands, it has become the burning mother of transparency. Sand. No longer the fast sky; the coughing wave. Girdled in a grey fastness of masonry, welkined with crasser substance than the clouds, it has found its purpose. And from its huge transmutation lucence breaks.
>
> (*Convoy* 27)

The imagery combines not just the 'grey fastness' of Gormenghast, the sky and clouds of this moment of Steerpike's transformation, but even the cry of the gull, which is what he thought he heard when the infant Titus was being carried to the library (TG226). What is more, the glassman's final act is to knock the vessel from the end of his blowpipe 'with frightening ease' (*Convoy* 25). The object he has created becomes separate and independent. Like Steerpike, 'it has found its purpose' (*Convoy* 27).

Following this new departure, Steerpike has no more to do with the Flay–Swelter feud, and never returns to the peephole opposite the Countess's room. But the stone skyfield itself, which he wishes to exploit the moment he discovers it (TG130), becomes a means to manipulate Fuchsia (TG158–59). Furthermore, the bird's eye view that it affords feeds his desire to dominate and shows him two things: Fuchsia's attic window – his only means of re-entering the castle – and the Twins on their tree, so distant that they seem to be 'about the size of those stub ends of pencil that are thrown away as too awkward to hold' (TG137).

The Twins are Steerpike's first victims – and the cause of his downfall. He uses them as stooges, stand-ins for himself, feeding their jealousy and their desire for power, promising them golden thrones and making them set fire to the library. But he overestimates his ability to control people and events. Unable to prevent the Twins from talking about the burning, and realizing that 'through terrorism and victimization alone could loose lips be sealed' (TG479), he pays them a nocturnal visit in the guise of Death. With Sourdust's skull stuck on the end of his swordstick, he threatens them with 'strangling in a darkened room' (481) if they cannot hold their tongues. He enjoys playing Death, savouring the phrase, 'I murder in a darkened room' (480). In the end, sensing that he is losing his grip on them, he carries out his threat by starving them in a window-less apartment, heartlessly discarding them like those pencil stubs that have become 'too awkward to hold'.[2] Like every murderer respectful of literary tradition, he returns to check that all has gone according to plan, unwittingly leading investigators to the scene of his crime.

With the Twins Steerpike discovers sadism. When he makes them sit in the lake, the 'twist of his lips' reveals 'the vile, overweening satisfaction he experienced' (TG475). At this stage he can still restrain himself. 'Directly he had seen, tasted and absorbed the delicious essence of the situation, his voice rapped out: "Go back!"' (TG475). Later, he becomes addicted to humiliating them, making them crawl beneath a carpet. Were it not for the sick pleasure this gives him, 'it is to be doubted whether he would have gone to all the trouble which was involved in keeping them alive' (G48).

At first it seems as though Steerpike might have a soft spot: as he prepares to burn down Lord Sepulchrave's library we learn that

> destruction in any form annoyed him. That is, the destruction of anything inanimate that was well constructed. For living creatures he had not this same concern, but in a well-made object, whatever its nature, a sword or a watch or a book, he felt an excited interest.                    (TG264)

But even this scruple is swept away in pursuit of his aim. He pushes a priceless vase off a mantelpiece merely to impress the Twins; with evident satisfaction he breaks a 'long oval window of blue glass' that blazes 'like lazuli – like a gem hung aloft against the grey walls' (G257) of the castle. As Mr Pye discovers, feeding one's vices stimulates the appetite to the point where it becomes more natural to do evil than good.

In *Titus Groan* Peake avoids all reference to Christianity (except for

---

2. There is a similar macabre ominousness about Steerpike's dismissal of Nannie Slagg. 'Leave her to me,' he repeats in his first conversation with Fuchsia. 'Leave her to me' (TG165). In *Gormenghast* he dispatches her with poison purloined from Prunesquallor's dispensary.

the name 'Pentecost'). Steerpike is assisted by Hardyesque 'questionable gods' (TG144). *Gormenghast*, on the other hand, includes specific references not only to Satan – Barquentine swears at Steerpike 'by the piss of Satan' (G166) – but also to God, Heaven and Hell. The concept of sin (not mentioned in *Titus Groan*) is there too: in leaving the Ceremony of the Bright Carvings to seek out the Thing, Titus knows that he commits 'the sin to cap all sins' (G407). In this novel, 'to sin was to sin against Gormenghast' (G267). What is more, Peake conceived this book on an epic scale: 'Surely so portentous an expanse should unburden itself of gods at least; scaled kings, or creatures whose outstretched wings might darken two horizons. Or dappled Satan with his brow of brass' (G15).[3] The language here recalls Milton's depiction, in the opening lines of *Paradise Lost*, of the Holy Spirit, 'with mighty wings outspread' (I: 20; NAEL 1: 1818) and later on of Satan's 'contemptuous brow' (IV: 885; NAEL 1: 1892). As *Gormenghast* progresses, Milton's influence becomes apparent.

In rising to become Master of Ritual and challenging the young Earl, Steerpike may be compared with Milton's Satan, who starts out as God's right-hand man, but loses this enviable position to the newly promoted Son. In protest Satan organizes a revolt in Heaven; defeated by God he is thrown down into Hell, which is specially created to receive him and his acolytes. Refusing to acknowledge defeat, Satan rejoices in his infernal kingdom. In *Gormenghast* Steerpike shares Satan's pride and desire for power. On his way through the uninhabited part of the castle where he has incarcerated the Twins, he

> exulted in it all. In the fact that it was only he who had the initiative to explore these wildernesses. He exulted in his restlessness, in his intelligence, in his passion to hold within his own hands the reins, despotic or otherwise, of supreme authority.                                         (G257)

Like Satan, Steerpike savours all the hellish qualities of the place:

> The air was chill and unhealthy; a smell of rotten wood, of dank masonry filled his lungs. He moved in a climate as of decay – of a decay rank with

---

3. The 'brow of brass' was a favourite with Nonconformists; it derives from 'thy brow [is] brass' (Isaiah 48.4) via Cowper's 'Self-Acquaintance', one of his Olney hymns, where it represents Presumption.

its own evil authority, a richer, more inexorable quality than freshness; it
smothered and drained all vibrancy, all hope.

　　Where another would have shuddered, the young man merely ran his
tongue across his lips. 'This is a *place*,' he said to himself. 'Without any
doubt, this is *somewhere*.'　　　　　　　　　　　(G258; Peake's emphases)

That Peake was thinking of Hell is confirmed by terms like 'evil authority'.
He even alludes to Dante's famous phrase, 'Abandon hope all ye who
enter here'. When Steerpike is finally surrounded by the flotilla of makeshift craft, he sees with 'overweening pride … in this concentration of the
castle's forces a tribute to himself' (G471). Although he is no fallen angel,
for he starts from the kitchen rather than an elevated place in Heaven
(which suggests a parodic intent on Peake's part, as does the fact that
Lord Sepulchrave has died while the son is yet an infant), there is often
little to choose between Steerpike and Satan.

　　Peake's most Miltonic passage is also one of the most extraordinary in
*Gormenghast*, a four-page account of Steerpike's journey across the castle,
during which his shadow seems 'every whit as predatory and meaningful
as the body that cast it'. Even when it disappears for a moment, it remains
'like the evil dream of some sleeper who on waking finds the substance
of his nightmare standing beside his bed – for *Steerpike* was there' (261;
Peake's emphasis). The narrator wonders why this should be, and why
this particular shadow should evoke a sense of darkness:

> Shadows more terrible and grotesque than Steerpike's gave no such feeling.
> … It was as though a shadow had a heart – a heart where blood was drawn
> from the margins of a world of less substance than air. A world of darkness
> whose very existence depended upon its enemy, the light.　　　(G263)

In *Paradise Lost* the existence of Hell depends on God, 'the Celestial
light' (I: 245), whom the fallen angels consider as their enemy. Steerpike's
shadow likewise depends on light for its existence.

　　At this point Peake causes an 'almost unprecedented' darkness to fall
over Gormenghast (as occurred at Christ's crucifixion). A phrase like 'the
world had been swathed away from the westering sun as though with
bandages' harks back to Steerpike's revelation on the stone skyfield.
Although Peake declares it to be 'a freak of nature and no more' he simultaneously suggests that it might have a supernatural origin, 'as though the
sense of oppression which the darkness had ushered in had more than
a material explanation' (G262). ('More than material' is Mr Slaughterboard's euphemism for the spiritual in man.) To drive off this darkness,

the inhabitants of the castle light 'every available lantern, burner, candle and lamp' – a scene that is paralleled at the killing of Veil in *Titus Alone*, which takes place by the light of multiple lamps (131). As a result,

> The walls of Gormenghast were like the walls of paradise or the walls of an inferno. The colours were devilish or angelical according to the colour of the mind that watched them. They swam, those walls, with the hues of hell, with the tints of Zion. The breasts of the plumaged seraphim; the scales of Satan.                                                     (G263)

In addition to all the verbal echoes of *Paradise Lost* in 'devilish', 'angelical', 'hell', 'Zion', 'seraphim' and of course Satan himself, the central statement about perception repeats Satan's claim that 'The mind is its own place, and in itself / Can make a Heav'n of Hell, a Hell of Heav'n' (I: 254–55; NAEL 1: 1823), which in turn reminds us of *Hamlet*: 'There is nothing either good or bad, but thinking makes it so' (II.ii). Peake would have us believe that Steerpike's evil derives, at least in part, from Hell itself and participates in the eternal battle between God and Satan.

The following paragraph sees Steerpike 'come to something very like an isthmus … that joined one great mass of sprawling masonry to another' (G263). The image of the isthmus, followed by references to 'continents of stone', shows that Peake is thinking in terms of womb and tomb, life and death; indeed, Steerpike is on his way to kill Barquentine. His shadow moves 'a little forward of its caster', as though to anticipate the act, leading the way 'towards those rooms where its immediate journey could, for a little while, be ended' (G264) – as will Barquentine's life. But Steerpike bungles the murder. Outwitted, he saves himself by leaping out of the window with the burning Master of Ritual still clutching him; they fall into the stagnant moat below, where Steerpike drowns Barquentine. Above them, 'the moon like a nail-paring floated unsubstantially in the low north. It cast no light upon the earth' (G275). This sliver of moon is Sin, and the light that casts no light repeats Milton's celebrated oxymoron describing hell, where there is 'no light, but rather darkness visible' (I: 63; NAEL 1: 1819).[4] Then Peake evokes the epic simile with which Milton compares Satan, after his fall into the burning lake of Hell,

---

4. One of Peake's potential titles for *Gormenghast* was actually 'By the Light of Darkness', along with countless variations around the word 'Chaos' (on the endpapers of notebooks 3: v and 3: vi).

with Leviathan, 'in bulk as huge / As whom the fables name of monstrous size' (I: 195–96; NAEL 1: 1822).

> Deep in the horrible waters of the moat the protagonists … still moved together as one thing, like some foul subaqueous beast of allegory. Above them the surface water through which they had fallen was sizzling and steam drifted up invisible through the darkness.                    (G275)

In this episode Steerpike is badly burned, so that he himself suffers what he threatened to inflict upon the Groans and the Prunesquallors in the library fire; in addition to the post-traumatic stress that racked them, he experiences the physical pain that they were spared. Peake has a sense of poetic justice – and punishment by fire is traditionally what Hell is all about.

A few pages later, Satan returns as the name of the monkey that Steerpike acquires and dresses for Fuchsia (G355). What, one wonders, was Peake's intention here? Was it only so that, after Fuchsia has refused the gift, Steerpike can say that the monkey wants to know who he belongs to, which immediately tells us who Steerpike belongs to? At any rate, the monkey serves later as a literal stand-in for Steerpike, its tail being cut off by the Twins' great axe. Thereafter both tail and monkey disappear entirely from the story – except perhaps for the moment when the search for Steerpike begins: there is hope that 'sooner or later, in the corner of some eye, the tail of his shadow would be seen' (G389), thus ensuring that Steerpike's diabolical nature is kept before the reader's eye.

Meanwhile, Fuchsia's rejection of Steerpike and her accusation that he is 'going soft' (G357) bring home to him the precariousness of his situation: 'there was that in Gormenghast that, with a puff, could blow him into darkness'. And in his mind's eye his future takes the shape of a pit into which he stares helplessly. 'What then was this pit, wherefore was its depth, and why its darkness?' he wonders (G361), echoing Satan's self-question on seeing Hell: 'Into what pit thou seest / From what height fall'n' (I: 90–91; NAEL 1: 1820). It's not only in Steerpike's mind that the pit – a traditional meronym for Hell and a favourite of Milton's – is present, for by the time he has reached the Twins' apartment 'his dark-red eyes were like small circular pits' (G384) – and it's tempting to add (remembering the burning of the library) 'through which the Night was pouring' (TG319).

By now Steerpike has lost all self-restraint and thrills with 'the evil knowledge of the power [of life and death] that was now his' (G345).

He shudders with 'a kind of lust' for 'unbridled evil' (G385), 'a lust for killing' (G442). Just as Satan rejoices in having brought Death into the world, so Steerpike celebrates his success with a war dance around the skeletons of the Twins. It is the climax of his career, for he is observed; from this point on he can only go downwards towards that pit.

When Prunesquallor attempts to arrest him, Steerpike thinks he makes a choice, but Peake points out that his lust for evil is such that he has now passed beyond choosing. To capture, trial and punishment he prefers 'a nether empire … the dark and terrible domain – the subterranean labyrinth – the lairs and warrens where, monarch of darkness like Satan himself, he could wear undisputed a crown no less imperial' (G386). In other words, he adopts Satan's motto: 'Better to reign in Hell, than serve in Heav'n' (I: 263; NAEL 1: 1824).

Following Milton like this leads Peake to use terms like 'empire', 'monarch' and 'imperial' that are incongruous in the world of Gormenghast. We can accept that Steerpike should disappear 'like a snake into a rock' (G446) and that Titus should think of him as a 'lithe and ingenious fiend' (G489), recalling the serpent in the Garden of Eden (and the snake in the grass of Virgil's *Eclogue* III), because there has been a snake writhing beneath Steerpike's ribs ever since his first meeting with Fuchsia (TG163). Likewise the evocation of 'the long-drawn hiss of the reptilian rain' (G264) takes us to that moment in *Paradise Lost* when all the fallen angels are transformed into snakes and can only hiss their approval of Satan (X: 508–21). But *Gormenghast* contains military images quite alien to Steerpike's experience yet characteristic of *Paradise Lost*, which repeatedly evokes the vast armies of myth and history. For instance, realizing that all his plans are ruined, Steerpike shudders with 'the glory of knowing himself to be pitted, openly, against the big battalions' (G385). 'It was war, now. Naked and bloody' (G443). Thus we find his mind engaged in 'a warfare of the gods'. It paces 'over no-man's-land, over the fields of the slain, paced to the rhythm of the blood's red bugles. To be alone and evil! To be a god at bay! What was more absolute?' (G444). This leads to his hope that, in his last stand, he will be able to

> create some gesture of supreme defiance, lewd and rare; and then, with the towers of Gormenghast about him, cheat the castle of its jealous right and die of his own evil in the moonbeams.                              (G495)

The military metaphors are pure Milton, and that final phrase, 'jealous right', is typical of Satan's view of God. *Gormenghast* becomes Peake's *Paradise Lost*.

T HE IMPLICATIONS OF WHAT he had done were not lost on Peake. To start with, by making Steerpike the antagonist, not to say the hero of *Gormenghast*, he had been celebrating him, or at least celebrating what made him diabolical. Satan invented Sin by imagining revolt against God in Heaven (II: 760) and brought it into this world; Steerpike, with 'his restlessness … his intelligence' and 'his initiative' (G257) brought evil into the world of Gormenghast, where 'Evil and doubt were one. To doubt the sacred stones was to profane the godhead' (G267). What they share is their inventiveness, their ability to imagine the unthinkable, and the energy with which they pursue their malevolent aims. So Peake's 'poetical character' placed him in a position much like Milton's: as Blake observed, Milton 'was a true Poet and of the Devil's party without knowing it' (*The Marriage of Heaven and Hell*). Having recognized his camp, Peake began to write explicitly about the conflict between art and religion.

His plays of the 1950s dramatize the making of works of art and the fears that they awaken. In a radio play first broadcast in 1954 as 'A Mural for Christmas', then revised and broadcast two years later as 'A Christmas Commission',[5] an artist is invited to paint 'a fresco of Christ's Nativity' (W&D106) on the wall of an English country church. The large white wall 'yawning to be filled' (106) by the artist's imagination rehearses the images and sense sequence of Peake's creative process identified in the opening chapter. The artist feels 'frightened' because the commission challenges his confidence in himself, 'as an artist and as a man', and in his faith – 'or lack of it' (111): he paints out of love for painting, not love of God. He is also afraid of how 'the Little Men' (112) of the congregation will react to his work. They correspond to those 'countless apes' (D8) that Peake opposes to the rebel artist; in *Mr Pye*, for instance, Thorpe has fled from 'the jungle of London with its millions of apes' (184). Here they are likened to 'the hippopotamus, the scorpion, the gadfly and the python' – people who, for lack of awareness, are impervious to beauty and aggressive towards artists. 'How would you like them in your congregation?' asks the painter. 'They'd be a change from sheep,' returns the vicar, dropping his voice (114). For all their protests, the Little Men are

5. A conflation of the two scripts is available in PS 9 (April 2005), ii: 5–31.

not interested in 'the glory of God' either; they only want the even tenor of their lives, the 'winter sleep' (114) of their self-absorption, to continue undisturbed. The artist's work will inevitably shake them up.

These Little Men are largely inspired by fear. They fear all art that departs from their Christmas card stereotypes and 'distracts' (113) them from their worship. They also fear that, because art depicts evil, it may offend God and 'blacken' (*Cave*, Act II) them in His eyes. In another of Peake's plays on this theme, an artist has carved a gargoyle for the local cathedral. His father hates it and protests that he

> would not be surprised if Our Lord came down those steps and beat you to the ground and trod upon your evil, blasphemous throat. I would not be surprised if He should burst apart this vile, unnatural Beast, this graven image. ... It is revolting to think of it upon God's house – crouched on some buttress, leering like a devil.          (Act II)

His artist son responds that a devil is just what it is meant to be – but 'a happy devil. ... Happier than many of us'. The Little Man's basic fear is summed up by the first Warden in 'A Christmas Commission':

> I am an ordinary man. I have no pretensions. I am not a highbrow. But by God's grace I know when I am right. I know when there is danger to our church. I know the devil when I see him. I can smell him out. And this [mural] ... this is one of his works.          (W&D116)

For the Little Man, art brings with it a whiff of hell; it awakens fears of damnation.

Here Peake is revisiting Christianity's age-old quarrel with art. When the painter confesses that he feels that his 'power to create is deeply challenged', the response is:

> Warden 1   'To create.' Listen to him!
> Warden 3   Creating should be left to the Creator.
> Warden 1   He talks as though he were God.
> Warden 3   Who is the only Creator.          (W&D114)

But the artist knows that his God, as a fellow creator, would approve. In *The Cave*, the sculptor finds himself in the same camp as the heretic, Mary, who judges his gargoyle quite differently:

Three 'gargoyles' – human, animal and angelic.

> God will enjoy it. Not the God of vengeance and torture. Not your great
> bully who sits astride the sky. It will make *him* angry. He will ask what it
> means. The great and impossible fool.                    (Act II; Peake's emphasis)

In short, Christianity equates the creative energy of the imagination that
is expressed by art with the 'quenchless vitality' of evil (BiD191). Peake
concludes that 'Art and religion sail on separate keels / Through separate
waters' (W&D111) – the maritime metaphor reminding us that both are
also responses to man's solitude. So their respective definitions of evil are
equally different.

 Art is procreative and forward-looking: it brings about change by
imagining the new and different. Religion is reactionary and backward-
looking; it clings to sameness and the past. In art, today's revolution is
tomorrow's cliché – which the Little Men love. Peake's artist observes
sorrowfully that Van Gogh's sunflowers 'were high explosive once. They

made men angry. But now they are almost tame ... the shock has gone'
(118). Out of their fear of change, the Little Men find the innovative
art of their own time evil, and so the artist suffers from rejection of his
work.

In 'A Christmas Commission', the congregation's immediate response
to the new fresco is horror and hatred. Only a child finds it exciting and
greets it with delighted laughter. After 10 years, though, familiarity makes
it seem comfortingly banal, at which it's the artist's turn to protest:

> Did you hear what they said? They find my mural 'soothing'. O God, it
> used to live when it was hated. When people mocked it and spat at it.
>
> (118)

He draws a parallel (already implied by the mocking and spitting) between
Christ, whose revolutionary message has become soothingly conventional, and his painting, whose shocking originality is now perceived as
'charming' and 'restful'.

> Restful? Was Christ restful? I would rather have returned to find my fresco
> scraped to the plaster in a fit of passion. I would rather it was smashed by
> vandals, than to find this apathy ... this unawareness.          (118)

The Little Man's 'unawareness' is the animal side of man, his tendency
to fall back into 'the morasses of the valleys' between 'the giant crests of a
mountain range that links the great rebels' (D8). Art should offend and
make people think differently, about God as well as about life, but the
apes would rather not think – or feel (W&D118). The evil they see in art
leads them to reject it.

This not only confirms that Peake was aware of being of the Devil's
party, it also supports my view that the Titus books are about the creation
of a work of art which experiences social rejection in *Titus Alone*. Starting
as a revolutionary idea that is in itself change in a society dedicated to
changelessness, it is 'exhibited' at the Black House.[6] There Titus suffers
'the supreme degradation' (214), exposed, mocked, spat at and scratched

---

6. The second edition of *Titus Alone* contains a surprising misprint. The narrator
   stated that an 'exhibition', instead of 'expedition', 'had been mounted' (202)
   to the Black House. As this reading was supported by neither manuscript,
   typescript, nor first edition, it is corrected in all editions since the early
   1980s.

EVIL                                    189

by Cheeta in a fit of passion. Around 1950, while Peake was reflecting on this topic, he produced a series of paintings and drawings depicting the mocking of Christ. The artist might wish the shock value of his work to endure, but it makes for persecution to be of the Devil's party. Being a creative artist not only parallels the work of God but leads to being treated as His Son was.

Nor is this all. Out of fear, the Little Men themselves bring evil into the world by inventing. In *The Cave*, the artist, Harry, has a conventional and rational brother, Miles.

Miles   There is only one creator. It is not for Man to create. Invention is a cleaner thing. The copestone, the lever, the wheel.
Harry   And the rack.
Miles   And the rack.
Harry   And the black instruments of modern war.                    (Act II)

From *Gormenghast* onwards, Peake sees man's inventions as potentially evil. Art may be explosive, but the shock of its vision and beauty has a vivifying power; it awakens man from his lethargy and jolts him into lively awareness. 'The black instruments of modern war' enable those who wield power (or usurp it, like Steerpike) to inflict pain and dominate or enslave the apes of the valleys. The artist's creations work for good; invention for evil. So Peake sets art back to back with technology, as he does art and religion.

The three are linked in Peake's mind. In *The Cave*, he illustrates his claim that man has always had 'something to worship and at the same time something to fear'. Primitive man imagines a moon goddess and dreams of improved spears the better to defend himself against wolves; medieval man fuses worship and fear in 'God & Hell fire & Witchcraft' (PS 5 (October 1997), iii: 29); modern man, for lack of a God, fears loneliness and the applied science of the hydrogen bomb. Art, religious belief and technology are all responses to fear. With vision and courage the artist transforms his fear into works of beauty; the religious believer turns his into cowardly worship, and the scientist invents 'the instruments of modern war'. This explains the capitalized 'Fear' that Titus feels shortly before encountering the product of his imagination, the Thing (G132). It also leads us straight to the world of Peake's fiction of the 1950s.

In 'Boy in Darkness' the Lamb reigns at the foot of a mineshaft or pit amid the wreckage of an industrial society. Enslaving men and turning them into animals, he is the antithesis of art. In fact he unites all the evils of religion and technology, down to his blindness that contrasts with the artist's vision.[7] Then comes the world of *Titus Alone*, where Peake uses the demonic power of his imagination to denounce the evil of man's inventions. Abuse of power and technology is epitomized by the scientists who annihilate all the animals in Muzzlehatch's zoo with some kind of death ray, and by their 'factory' where vast numbers of unidentified men and women suffer and die.[8] Evil characters believe in the value of revenge and the infliction of pain; they also believe in that 'great bully' in the sky, 'the God of vengeance and torture' (*Cave*, Act II).

Peake associates all the evil characters of *Titus Alone* with the image of the pit, along with the fumes of hell and – a new motif that is loaded with physical revulsion – *slime*. This is most evident when Veil cruelly reminds the Black Rose of how he has bound her to him in an abuser/abused relationship. 'O slime of the slime-pit!' she retorts in scorn (TA127). Later, as Titus fights to release her, 'Veil's face seemed to expose itself as though it were vile as a sore: it swam before his eyes like the shiftings of the grey slime of the pit' (TA136). The scientist's 'factory' is qualified as a 'ghastly hive of horror; a hive whose honey was the grey and ultimate slime of the pit' (TA199). Until the Black House episode, Peake leaves 'the pit' undefined. Then he brings his motifs together in the image of the 'great and horrible' *fleur du mal*: 'a flower whose roots drew sustenance from the grey slime of the pit, and whose vile scent obscured the delicacy of the juniper. This flower was evil, and its bloom satanic' (TA225). Thereafter, 'fumes' serve as a shorthand for the evil that fills Cheeta's 'inventive brain' (199) and 'her vision, as a pit can be filled with fumes' (TA246). Because she is utterly heartless, she is 'all sophistication; desirable, intelligent, remote. Who could have told that joined in deadly grapple beneath her ribs were the powers of fear and evil?' (199). 'An evil thing borne on an evil draught' (250), she is the epitome of the intelligent person 'gone wrong': her parody of Gormenghast is an instance of the 'mimic art' that Peake denounced in his Introduction to *Drawings*.

Veil, on the other hand, embodies 'the ape' who is 'wrong' from the start. His evil stems not from misuse of the brain and its inventiveness, nor from lack of heart. So, 'what is it threads the inflamed brain of the

---

7. His eyes are regularly described as 'veiled' – e.g. pages 189, 191, 201 and 204. All three animals, Lamb, Goat and Hyena, are qualified as 'vile'.

8. The chief scientist recalls Dr Mengele, who experimented on prisoners at the extermination camp associated with a factory, Auschwitz.

one-time killer?' asks Peake. 'Fear? No, not so much as would fill the socket of a fly's eye. Remorse? He has never heard of it.' Having no awareness, he has no conscience to fling away. 'It is loyalty that fills him, as he lifts his long right arm. Loyalty to the child, the long scab-legged child, who tore the wings off sparrows long ago.' So he was evil even as a small boy.[9] Loyalty, we might recall, keeps Prunesquallor faithful to his animal companion, which suggests that Veil's childhood self may play a similar role for him. Finally, it is 'loyalty to his aloneness' that motivates him, along with

> loyalty to his own evil, for only through this evil has he climbed the foul stairways to the lofts of hell. Had he wished to do so, he could never have withdrawn from the conflict, for to do so would have been to have denied Satan the suzerainty of pain.                                   (TA136)

Inhabited by evil from the moment of his inception, Veil has made evil his companion in solitude, and to that evil self he remains faithful.

In *Titus Alone* Peake mourns the passing of innocence and the desecration of the planet:

> Once there were islands all a-sprout with palms: and coral reefs and sands as white as milk. What is there now but a vast shambles of the heart? Filth, squalor, and a world of little men.                                   (TA250)

He could be thankful that he had his art, painting and above all the novel, in which to express in all innocence the demonic power of his imagination and suffer only the scorn, or neglect, of Little Men.

---

9. Psychologically, this is quite correct: cruelty to animals in childhood is a high-level predictor of criminal behaviour in adulthood. Cf, for instance, K.D. Becker, J. Stuewig, V.M. Herrera, and L.A.A. McCloskey, 'A Study of Fire-setting and Animal Cruelty in Children: Family Influences and Adolescent Outcomes' in the *Journal of the American Academy of Child and Adolescent Psychiatry*. 2004; 43(7): 905–12.

# Perspective

> Whether the scouring, sexless eye of the bird or beast of prey disperses and sees all or concentrates and evades all saving that for which it searches, it is certain that the less powerful eye of the human cannot grasp, even after a life of training, a scene in its entirety. No eye may see dispassionately. There is no comprehension at a glance. Only the recognition of damsel, horse or fly and the assumption of damsel, horse or fly; and so with dreams and beyond, for what haunts the heart will, when it is found, leap foremost, blinding the eye and leaving the main of Life in darkness. (TG136–37)

> The moon 'can see us from above. We are nothing but moles.' (*Cave*, Act III)

WHENEVER PEAKE WRITES OF visual perception, he underlines its selectiveness: what we see depends not upon the optical qualities of the eye but on the heart and mind behind it. 'We do not see with our eyes but with our trades.' To a poet, a tree may be 'a green fountain', to a carpenter the same tree is 'potential timber' and to a child it is 'a world of boughs' to climb into (AW3). Because this subjectivity is fuelled by emotion, 'no eye may see dispassionately': 'what haunts the heart' blinds the eye and leaves 'the main of Life in darkness' (TG136–37; Peake's capital). The world we live in is ultimately defined by the heart, so if we examine how Peake sees the worlds that he creates, taking *perspective* as our theme, we may learn more of what haunts his heart.

In everyday life, as we look out upon the world, our point of view corresponds to the height of our eyes above the ground. This standpoint

Sebastian, Peake's elder son, drawn from the level of a child's eye.

in space creates perspective. Change the point from which you view the world, and it will look and feel different. A tall building – the roof of Gormenghast – a mountain or a plane affords us with a bird's eye view, which can feel godlike, reducing people on the ground below to the insignificance of ants (as it does for Fuchsia (TG82)). The opposite is the worm's eye view, looking up from below, which vastly increases the apparent size of objects, so that they may seem to threaten the viewer. It can make a giant of a small man. The other factor governing perspective is the distance from the eye to the thing observed; this ranges from the close-up to the long view. Every departure from the familiar, everyday standpoint, whether of angle of view or proximity, increases emotional impact. At the extreme, our feelings can be so powerful that we no longer *see* at all.

In Peake's graphic works, his portraits respect the classic distances – head-and-shoulders, seated or full length – and the angle of view is slightly raised or lowered. His illustrations, on the other hand, frequently introduce a sense of tension and drama by raising the point of view to 12 or 15 feet above the ground. One thinks of Long John Silver, cleaning his knife on a wisp of grass after killing poor Tom, for instance, or (in *Household Tales* by the brothers Grimm) Our Lady's Child in the midst of the wilderness, surrounded by thorn bushes. Both these scenes are highly theatrical, with the spectator's raised viewpoint, vegetation framing the scene like a proscenium arch, the level floor of the 'stage' and the artfully directed lighting. Increasing the height of the viewpoint (higher than the gallery called 'the gods' in a theatre) and looking down more steeply pushes the horizon up toward the limits of the frame. Peake does this in his illustrations for *The Rime of the Ancient Mariner* – and even out of the frame altogether in *Treasure Island*, with the superb fall of Israel Hands from the rigging of the *Hispaniola*.[1] He also uses the worm's eye view: out in the street Tom Thumb flinches from the boots that threaten to crush him. Illustrating other people's writing, Peake uses a wider range of perspectives than for his portraits.

In his own books, he employs an equally wide range of viewpoints, with significant variations: the longer the text, the more extreme the

1. The complete absence of reference points in this illustration caused it to be printed upside down on one occasion when it was borrowed for a theatre programme. These illustrations for *Treasure Island* can also be found in MPMA 120–23.

Portrait of Jenifer Pink. The point of view is slightly raised, emphasizing the broad forehead and narrow chin.

A plunging view of a 'Creature with thatch-like hair'.

One of Peake's illustrations for *Tom Thumb*.

Illustration for 'Our Lady's Child' in *Household Tales*.

*Facing page:* Long John Silver cleans his knife on a wisp of grass.

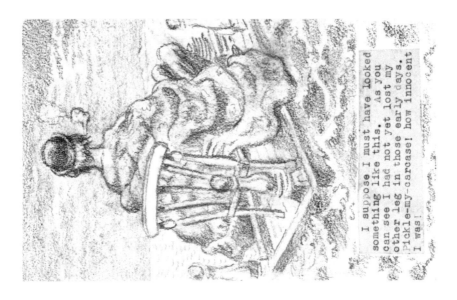

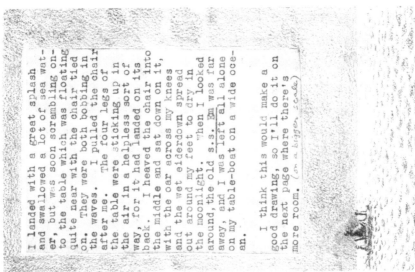

An opening from *Letters from a Lost Uncle*, showing
two views of the Uncle in mid-ocean on his table-raft.
The left-hand page is 80 per cent sky.

views. *Figures of Speech* contains no text, and all the pictures adopt an everyday standpoint and distance. *Rhymes without Reason* varies the distance, but not much the angle. *Captain Slaughterboard* presents greater contrasts: the horizon dips to the bottom of the frame or disappears over the top; distance varies from page to page, shifting from close-up to long view, and several views are subjective. Visually the book is like a trip in a small boat on a rough sea. In a word, Peake observes his own injunction to the artist: 'leave the spectator with no option but to see what *you* liked' (CLP4; Peake's emphasis), and what he liked here was graphic variety.

*Letters from a Lost Uncle* combines Peake's visual and verbal arts on the same page at much greater length than *Captain Slaughterboard*; its illustrations approach the extreme, with frequent changes in distance and angle. Opposite a conventional 'full-length self-portrait' of the Uncle we find a dizzying contrast: an aerial view of his igloo on an ice floe 'the size of Kent' (4–5). Also on facing pages are two pictures of the Uncle on his raft: a long view from the side, eight tenths of which is sky, followed by a rear three-quarter view from only a few feet away (34–35). We also find ultra-close-ups (a footprint, an eye) and distant views in which the human figure, relegated to the very edge of the picture, shrinks to a mere speck; aerial views and walrus's eye views. (There are no worms in the polar ice, particularly not worms with eyes to view with.) There are even cross-sections through the pack ice, with the Uncle and Jackson or just the Snow Lion's paw on the surface, and all the sea creatures in the water below. Several illustrations are resolutely subjective, such as the view over the Uncle's knees, as he sits looking at the interior of his igloo. Jackson's point of view is rendered indirectly by a footprint and stains of coffee and washing up water on the page. The *Lost Uncle* takes Peake's pencil towards the limits that drawing can accommodate.

In the Titus books Peake alternates action with tableaux, interspersed with passages during which time passes or the scene changes. For all three he generally places his readers in the position of a theatre audience. In *Titus Groan* this metaphor is generally implicit, but one scene, complete with the diminutive figure of the infant Titus, spells it out:

From the sky's zenith to where he sat upon the strip of sand it seemed that a great backcloth had been let down, for the heat had flattened out the lake, lifted it upright on its sandy rim; … balanced in a jigsaw way upon the ragged edge of this painted wood was a heavy, dead, blue sky, towering

I had left my harpoon behind the
door of the cave - which
was a very silly thing to
do - but it wouldn't have
been much use against so
huge a beast. Nor could
my leg-spike jab him any
higher than his knee. I
knew the way that bears killed people. They take
them in their huge white hairy
arms as though they are going to kiss them and then
they hug them to death.

    I knew it was no good to
turn round and run, because
with my leg-spike I wouldn't
be fast enough to escape. So
I waited and hoped for inspiration.

Jackson dwarfed by the paw of a polar bear.

to the proscenium arch of the vision's limit – the curved eyelid. At the base
of this staring drop-cloth of raw phenomena he sat, incredibly minute.

(TG463)

In *Gormenghast* many scenes – the golden oak wood examined in the
first chapter, or the heronry, which 'seemed stage-lit in the beams of the
westering sun' (17) – are set like this. The furnishings of Steerpike's room,
'that tasteful and orderly trap' (350), are theatrically composed, as are the
scenes leading up to his death. At the last, 'his lust was to stand naked
upon the moonlit stage' (496). In *Titus Alone*, the metaphor becomes
increasingly explicit. When Titus enters a room we are told that immediately to his left 'was a striped couch and on the other side of the room,
down-stage as it were, supposing the night to be the auditorium, was a
tall screen' (57). The same occurs in scenes mediated through his eyes:
'From where he stood, Titus could see, as though on a stage, the protagonists' (244). Finally, in *Mr Pye*, Peake jokingly foregrounds his technique:
the seaward opening of the tunnel to the port of Sark, 'like a proscenium
arch, contained this morning a harbour set, as lovely and inventive as you
could wish. The props were all in place' (15).

When he abandons the perspective of the theatre, Peake's narrative
standpoint is mobile and dynamic, liable to shift to any conceivable angle,
point of view, or perceiver, way beyond the limits of drawing. His eye can
zoom in on horses swimming in a tower-top lake, seen from so great a
distance as to be as small as insects, or accommodate the microscopic
and the macroscopic simultaneously. In *Titus Groan*, the opening of the
chapter called 'By Gormenghast Lake' combines 'the motion of minutiae'
(455), a distant view of the castle and the whole of summer in 'the belly'
of a single drop of water (456). Peake focalizes erratically. For instance,
the first two pages of *Titus Groan* present the castle from the outside,
somewhat in the manner of a guidebook,[2] and then suddenly adopt the
point of view of an observer who 'from a window in the southern wall of
Gormenghast' might watch 'the minute moonlit figures' of prize-winning
Bright Carvers 'moving to and fro along the battlements' (16). Neither
this observer nor this particular standpoint is ever revisited in the book.

On other occasions Peake suddenly shifts to literal bird's eye views,

---

2. In 'Peake, Knole, and *Orlando*' I showed how these pages are immediately
comparable to the opening of Vita Sackville-West's guide to her ancient stately
home, *Knole and the Sackvilles*.

wondering 'Who can say how long the eye of the vulture … requires to grasp the totality of a landscape' (TG136) or enjoying 'space, such as the condors have shrill inklings of, and the cock-eagle glimpses through his blood' (TG80). He can adopt the draughtsman's perspective: describing the movement of Irma's hips, he presents a 'bird's eye view, cross-section' of their 'figure-of-eight patternations' (TG460). The cartographer takes a similar vertical view. Captain Slaughterboard maps his discoveries. Flay struggles for months to gain an overview of the labyrinthine cellars of Gormenghast by mapping them. Peake sees both landscapes and maps in human faces, and in both cases he views them from above, like a bird.

He is also a frequent user of internal perspective, rendering what the narrator or character thinks and feels, which of course cannot be represented in a picture. It's what the novel does best. Yet his habit of unexpectedly slipping in and out of various minds can confuse the reader. At the christening ceremony, Titus slips and clutches at the Book of Baptism on which he has been laid, committing 'his first recorded act of blasphemy' (119) by tearing the corner of a page. Failing to appreciate that the perspective of this passage is that of the castle, not the narrator, Colin Manlove singled this out as an example of what he called Peake's illogic (Manlove 233). Sometimes words liberate Peake's eye from the fixed perspective of a drawing faster than the reader can accommodate.

In fact, what characterizes much of Peake's work is the stunning abruptness of his shifts of perspective or viewpoint. Take the scene in *Titus Groan* of Flay looking through a lighted window and discovering Swelter giving his pet cleaver an even finer edge. It is focalized through Flay's eyes: we see what he sees and no more. Then he moves his head 'further into the light in order to obtain a clear view of the floor of the room'. The following paragraph reads:

> The light that seeped in a dull haze through the window dragged out as from a black canvas the main bone formation of Mr Flay's head, leaving the eye sockets, the hair, an area beneath the nose and lower lip, and every-thing that lay beneath the chin, as part of the night itself. It was a mask that hung in the darkness.                    (208)

Because we assume that we are still looking in with Flay, we do not realize at first that 'through the window' refers to the light shining *out*. Flay's head is being viewed *as from inside the room*. Swelter does not notice him, so this new point of view is that of the narrator alone, a disembodied artist's eye looking at a painting. Then the narrative returns to Flay's subjective experience. This particular kind of confusing transition resembles 'crossing the line' in film making; it occurs more frequently in *Titus Groan* than in Peake's later works, probably as a result of inexperience. On the other hand, unexpected shifts of point of view continue to occur throughout his work.

There is a sudden vertical view when Steerpike reaches the stone skyfield at the climax of his climb over the roofs of Gormenghast. For three pages, Peake has foregrounded what Steerpike sees, thinks and feels as he climbs; the narrator's comments serve only to enhance the intensity of the internal perspective.[3] 'It took him perhaps seventeen minutes by the clock, but by the time of his beating heart he was all evening upon the swaying wall' (TG128). Objectivity is there in the reference to clock time, but with 'his beating heart' and 'the swaying wall' the narrator rejects it in favour of the subjective experience of time and space. When at last Steerpike looks over the parapet of the high terrace, his field of view suddenly opens up:

> a crane arose at a far corner of the stone field and, with a slow beating of its wings, drifted over the distant battlements and dropped out of sight. The sun was beginning to set in a violet haze and the stone field, save for the tiny figure of Steerpike, spread out emptily.                          (130)

The whole passage is mediated through Steerpike's perceptions – except for that interpolated observation about his 'tiny figure'. Suddenly Peake has thrown in an aerial, god-like perspective. We might call it 'the creator's view', for Peake has stepped back, or rather *up*, to view Steerpike as a minute creature in the vast world of his imagining. It happens again early in *Titus Alone*: suddenly we have the statement, 'seen from above Titus must have appeared very small as he ran on and on' (TA35).

The experience of reading a novel may be thought of as progression on a horizontal axis, a word-by-word sequence of impressions. Only when we have finished reading can we accede to the vertical axis and entertain a view of the work as a whole, and thus enjoy something of the writer's perspective. Because Peake is anticipating this moment, and dramatizing the creator's view before we can yet share it, his switch to the vertical is disorientating. It is similar to the shock effect of the opening of *Titus*

---

3. Roger Fowler noticed the abruptness of Peake's shifts when he used this passage (i.e. pp. 126–31) to illustrate his multi-category approach to point of view (Fowler 213–35).

*Alone* when the author/narrator apostrophizes his character: 'Come out of the shadows, traitor, and stand upon the wild brink of my brain!' (TA9). Most of the time, though, his creator's all-seeing eye remains implicit.

On the other hand, Peake is always explicit as to the colour and appearance of his characters' eyes. Some are quite striking: 'pure violet' (TG96) for Titus and 'small, dark red', the colour of 'dried blood' (G14) for Steerpike. (Violet and dark red are at opposite ends of the spectrum.) Predictably, the Countess's eyes are 'of the pale green that is common among cats' (TG54), and Bellgrove is memorable because

> his eyes were disappointing. They made no effort to bear out the promise of the other features, which would have formed the ideal setting for the kind of eye that flashes with visionary fire. Mr Bellgrove's eyes didn't flash at all. They were rather small, a dreary grey-green in colour, and were quite expressionless.                                                      (G59–60)

Eyes reflect personality. Dr Prunesquallor's 'great vague eyes … like a pair of jellyfish' (TG49) behind the thick lenses of his glasses may seem comic, but ultimately they reveal how easily his heart can be moved to tears.

Peake makes his characters' eyes the *subject* of many sentences, as if they had a will and a life of their own. The Poet's eyes, for instance, 'travelled rapidly in every direction before they came to rest' (TG140). Flay's eyes *travel* frequently too; Prunesquallor's *swim*, of course. As for Rottcodd,

> his eyes behind the gleaming of his glasses were the twin miniatures of his head. All three were constantly on the move, as though to make up for the time they spent asleep, the head wobbling in a mechanical way from side to side when Mr Rottcodd walked, and the eyes, as though taking their cue from the parent sphere to which they were attached, peering here, there, and everywhere at nothing in particular.                           (TG17)

This relationship of Rottcodd's eyeball to his cannon ball shaped head repeats Peake's homomorphic pattern of part to whole, island to continent and created world to creator's universe. These eyes are still attached, taking their cue from the 'parent sphere', but like rebellious offspring they act independently of it. The result is comic: they run 'up and down and all over' each carving (18) and also have 'the run of the ceiling' (20). Rottcodd has roving eyes for everything except women.

For Peake, the independence of his characters' eyes is no joke. The narrative eye of his imagination – what he calls 'the brain in the eye and the eye in the brain' (D7) – can hover or whiz where and how it pleases. It can go where the body cannot, affording sudden and unexpected perspectives, but it remains subordinate to his head and his heart. However, when his characters' eyes take excursions of their own, he disapproves. Departure from the norm heightens the emotions of both narrator and character. Here's Swelter peeping at his apprentices:

> he opens the door the merest fraction of an inch and applies his eye to the fissure. As he bends, the shimmering folds of the silk about his belly hiss and whisper. … His eye, moving around the panel of the door, is like something detached, self-sufficient, and having no need of the voluminous head that follows it. … So alive is it, this eye, quick as an adder, veined like a blood-alley. … As the eye rounds the corner of the door it devours the long double line of skinny apprentices as a squid might engulf and devour some long-shaped creature of the depths. As it sucks in the line of boys through the pupil, the knowledge of his power over them spreads sensuously across his trunk like a delicious gooseflesh.        (TG361–62)

That *self-sufficiency* says it all: the autonomy of a part that becomes detached from its 'parent sphere' opens the door to evil, hence the 'hiss and whisper' of the snake and the release of sordid passions from the depths. Yet more is to come, an extraordinary flight of fancy summing up the feud between Flay and Swelter:

> Had the flesh, the fibres, and the bones of the chef and those of Mr Flay been conjured away and away down that dark corridor leaving only their four eyes suspended in mid-air outside the Earl's door, then, surely, they must have reddened to the hue of Mars, reddened and smouldered, and at last broken into flame, so intense was their hatred – broken into flame and circled about one another in ever-narrowing gyres and in swifter and yet swifter flight until, merged into one sizzling globe of ire, they must surely have fled, the four in one, leaving a trail of blood behind them in the cold grey air of the corridor, until, screaming as they fly beneath innumerable arches and down the endless passageways of Gormenghast, they found their eyeless bodies once again, and re-entrenched themselves in startled sockets.        (TG364–65)

After this 140-word sentence, whose sockets are the more startled, the characters' or the reader's? Notice how astronomical metaphors come naturally to Peake when he writes of autonomous ocular globes: they are like the world that the artist 'fling[s] out into space, complete from pole to pole' just as 'the earth was thrown from the sun' (D11). He may accept the independence of his works, but he disapproves of the independence of these characters' eyes within his created world.

Peake's roving creator's eye could be indiscreet and awaken salacious ideas like Swelter's; after all, it could tell us everything that he can imagine. In the event, he never allows it to be a peeping Tom; his moral code is strict in this respect. But his characters are less restrained. In fact, the Titus books contain a whole catalogue of peeping and spying of increasing indiscretion, invasiveness and technological complexity.

*Titus Groan* begins innocently enough: before entering the Hall of Bright Carvings, Flay rattles the door handle. Wondering who is there, Rottcodd looks through the keyhole, striving to control 'the vagaries of his left eye (which was for ever trying to dash up and down the vertical surface of the door).' He discovers 'an eye which was not his'; if it's Mr Flay's, then 'presumably the rest of Mr Flay [is] joined on behind it' (19–20). The playful tone and comic situation of two men peeping at each other through a keyhole should not blind us to the fact that Rottcodd's eye is barely under control and the connection between Flay's eye and his body is merely deduced, not a foregone conclusion. Here, however, the spying is mutual, unlike the more reprehensible activities that follow.

Paradoxically, it's Flay who sets it all in motion; he peeps through the hole in the wall of the octagonal room to find out whether he should return to Lord Sepulchrave's side. He does this the better to fulfil his duty, which remains his motivation for spying throughout the books; he literally 'watches over' Fuchsia. Steerpike's motives are quite other. Once Flay has allowed him his first glimpse of his social superiors through the spyhole, he makes peeping and prying his main means of gaining information – and power. He starts at once: no sooner has Flay locked him in than he 'glue[s] his eye to the keyhole' (TG126). Having escaped and climbed to Fuchsia's attic, he peeps through the doorway there and sees her approaching, which just gives him time to fake a faint, his first step in manipulating her.

All the spying in *Titus Groan* is horizontal, through what we might call 'natural' apertures like keyholes, windows and door chinks. In *Gormenghast* it turns vertical, employs contrivances and implies power. Steerpike uses an ingenious system of mirrors, installed in a disused chimney, to see into rooms on higher floors, realizing his desire to 'pry into the affairs of those [literally and figuratively] above him' (TG53). From a dark curtained alcove and through peepholes made by cutting out the pupils of the eyes of both horse and rider in an equestrian painting, he can spy

on Barquentine.[4] He can also see into the rooms of the Countess and
Fuchsia – but at this point Peake hastens to close the chapter, refusing
the lubricious possibilities that this affords. Steerpike may be like Satan
spying on Adam and Eve in *Paradise Lost*, but Peake does not permit the
reader to be prurient. He will not tell us what Steerpike sees in the ladies'
rooms, yet he seems to like the idea of setting up such a surveillance
system, for without a hint of irony he underlines the trouble Steerpike
takes to install it. He does not mention this set-up again. At the end of
the book, though, he neatly turns the tables on Steerpike: his final hiding
place is discovered by the Countess through a 'huge spy-hole' (G487) cut
in the ceiling above him. In Peake's world, true power comes from above,
and is not to be usurped.

Neither of Peake's following stories, 'Boy in Darkness' and *Mr Pye*,
contains devices for spying, but both stories feature characters usurping
power on the vertical axis. From the foot of his disused mineshaft, the
infernal White Lamb controls everyone for miles around. In *Mr Pye*, the
'normal' man, Thorpe the painter, is seen mostly around the base of the
island, at the harbour or on beaches; he dislikes the idea of having God
look over his shoulder (88). For him, a natural chimney in the cliffs is
merely something to paint, 'looking up. T-terribly d-difficult, with that
little circle of light at the t-top' (87). Mr Pye, on the other hand, goes up
and down all over the island, particularly its 'back'. He plans to convert
the Sarkese to his faith by staging a midnight miracle: his designated
martyr, Miss George, is to descend that self-same chimney, wearing a
nightdress as a 'symbol of chastity' (90). The advent of the floating dead
whale forestalls this theatrical trick. Unlike the moon, that 'little circle of
light' is not to be gained by artifice.

It's in *Titus Alone* that Peake most vigorously expresses his feelings
about spying and misappropriation of the vertical axis. It begins with
Titus observing through a skylight the animal-like guests at Lady Cusp-
Canine's cocktail party; it ends with animals watching the glitterati at
Cheeta's party at the Black House. In between we learn that Cheeta's
mother likes to watch a CCTV screen (as we should call it today), like a

---

4. How appropriate: it's the pupils of Steerpike's eyes that reveal his evil. Notice
   also the punning link between pupils and power in the passage about Swelter,
   quoted above. Furthermore, Steerpike plays a double game in the book,
   pretending to serve the castle while attempting to control it – both horse and
   rider at the same time. Here they serve as masks for him.

fisheye on the wall in her husband's 'factory'. Exactly what she sees we are not told, but one deduces that it is the poor prisoners in their cells and the tortures inflicted on them. Peake does not develop the point, just as he withholds comment on the helmeteers; their spying, chilling though it be, is mainly horizontal. What really incenses him are remote-controlled planes and spy globes that can watch people from above. On one occasion a 'small green dart' of a plane, an observation drone, starts to circle Titus. This makes him laugh, 'though his laughter was not altogether without a touch of hysteria'. In the lines that follow, it's the narrator who appears hysterical:

> This exquisite beast of the air; this wingless swallow; this aerial leopard; this fish of the water-sky; this threader of moon-beams; this dandy of the dawn; this metal playboy; this wanderer in black spaces; this flash in the night; this drinker of its own speed; this god-like child of a diseased brain – what did it do?
>
> What did it do but act like any other petty snooper, prying upon man and child, sucking information as a bat sucks blood; amoral; mindless; sent out on empty missions, acting as its maker would act, its narrow-headed maker … and having no heart it becomes fatuous – a fatuous reflection of a fatuous concept – so that it … gobbles incongruity to such an outlandish degree that laughter is the only way out.                                   (TA34)

This outburst is followed by a second in which Peake denounces the man who controls a spy globe that follows Titus about. Like Steerpike in his curtained alcove, he's 'a backroom boy, his soul working in the primordial dark of a diseased yet sixty horse-power brain' (TA106).

When Peake wrote *Titus Alone* in the mid-1950s pilotless spy planes did not exist and satellites were completely blind – Sputnik 1 dates from autumn 1956; he *created* them with his imagination. Within his work the Little Men that he imagines *invent* their devices, those 'miracles' (108) of modern technology. Just as any part of a creation reflects its maker's mind, taking 'the colour of the globe it flew from' (D11), so these inventions reflect the minds of the Little Men. But the Little Men themselves reflect the author's mind; consequently much of the powerful affect in these passages stems from Peake's desire to dissociate himself from the acts and inventions of his characters. As 'Authorjehovah' he leaves them free, while deploring their evil acts in his created world.

Peake creates with the imagination of his heart, with love; the Little Men invent out of fear, fear of the independence of other people. Their need to control other people, particularly social misfits like Titus, who 'little relished the idea of being singled out, pinpointed, and examined by a mechanical brain' (35), causes their minds to become diseased. Moreover, their spiritual condition is impoverished, for their souls work 'in the primordial dark'. So while Peake can admire an 'exquisite beast of the air', a 'wingless swallow' like the Thing, he denounces the drone as a 'metal playboy' like the London playboys that Thorpe briefly envies. Worse, it is a 'threader of moon-beams' and therefore misguided, if not downright evil.

Furthermore, because the drone and the spy globe are remotely controlled – physically detached from the brain and heart of their maker – they view dispassionately. For the human eye 'there is no comprehension at a glance. Only the recognition of damsel, horse or fly and the assumption of damsel, horse or fly' (TG136–37). Our perceptions are subject to both the brain and the heart, whereas machines are 'mindless', loveless parasites. Think of them as the antithesis of Keda, when she says, 'I am in love with all things … because I can now watch them from above' (TG242). Their vertical observation is loveless.

Finally, there's the 'god-like' quality of these devices: by usurping the creator's prerogative of viewing his creation from above, they violate his creatures' intimacy and privacy. So what haunts Peake's heart is the belief that the creator can rightfully view his work from above because he loves it. The negative emotion that inspires the Little Men debars them from any such right. Only a character like Flay, who adopts the vertical view to make maps in his selfless search to save the starving Twins, is justified in his use of it. The Little Men are doubly evil in that they misappropriate this perspective for inventions that are divorced from the heart.

P EAKE RARELY USES THE word 'perspective'; when he does it is more often qualified by negative sensations (chill, cold, dark or wet) than with visual attributes (long, narrow or, his favourite, dwindling). On the other hand, he has another use for the term, one that relates to the ordering of events in his fiction.

A classic story-writing technique is to open *in medias res* and then, after a chapter or two, backtrack to an earlier time to show how this situation came about. Once the reader has been been 'brought up to speed', the plot moves on (possibly with more flashbacks along the way) towards resolution. This ordering might be expressed as C and D, followed by A, B, E, F and so on (in which alphabetical order corresponds to the chronological sequence of events). Peake favoured this gambit. For example, the

Lost Uncle's first three letters describe how he is living in an igloo in the polar waste, and then the fourth summarizes his life from birth. By telling how he started his 'wandering life', the Uncle provides 'what old men call perspective, which only means that you can understand why I do certain things because you know the sort of things I did before'. He intends to dispose of this part as fast as he can because 'the real reason for this talk is the Lion on the Stamp and everything else is only padding' (21). In the event, the fourth letter proves to be a long one, so the Uncle promises not to talk of his past again, only to break his promise a page or two later. The 'padding' provides story, not just perspective. To coin a phrase, the proof of the padding is in the reading.

The structure of 'Mr Slaughterboard' is similar: after setting the scene and describing the principal characters in chapter 1, Peake devotes chapter 2 to an account of how the pirates discovered and captured the Yellow Creature some three years previously. This episode became the independent storybook of *Captain Slaughterboard Drops Anchor*. Detaching it from the original context, he had difficulty in finding a new ending, and on this occasion his friend Gordon Smith helped him out. This is typical of Peake: when a dramatic scene presented itself on the stage of his imagination, he found it easier to recount the events that led up to it than to resolve it. In other words, he was often happier answering the question, 'How did this come about?' than 'What happened next?' This is what gives the story of Titus Groan its structural characteristics.

From the notes in Peake's manuscripts and from his correspondence, we know that he used the flashback technique to start the first version of *Titus Groan*. It opened with two chapters, 'A Room by the River' and 'Goodbye to Stitchwater', which introduced Titus Groan (as Lord Groan, already characterized by his violet eyes) in his 40s along with his manservant Stewflower. Chapters 3 and following went back to the birth of Titus to recount his life up to 'the present' of the opening chapters or prologue (as Graham Greene called them in a letter to Peake – see *Vast Alchemies*, pp. 168–69). In the event, however, the flashback swelled to such an extent under Peake's pen that, as he reached the end of the book with his hero little more than a year old, he decided to discard the prologue altogether. At the same time, he cheerfully announced that this was but the first of three volumes. By the end of the third, Titus still hasn't caught up with his middle-aged self; in fact he's less than halfway there, being still a teenager. The 'padding' took over entirely. No copy of the prologue seems to have survived; the couple of drafts published in *Peake's Progress* as 'The House of Darkstones' (PP105–09) antedate it, and the extant manuscripts start at chapter 12. So we could schematize the overall structure of the Titus books as [Y, Z], A, B, C, etc., in which Y and Z are missing. It is all one long flashback, from which the 'real reason' is absent.

For the reader, the omission of the original opening chapters has a disorientating effect. As the Lost Uncle says, the flashback serves to answer virtual questions like 'How did this situation come about?' and 'Why are you doing these things?' In *Titus Groan* we are supplied with answers without having any of the corresponding questions. Why, for instance, should the narrator, opening chapter 12 ('Mrs Slagg by moonlight') already recapitulate, saying 'These [characters] then ... have been discovered at their pursuits on the day of the advent, and have perhaps indicated the atmosphere into which it was the lot of Titus to be born' (TG86)? Advent and atmosphere! The reader can but feel a discrepancy between this portentous formulation and the puny infant whose first hours have just been described. So we are inclined to ask something like, 'What's the point of it all?' – exactly the opposite of what Peake originally intended. The story has a teleology that is never revealed.[5] To use Peake's term, its *perspective* is skewed.

The reordering of events into a C, D, A, B sequence lies at the heart of the Titus books. Take, for instance, the sequence of announcements of the birth of Titus. We first get to hear of it (A, page 22), when Flay tells Rottcodd, the only person in the castle who does not already know – a classic opening gambit. Then, through the eyes of Steerpike at the spyhole (B, page 52), we witness the doctor informing Fuchsia that she has a little brother – but she had already been told by Nannie Slagg, as we learn on page 86 (C). The first event is the last narrated, giving the chronological sequence C, A, B.

Peake reorders like this at every level of the text, right down to the individual sentence, where he creates a comic effect by placing key information at the end:

5. In her Introduction to *Stuckness in the Fiction of Mervyn Peake*, Alice Mills reveals that of the books she read as a child, only Peake and Homer 'repeatedly thwarted' her reading pleasure 'by exasperating, insolvable problems. Who, or what, were these characters? What were they up to, and why?' Her book honours a promise she made to her 'eight- or nine-year-old self ... that one day [she] would find a way to understand' the Titus books.

> Of the three professors, the first to have reached the room that morning in
> order to establish himself securely in the only armchair (it was his habit to
> leave the class he was teaching – or pretending to teach – at least twenty
> minutes before its official conclusion, in order to be certain that the chair
> was free) was Opus Fluke.                                              (G52)

Opus Fluke leaves nothing to the work of chance – which is perhaps how
he got his name (and his favourite armchair).[6] The same goes for the
structure of the sentence. It is Peake's favourite narrative sequence.

   Now let me direct your attention back to the first verb in that quotation, 'to have reached'. Was it really necessary for Peake to use a past
infinitive? A plain infinitive would have done just as well. Traditionally,
plot-advancing events in a novel are expressed in the simple past. 'She
*carried* the child towards the bed and *turned* the little face to the mother,
who *gazed* right through it' (TG58; my emphasis, as in all the following
quotations unless otherwise indicated). Each simple past corresponds to
the advancing 'now' or 'present' of the narrative. The past perfect situates
an event before this 'present', just as the present perfect does in relation to
the grammatical present. This can be illustrated with two examples from
the Titus books:

> 'No, no, my lord, do not get up yet.' (Lord Sepulchrave *has made* an
> attempt to stand.)                                                     (TG381)

> 'Your mistress's maid; a stretcher; and a couple of men to handle it.' (A face
> *had appeared* in the doorway.)                                        (G34)

In both cases, the parenthesized action took place before the words were
spoken, so we have a present perfect when Peake is narrating in the
present (as in the first example) and a past perfect when he is narrating
in the past. This is so unremarkable that we pay no attention to it. But
Peake plays strange games with his tenses. In fact, the superfluous past
perfect is a hallmark of Peake's work. It identifies his earliest published
poem, and in his last writings we find: 'Titus, who was about *to have risen*
to his feet, remained immobile' (TA226).[7]

---

6. John Donaldson tells me that when Peake was a schoolboy at Eltham, 'fluke'
   was a slang term for laziness.
7. *Uriel for President* (1938) by a certain 'M. Peake' has sometimes been attributed to Mervyn; it contains not one instance of a superfluous past perfect.

Take the chapter called 'The Stone Lanes' in *Titus Groan*; it opens with a double flashback. At the sight of Swelter,

> Mr Flay's gorge *had risen* steadily and … he *had been filled* with revulsion.
> … He *had turned* his head away at last and … *had made* his way … to a
> narrow doorway in the wall opposite that through which *he had entered*.
>
> (TG39)

The last of these past perfects is not, chronologically speaking, the last in the sequence; it is the first, since it relates to Flay's entry into the kitchen, before he started to feel such disgust at Swelter's 'crapulous' monologue. It might have been clearer for us if Peake had used the simple past for the first four verbs, keeping the past perfect for the last. But he did not, for in his mind Flay is already in the Stone Lanes and everything that led up to this moment is anterior and therefore subordinate to it. However, the reader knows nothing of the Stone Lanes as yet; Peake introduces them a couple of pages later, after Steerpike '*had viewed* … *had gazed* … [and then] *had made* for the door through which Mr Flay *had passed*' (TG40) – again, three past perfects followed by a fourth that took place even earlier. A simple past would merely have indicated a further step in the action; the past perfect signals that the narrative is lagging behind the author-narrator's 'now' in which some as-yet-undisclosed event has already happened. Sometimes Peake does not identify this event even when it actually happens, for in his mind it has already been supplanted by another future unknown event. Thus the tenses often tell the reader that he is a step behind the author-narrator, repeating in small the larger [Y, Z], A, B, C pattern of the work as a whole.

This applies whether Peake is narrating in the past or the present. He wrote whole sections of *Titus Groan* in the present and then transposed them into the past during revision. Chapters 52 to 58 (pp. 360–407), which include the stream-of-consciousness passages called 'the reveries', remain in the present. From the moment when these reveries are interrupted by the thud of Fuchsia's head hitting the table as she faints, Peake shifts into the present perfect. For instance 'Prunesquallor has dabbed a quantity of water over Fuchsia's face with a napkin' and 'Barquentine has not ceased a moment in the administration of his duties' (404). This is followed by running commentary ('He is laying his tomes aside') with more present perfects, such as 'Doctor Prunesquallor has staggered away with Fuchsia in his arms' (405). The 'sliding moment' of the now, the reference point in time, is forever advancing, just ahead of the reader who is left in permanent 'catch-up mode'.

Let me illustrate this with a more complex example. In the climactic scene where Titus meets the Thing in Flay's old cave, she leaps up all of a sudden onto a ledge. Let us call this act A, and give a fresh letter to each subsequent main verb.

> Once there, she *tore* (B) at Titus's shirt, hauling it over her head as though she were freeing herself of a sail, but somehow it *had become entangled* (C) about her, during her leap, and, blinded for a moment by its folds across her face, she *had*, in a momentary panic, *shifted* (D) her foothold and, misjudging the area of the ledge, she *had overbalanced* (E) in the darkness and, with a muffled cry, *had toppled* (F) from the height.          (G422)

Only the first past perfect (C) antedates her leap to the ledge, so the chronological sequence is A, C, B; actually, C takes place *during* A. The following actions (D, E, and F), although expressed with the same tense, are in fact subsequent to both A and B. Some other event that we have not yet heard about happens first. The implied sequence, in which [?] represents the unknown event, is: C during A, B, [?], D, E, F. The narrative continues with a fresh paragraph, in which the first two verbs (G and H) turn out not to be [?], for they too took place during action A:

> Involuntarily, as she *had leapt* (G) to the broader shelf of rock, Titus *had moved* (H) after her, as though drawn by the magic of her mobility, so that as she *overbalanced* (I) he *was* (J) within a few feet of where she *would have struck* (K) the floor. But before she *had fallen* (L) more than her own length he *was stationed* (M) beneath her, his knees flexed, his hands raised, his fingers spread, his head thrown back.
>
> But what he *caught* (N) was so unsubstantial that *he fell* (O) with it to the floor from the very shock of its lightness.          (G422)

Finally we discover that the Thing's loss of balance and fall (D, E, and F) were indeed preceded by Titus's movement (H) – but all four are placed on the same level as far as tense is concerned. The simple pasts tell us that the [?] which is paramount in Peake's mind is the M–N–O sequence: Titus was just below the Thing at this moment and therefore able to catch her as she fell. Everything else is subordinate to it. Consequently the chronological order of the complete action proves to be: C, G and H during A; B; J during D, E & I; F, M, L; N and O, with a hypothetical K had not M and N taken place. Actions D, E and F could equally well have been expressed with a simple past, but this would have had a rather different effect on the reader.

This analysis confirms Peake's creative process. His imagination stages a dramatic moment that becomes the 'now' in his mind; then he creates a sequence of actions that lead up to it. This accounts for the sequence of composition of *Gormenghast*: the first three chapters that Peake wrote are preceded by more than a dozen chapters in the published version. In his mind this 'technique' produces perspective by foregrounding the climax – the 'real reason' – and relegating the narrative of how it is reached – the 'padding' – to the background, as expressed by the past perfect tenses. At the same time, however, because he allocates many more pages to the 'padding' than to the 'real reason' – which he may not even mention – he produces the opposite perspective in the reader's mind. Despite the tenses, the narrative is foregrounded while the climax diminishes or even disappears entirely. As a result, the reader concludes (as Peake put it with reference to the practice of drawing), 'The end is hypothetical. It is the journey that counts' (CLP17).

This difference in perspective orchestrates the cave scene. In Peake's climax Titus falls to the ground as the Thing tumbles into his waiting arms: 'He had caught at a feather and it had struck him down' (G422–23). From first glimpse to this moment when he holds the Thing in his arms, with 'his body and his imagination fused in a throbbing lust' (G423), Titus has waited for something like 10 years (and the reader for 300 pages). This, he thinks – and the reader with him – is the big moment. He grips her more tightly, tears the cloth from her face, and prepares to kiss her – but her face is

> so small that he began to cry. … His whole body weakened as the first wild virgin kiss that trembled on his lips for release died out. He laid his cheek along hers. She had ceased to move. … He had become far away and he knew that there would be no climax. (G423)

The perspectives of writer, character and reader collide and collapse; she is 'so small' and he is 'far away'. The big moment turns out to be such a thorough anticlimax that it takes an oxymoron to express it: like Titus, we are 'sick with a kind of glory' (G423).

PUTTING THE TWO TYPES of perspective together – visual and structural – shows that, as a creator of worlds, Peake enjoys the god-like prerogative of having control over both time and space in his work. For him it reflects who he is and what he does. Flaubert's celebrated definition of the narrator, 'present everywhere, like God, but visible nowhere', obviously chimed with Peake, for he copied it into the MS of *Gormenghast*. At the same time he is a creature in God's created world, which enables him to shift between the bird's eye (or divine) and the worm's eye (or human) points of view. As we saw previously, the two form 'an astral and at the same time a solar province' (G49), and he switches between them.

The vertical view is realized in map-making. At the beginning of 'Boy in Darkness', Titus feels that he is powerless, the victim of inferiors who order him around. Lying on his bed and looking up at the ceiling above him, he sees a map in the pattern of damp stains; this moves him to escape from the castle, explore the outer world and have an adventure, thus taking control of his life. The vertical perspective liberates and empowers. Because freedom and power open the door to evil-doing, Peake objects to his characters gaining this perspective of the world they inhabit, unless their motives come from the heart (as they do in Titus, in Flay and in Slaughterboard, who is seeking a life partner). In fact, his notion of evil might be defined as misuse of the creator's perspective.

Whether he was aware of it or not, Peake hinders his readers from sharing his god-like overview. Taking the omission of the prologue as a paradigm, we now know that the Titus books constitute a part detached from a whole that we can only guess at. Thus our experience of his created world parallels Peake's experience of the world that he lived in: in both the 'real reason' or first cause has disappeared down a black hole. Looking back horizontally, both Peake and reader can appreciate how the situation came about, but neither can know the finality of the work, the teleology of the whole. Only God can know such things. Looking down from above, He remains one step ahead. No wonder it has taken 60 years to work out what's going on in Peake's created world. To illumine it, we have to learn what haunts his heart.

# Voice

Art is the voice of man, naked, militant, and unashamed.                                          (D10)

'Stones have their voices and the quills of birds; the
anger of the thorns, the wounded spirits, the antlers,
ribs that curve, bread, tears and needles. Blunt
boulders and the silence of cold marshes – these have
their voices – the insurgent clouds, the cockerel and
the worm. …
    'Voices that grind at night from lungs of granite.
Lungs of blue air and the white lungs of rivers. All
voices haunt all moments of all days; all voices fill the
crannies of all regions.
    'Voices that he shall hear when he has listened, and
when his ear is tuned to Gormenghast; whose voice is
endlessness of endlessness. This is the ancient sound
that he must follow. The voice of stones heaped up
into grey towers, until he dies across the Groan's [sic]
death-turret.'                              (TG112–13)

A style is the result of an artist's development.  (D11)

IN THE PREVIOUS CHAPTER, we noticed how precisely Peake describes
the eyes of his characters and how, following his own narrative eye,
they are liable to become disembodied and autonomous. These qualities
are also enjoyed by the voice, with a significant difference: Peake's characters came to him first of all as voices, and as he wrote he made sketches
to check whether his writing was faithful to what he had heard. These
drawings 'were never exactly as [he] imagined the people, but were near

enough for [him] to know when their voices lost touch with their heads' (HRNE) – the sound, sensation, sight sequence of his creative process. Given that seeing and sequencing (which we can assimilate to sensation and the physical act of writing) affect – effect even – the narrative structure and technique of Peake's writing, we can expect sound, being the primary sense, to have at least as great an impact on his style.

In the course of his stories, the information that Peake provides about the sound of his characters' voices is more richly detailed, especially in imagery, than any other aspect of their appearance, eyes included. The individual quality of a voice identifies the speaker, both physically and as a personality, and Peake alludes to it frequently, with variety and inventiveness. We come away from *Titus Groan* remembering the deep, heavy and sometimes husky voice of Lady Groan, 'like a laden ship upon a purring tide' (297); the identical voices of the Twins, so flat that they are 'like the body of a plaice translated into sound' (250); Lord Groan's brooding voice 'of unutterable mournfulness' (426); and Swelter's 'sponge-like' (432), 'moss-soft' voice (421) that seems 'to seep out of dough' (104) and becomes 'murderously unctuous' (102). In *Gormenghast* Bellgrove's 'fruity' (171) paternal voice can be 'deep and subterranean' with 'sepulchral authority' (248), whereas the unpleasant, 'loveless, didactic voice' (TG391) of Barquentine forces its way between his teeth (G174) and 'rises to a shriek' (TG407) at moments of frustration. Then there's Steerpike, whose 'clear, neat and persuasive voice' (G352) is generally calm, confident and controlled, but at critical moments it betrays his true character, with a 'weird and horrible pitch' (TG480) and 'so savage and cruel' a tone (G352). In *Titus Alone*, 'a voice like a cracked bell' (123) gives a character his name, and Muzzlehatch's rusty voice 'like sandpaper' (23) contrasts with Cheeta's, which is 'dry and crisp as an autumn leaf' (223), 'quite horrible in its listlessness' (208) and 'as laconic as a gull's' (185). The Lamb in 'Boy in Darkness' has 'the sweetest voice in the world' (222); it is 'flute-like' (209), 'like a chime of little bells' (223) and yet 'like a knife in a velvet sheath' (201). Mr Pye possesses the 'gentlest voice imaginable' (8), 'as gentle as the cooing of a dove' (196); it has 'so devastating' a charm that 'there were few who could resist it for more than a few sentences' (76). Tintagieu's charms include her 'deep, sexy voice' (70), 'half purr, half growl' (180), that can be 'hoarse as a raven's' (239) but is generally 'husky enough to dissolve any man's knee-caps' (155). One of my favourites is the sailor's 'deep-sea voice' (22) in *The Rhyme of the Flying Bomb*: it's 'as gruff as a gun' (17). When it comes to images qualifying the voices of his characters, Peake's inventiveness seems inexhaustible. In fact, there's material enough for a doctoral dissertation on the taxonomy of voice in Peake.

Moreover, the manner of delivery (whether timid, hesitant, confident or blustering) is generally less important to him than the individual quality and tone of the voice. He reserves the word 'tone' for this specific purpose. One might have expected him, as an artist, to use it to qualify colour, but I have found only one instance of that: a wine stain on Swelter's apron seemed 'to defy the laws of tone' (TG33). Otherwise, 'tone' always applies to voice – and not social life, or musical notes either. Conversely, I have found only one instance of the term 'colour' applied to a voice – 'it was not the voice of a single individual, so continuous and uniform appeared the flat colour of the sound' (TG215) – which puts paid to any notion that sight might have been Peake's primary sense.

For Peake, sound plays a vital role in the creation of character. When physical appearance (especially grotesque appearance) inspires him more than quality of voice, the character generally fails to come to life. Although he devotes a whole page to describing the respective faces of Spiregrain, Splint and Throd, the three disciples of the old philosopher, he tells us almost nothing of the sound of their voices, with the result that they fizzle out (unlike their master, whose beard is set aflame). Moreover, when sight outweighs sound, Peake repeats the same image every time the character appears, which leads to caricature. The trio's faces are reduced to glass, sand and water – and we forget whose is which. It's the same with Gormenghast's Poet. After one of Peake's most memorable paragraphs on the landscape of his face, we learn that he has 'a voice as strange and deep as the echo of a lugubrious ocean' (TG139). And that's it. Each time he reappears, he is identified by the wedge-shape of his head, not by the sound of his voice. He fails to fulfil the expectations raised by the opening description and simply falls into the background. Another damp squib. On the other hand, for characters whose voices come first, Peake continually invents fresh and original images. Hearing them keeps them alive, for him as for us.

Even with characters who make only the briefest of appearances, Peake is inspired if he individualizes them primarily by voice. Seeking a wet-nurse for Titus, Nannie Slagg – whose voice is 'thin as a curlew' (TG92) by the way – is greeted by a Bright Carver with a voice 'like the noise of boulders rolling through far valleys' (TG91). In *Titus Alone*, 'the croaking of the voice' of the man selling tickets to view the sunset 'seemed to hack its way out of [his] arid throat' (TA153). The Chief Constable who comes to arrest Mr Pye speaks to a little boy with that 'thin little extra voice which is often reserved for cats' (241). The variety and originality of these evocations make them one of the defining characteristics of Peake's writing.

This accounts for the strong link between voice and identity that we noticed in a previous chapter. For many readers, Titus himself never really comes alive, not in the way that Fuchsia, Prunesquallor, or Steerpike do, for instance. He differs from them in that we never learn what his voice sounds like – and he started out as one of 'a couple of characters leaning against one another, back to back, in a high room before dawn' (HRNE): seen rather than heard. However, Titus knows the sound of his own voice, for when it changes at moments of intense emotion – appealing to the Thing (G420), or mocking Muzzlehatch (TA61) – he barely recognizes it. This happens to other characters too: Flay is 'surprised to hear his own mirthless voice saying "Breakfast"' (TG378). Keda hears her voice 'sounding like that of another woman, it was so different and clear' (TG238). Tricked by Mr Pye, Miss Dredger exclaims '"Well, really!" … in a voice which she hardly recognized' (MP28). The change in voice quality alerts them when they act out of character, leading them to discover new facets of themselves. Just for once Irma acknowledges her true feelings and admits to being terrified of Steerpike, saying it 'so simply and so quietly that she [does] not recognize her own voice'. Nor, for that matter, does Bellgrove. 'He could hardly believe that it was she who had spoken' (G391). When other people hear these changes, voice becomes audible identity. Part of the problem with Titus is that no other character ever comments on his voice; on his behaviour and his attitudes, yes, even on the shape of his head, but not the sound of his voice. Without that sound he is barely credible, a mere concept. On the other hand, if he is as much a work of art as a character, as I have been suggesting, then he only truly exists when he finds his voice in *Titus Alone*.

How voice reflects identity and is perceived as such by others is comically illustrated by Irma Prunesquallor. Every time she affirms her femininity, she loses control of both herself and her voice.

> *'I'm a lady!* What do you think I want with *men*? The beasts! I hate them. Blind, stupid, clumsy, horrible, heavy, vulgar things they are. And you're *one* of them!' she screamed, pointing at her brother. …
>
>     Irma's throat was quivering like a bowstring.
>
>     'What have ladies to do with men?' she screamed; and then, catching

sight of the face of the servant at the door, she plucked a knife from the table and flung it at the face. But her aim was not all it might have been, possibly because she was so involved in being a lady, and the knife impaled itself on the ceiling immediately above her own head, where it gave a perfect imitation of the shuddering of her throat.

(G91; Peake's emphases)

In a repeat performance, Irma cries 'I *am* a woman, aren't I?' and ends with: '"I'll *show* them I am!" … her voice losing all control' (G95; Irma's emphases). At such moments, her 'sharp, unpleasant voice' (TG460) inflicts physical pain on the men who hear it. For her brother it rings disagreeably in 'the very middle' (TG187) of his middle ear, and it goes through Bellgrove's head 'like a knife' (G451), recalling the knife that planted itself in the ceiling above Irma's head.

Peake always treats Bellgrove with affectionate irony; his quintessentially male voice continually contrasts with hers.

What a deep and resonant organ the man has, he thought to himself, pretending for the moment that it was not his own voice he was hearing, for there was something humble in his nature which, every once in a while, found outlet.                                                                           (G231)

Irma responds more to the virility of that organ than to the physical man, who is past his best:

'Say it, my male!' cried Irma, forgetting herself. Her strident voice, quite out of key with the secret and muted atmosphere of an arbour'd wooing, splintered the darkness.

   Bellgrove shuddered. Her voice had been a shock to him. At a more appropriate moment he would teach her not to do things of that kind.

(G248)

Irma's voice proclaims identity to excess; the men around her would prefer that it didn't.

For all her aspirations to gentility, Irma screams in most unladylike ways, illustrating – with a voice 'as clipped as the sound of castanets' (G391) – a pathetic discrepancy between aim and achievement. Peake enjoys the shock value of disparity between voice and appearance or personality. Once he glimpsed a pretty girl in the street,

> And then I heard her speak
> And her shrill voice shattered

The alabaster of her brow's
Rare symmetry:
And her loveliness seemed to crumble, and break,
[…]
And the magic was scattered.

(Gb34)

This leads to Mrs Grass, in *Titus Alone*, who lacerates her beauty with
the edge of her voice (45), and to Crabcalf (Bellgrove's vocal counterpart
in *Titus Alone*) whose deep voice is 'so very much more impressive than
anything it ever had to say' (TA114). A similar discrepancy has a rather
different effect on Juno when she meets Anchor. 'There was something
in his voice that belied his mop of dark red hair and general air of brig-
andage. It was deep, husky – and unbelievably gentle' (TA149). At that
moment she begins to fall in love with him. (For the reader, he remains
a shadowy figure, one of those introduced by sight rather than sound.) A
voice at variance with its owner's appearance may be comic; of the Poet
we learn that 'never was a face so belied by its voice' (TG139). Or it may
be pathetic: Titus sees the head of an Old Testament prophet coming
up through the floor of his cell, but when Old Crime speaks 'his accents
were as soft as dough' (TA71–72) and his voice as 'soft as gruel' (75).
'Titus stared at the leonine head: the voice had robbed it of all grandeur'
(TA72), rather as Bellgrove's eyes undermine his physical appearance.
Disparities like these generate emotion, positive or negative; they leave
no one, neither Peake nor his characters, indifferent.

The voice being a sound that we generate, it can be more independent
and separate from the body than the eye. We regularly hear voices without
seeing (or being able to identify) their owners; so do Peake's characters at
gatherings like the christening of Titus or Irma's soirée. As the rainbow
curves over Gormenghast at the Earling, 'a voice' answers Titus's cry and
we realize only gradually that it must be that of Keda's daughter, the future
Thing. *Titus Alone* being Peake's novel of social life, it contains several
such gatherings, at which Titus is surrounded by unknown people with
unidentified voices, like the 'voice of curds and whey' (40) he hears at the
cocktail party. At first, he is equally unknown to these people, but by the
end, 'of all that multitude' at the Black House 'there was not one who
did not know him, yet for Titus there was not one to recognize' (225).
This makes it a mind-wrenching experience for him to hear 'a hundred
voices, like an incantation' telling him 'how much [they] love him' (231).
Separation of voice and identity is the means by which Cheeta intends to

drive Titus mad, quite as much as by the grotesque caricatures of figures from his childhood, many of whom are dead.

This torture is intensified by two of Peake's favourite spine-chilling devices: voices heard from unexpected angles (from behind, over the shoulder, suddenly very close, or very distant, 'as though from miles away' (G311), correlating to the unexpected angles of view of his narrative eye) and unknown voices heard in extremes of light and darkness. During Titus's appearance in court, rain begins to fall and with it comes 'a premature darkness' (TA80). At once an unidentified voice calls for 'More candles! ... More lanterns! Brands and torches, electricity, gas and glow-worms!' (81). Someone throws an emergency switch

> and the whole place was jerked into a spasm of naked brilliance. ... Everything was changed save for the roaring of the rain upon the roof. While this noise made it impossible to be *heard*, yet every detail had become important to the *eye*. ... There was a hush in the Court until an anonymous voice cried out – 'Switch off this fiendish light!'
>
> (81–83; Peake's emphases)

The hearing closes abruptly when yet another unknown voice breaks 'the stillness of the Court, asking permission to address the Magistrate. ... It was Juno', volunteering to adopt Titus as her ward (87). At the Black House, the only voice that Titus knows is Cheeta's but even that has 'an edge to it he had never heard before' (225). 'It was harsher with every order' (226) as she directs the masquerade, calling for more lights or for darkness.

It is one thing to hear voices and not see their owners at a crowded party or in a court of law; it is quite another to hear a voice when no person is physically present. Of course, the telephone makes it possible to hear a 'voice from the other side of the island' (MP64), just as Cheeta can press little levers in her father's factory and hear over a loudspeaker a voice 'with the consistency of porridge' (TA204). It is also possible in altered states of consciousness such as Keda experiences (e.g. TG351), and Titus too, either between sleep and waking (TA97–98) or in fevered states (TA163–65), but it is uncanny to be addressed when no person is visibly present. At the door to Steerpike's room, Fuchsia hears 'a voice out of nowhere' (G352) warning her to be careful. We know it is Flay, but she does not and it has a profound effect upon her.

Equally uncanny is to hear the voice of a present person, and be unable to attach it to that person's body, like witnessing a ventriloquist at work.

In 'Boy in Darkness', the Lamb screams, yet its face remains immobile, 'as though the head and the voice were strangers to one another' (BiD212). Greater discrepancy still is observed by Miss Dredger, watching

> the shadow of Mr Pye's head that was quite motionless. … The only things that moved were the shadow-lips and they opened and shut with a horrid precision, while the voice that kept pace with them came from another part of the landing.                                                   (MP160)

This reveals an unexpected parallel between Mr Pye and the Lamb: their voices belie their true identity.

Nor should we forget that in Peake's work, almost anything may have a voice of its own; the Tower of Flints and the stones of Gormenghast are two that we have noticed already, and there are countless others, animal, vegetable and mineral. Punningly, even 'adventure can be a voice' (BN83). Inanimate and animate frequently combine, as when a bridle creaks 'with the voice of a gnat' (TG503). Natural features like the wind, a river or an ocean, all have voices, as do the seasons:

> The autumn and winter winds and the lashing rain storms and the very cold of those seasons, for all their barbarism, were of a spleen that voiced the heart. Their passions were allied to human passions – their cries to human cries.                                                   (TG412)

Ultimately, all the media of Peake's expression – pencil, ink, chalk, paint or stone (D7) – are voicing the heart.

Consequently, detached voices are ubiquitous in Peake; he invariably makes us hear major characters before we see them, so that our experience as readers parallels his as creator. As Flay descends to the kitchen, after telling Rottcodd of the birth of Titus, he hears 'a great bellowing and clattering and stamping' (TG27); Swelter enters the story four pages later as 'a prodigious bellow outvoicing all [that] cacophony' (31). This spatial and temporal dissociation of voice from physical presence grants a degree of autonomy: voices can go off on little trips of their own. Sourdust's voice wanders through the library 'like something lost' (TG305), and at the christening of Titus, Lord Groan's voice 'moved down the corridor and turned about the stone corner' (TG115). It may even be that following the sound of the voice generates all those independent eyes, and the animus that goes with them, studied in the previous chapter. Certainly, a major function of the spying devices is to eavesdrop, to listen in on the voice of the heart at moments when the characters believe themselves to be alone. Nannie Slagg suffers from just this fear – that 'someone might be … listening to her thoughts' (TG87–88).

These independent voices bring us to a major aspect of Peake's writing, which we have already noticed on several occasions: he literalizes or materializes figurative expressions, even single words. He reduces the character called Crust to an animated word, 'something of five letters that walked on two legs' (G65). Voices also walk. When Flay wonders why he should wish to visit Rottcodd, it occurs to him that the curator must be the only person in the castle who does not yet know of Titus's birth, and he is relieved to realize that 'there was no question of his soul calling along the corridors and up the stairs to the soul of Rottcodd' (TG25). A few pages later a voice is animated in exactly this way: the Countess calls Prunesquallor up from the Coldroom. In her 'deepest and loudest voice' she bellows, 'SQUALLOR!'

> The word echoed along the corridors and down the stairs, and creeping under the door and along the black rug in the Coldroom, just managed, after climbing the Doctor's body, to find its way into both his ears simultaneously.                                                   (TG59)

Later on, a remark by the Twins, 'But we mustn't burn her, must we?' becomes animated. Entering Prunesquallor's ears it appropriates 'a long shelf at the back of [his] brain', throws out a 'ridiculous little phrase found squatting drowsily at one end' and stretches its body

> along the shelf from the 'B' of its head to the 'e' of its tail, and turning over had twenty-four winks (in defiance of the usual convention) – deciding upon one per letter and two over for luck; for there was not much time for slumber, the owner of this shelf – of the whole bone house, in fact – being liable to pluck from the most obscure of his grey-cell caves and crannies, let alone the shelves, the drowsy phrases at any odd moment. There was no real peace.                                                   (TG467)

In Peake's writing, there is indeed little peace for phrases; any image on one page is liable to become animated on the next. Hardly has he compared the castle to an island rising above the morning mist than it becomes a literal island surrounded by flood water. Halfway through *Gormenghast*, 'Titus and Steerpike were at daggers drawn' (G348); at the height of the flood they fight it out with real knives. Occasionally, Peake goes from the literal to the metaphorical: the knife that Irma throws becomes a metaphorical knife in Bellgrove's head. Most often though, he works in the reverse direction. Animating words and literalizing metaphor is a major source of inspiration for him, achieved by hearing sound before sense.

P EAKE'S ATTENTION TO THE sound of words accounts for both the quality and the defects of his writing, in prose as in verse. At its best, it is ideal for reading aloud; through assonance, consonance, alliteration and internal rhyme, associated with powerful rhythms, his finely tuned ear assembles intricate filigrees of sound. Interviewed in 1947, he confessed that while writing *Titus Groan*, he 'found that [he] was writing in five-feet lines over a large part of the book … in poem rhythm rather than prose rhythm' (RTO11). This is the form of several of his plays, including his Christmas plays for radio and his stage play, *The Wit to Woo*. When his verse goes wrong, as it does for me in 'A Reverie of Bone', the rhythm remains but sense has been sacrificed to sound.

Hearing words as sound detached from meaning liberates the mind from the constraints of context and leads to both punning and nonsense, both of which Peake greatly enjoyed. In his series of ditties about Uncles and Aunts, he draws Uncle George, who 'became so nosey / That we bought him a Tea-cosey' (PS 5 (April 1998), iv: 23), with the tea-cosey on his long sharp nose, which effectively prevents him from poking it into other people's business. Peake's book of *Figures of Speech* systematically depicts idioms taken literally and invites the 'reader' to guess what they are. Many involve puns. A smiling man carrying an equally happy bear on his back represents 'grin and bear it'; a couple striding across the page with their noses aflame are 'burning their bridges'; and a man using a sword to slice up people who look like him is 'severing relations'. *Mr Pye* is full of puns, and in his play *The Wit to Woo* Peake puns and quips so much that at times the speeches turn into little more than verbal froth.

Hearing words as sound allows them to take on lives of their own, in the mind as on the page, and contributes much to the humour of Peake's writing. Like him, his characters ponder over idioms: as the Countess enters Prunesquallor's house with her cats, she orders them to 'hold their horses'. 'How peculiar to have enjoined a swarm of cats to hold their horses!' thinks the doctor, and wonders if they expect to play 'mews-ical chairs' (G36). Animated idioms create a complex of images linking Dr Prunesquallor, his sister and Bellgrove. The latter has 'the melancholy grandeur of a sick lion' (G124) and would rather like to see himself as a lion – or at the least be lionized – but he comes through in the end as a tired old horse. This metaphorical transformation starts with Dr

Prunesquallor (who is something of a horse himself, for his laugh sounds like a whinny) literalizing an idiomatic expression:

> He had found relief in the notion that there were several worse things imaginable than being saddled with his sister metaphorically, and one of them was that he should have been saddled with her in all its literal horror. For his imagination had caught a startlingly vivid glimpse of her upon his back, her flat feet in the stirrups, her heels digging into his flanks as, careering round the table on all fours with the bit in his mouth and with his haunches being crosshatched with the flicks of her whip, he galloped his miserable life away. (G29)

So when Irma announces her intention of getting married, he wants to supply her with a horse for husband: 'You deserve a thoroughbred: something that can cock his ears and whisk his tail' (G89). Mention of 'cock' and 'tail' with reference to a prospective husband calls for no analysis

Uncle George with the tea-cosey on his nose.

'Grin and bear it' from *Figures of Speech*.

here; note simply that Peake does not let us forget them. To assert his
authority over one of his teachers, Bellgrove warns, 'Watch your step, sir.
… You have twisted my tail for long enough' (G125). Let us rather pursue
the horse itself. Even before Irma has put her metaphorical money on
Bellgrove, who fancies himself as a 'dark horse' (G200), her brother has
already repeated his initial image by imagining 'Bellgrove galloping like a
horse on all fours with Titus on his back' (G197). Indeed the headmaster
proves to be just the mount for Irma's dominant nature, although she was
rather hoping for one less broken-winded. Still, it doesn't do to look a gift
horse in the mouth – a saying that Peake does not actually use but repeatedly alludes to and plays with. Perch-Prism requests information from
Bellgrove because he wants it 'straight from the horse's mouth', although
he knows that Bellgrove's mouth 'was nothing like a horse's' (G124) – but
he does have bad teeth. So when his pupils 'looked this great gift-lion
in the mouth, it snarled … for its teeth were aching' (G153). With this
verbal horseplay, Peake maintains a running joke throughout the love
affair. Initially, the doctor was saddled with a spinster sister; by the end of
*Gormenghast*, Bellgrove complains, 'what a wife to be saddled with' (451),
and thus gallops *his* miserable life away.

Peake's characters share his hobbyhorse, hearing words as the interplay
of sound. At Irma's soirée, for instance, she hears

> voices at play; and as such it was novel and peculiar to her ears, in the way
> that shadow at play (as against the play of shadows) would have been to
> her eyes. She had, on rare occasions, enjoyed the play of her brother's brain
> – but … here was … language playing on its own; enfranchised notions
> playing by themselves, the truants of the brain.                      (G227)

Because their sound makes words autonomous for Peake, there is a sense
in which all his fiction could be qualified as 'enfranchised notions playing
by themselves', giving rise to the rich imagery we have examined in
previous chapters.

Certainly, while writing *Titus Groan* Peake made lists of unusual
words. They do not fall into any particular class; he was simply seeking
sounds (and rhythms) like *abactina* and *susurrous* that give his book its
unique texture. In this respect he placed a revealing comment in Steerpike's mouth:

> We are all imprisoned by the dictionary. We choose out of that vast, paper-
> walled prison our convicts, the little black printed words, when in truth we

need fresh sounds to utter, new enfranchised noises which would produce
a new effect.                                                    (TG287)

Rather than parade the usual suspects before us, Peake ransacked the
thesaurus for 'truants of the brain' and occasionally broke out of the
dictionary to forge neologisms. These he put mainly in the mouth of
Nannie Slagg: for her Titus is 'born in the lapsury' (TG86; a portman-
teau word, 'lap of luxury'); she suffers from the 'responsiverity' imposed
on her (severe responsibility) and from the 'justlessness' of life (injustice;
both TG485), and so on. In *Titus Alone*, he has Muzzlehatch comment
on the previous volumes, in terms of sound and sensation:

> Words can be tiresome as a swarm of insects. They can prick and buzz!
> Words can be no more than a series of farts; or on the other hand they can
> be adamantine, obdurate, inviolable, stone upon stone. Rather like your
> 'so-called Gormenghast'.                                      (TA145)

In the Titus books Peake was consciously building verbal structures,
'worlds of words' that his readers could, like Lord Sepulchrave in his
library, 'inhabit' and console themselves with (TG296–97).

In these worlds the most disembodied voice we hear is that of the
narrator who is 'present everywhere, like God, but visible nowhere'
(Flaubert). Just occasionally, this voice addresses the reader in the
ponderous manner of a nineteenth-century narrator: 'Tiresome in the
extreme for all those present, it would be hardly less tedious for the reader
to be obliged to suffer the long catalogue of Breakfast ritual' (TG390).
More frequently, though, it starts out by adopting the detached tone of
a guidebook and then moves in so close to the characters that its voice
commingles with theirs.

As a result it is sometimes unclear who is addressing us. In this passage,
which might be compared with the opening of Katherine Mansfield's
short story, 'The Garden Party', we have the impression that the speaker
might be one of the characters:

> The afternoon was perfect. The great cedars basked magnificently in the
> still air. The lawns had been cut and were like dull emerald glass. The
> carvings upon the walls that had been engulfed in the night and had
> faltered through the dawn were now chiselled and free in the brightness.
>
> The Christening Room itself looked cool and clear and unperturbed.
> With space and dignity it awaited the entrance of the characters. The
> flowers in their vases were incredibly gracious.            (TG101–02)

Sentence length, rhythm and lexis ('incredibly gracious') suggest character, but (rather as Mansfield surprises us in her story) this is immediately belied by reference to 'the characters'.

Likewise, it is often unclear to us whose thoughts are being presented. Take the moment, early in *Titus Groan*, when Flay is conducting Steerpike up to the Octagonal Room, passing through the roomful of white cats:

> 'Whose are they?' asked Steerpike. They were climbing stone stairs. The wall on their right was draped with hideous papers that were peeling off and showed rotting surfaces of chill plaster behind. … The plaster had cracked into a network of intricate fissures varying in depth and resembling a bird's eye view, or map of some fabulous delta. A thousand imaginary journeys might be made along the banks of these rivers of an unexplored world.
>     Steerpike repeated his question, 'Whose are they?' he said.        (TG46)

Does the description of the walls and the imaginary journeys, sandwiched between Steerpike's questions, belong to *his* mind – or the narrator's? Steerpike is discovering the castle and unlikely to be dreaming of another 'unexplored world' at this point. Ambiguities like this are rife in the first Titus books, but diminish as Peake gained experience. It is clearly Titus who sees the 'map' formed by cracks in the ceiling of his bedroom (BiD158).

Peake's frequent use of free direct and indirect speech complicates the issue. When the narrator's opinion coincides closely with a character's, an inattentive reader may find it hard to attribute their respective words correctly. The narrator dislikes Barquentine, for instance, dismissing him as a 'wrinkled and filthy dwarf' (G265); Steerpike voices similar sentiments:

> The time was almost ripe in Steerpike's judgement for the Master of Ritual to be dispatched. Apart from other motives the wiping out of so ugly a thing as Barquentine seemed to Steerpike, upon aesthetic considerations alone, an act long overdue. Why should such a bundle of hideousness be allowed to crutch its way about, year after year?
>     Steerpike admired beauty. … Dirt offended him. Untidiness offended him. Barquentine, old, filthy, his face cracked and pitted like stale bread, his beard tangled, dirty and knotted, sickened the young man. It was time for the dirty core of ritual to be plucked out of the enormous mouldering

> body of the castle's life and for him to take its place, and from that hidden centre – who knew how far his tangent wits might lead him? (G164)

Some readers, even supposedly educated ones (to judge from a recent dissertation), have attributed the final sentence of each of these paragraphs to the narrator, whereas they are (to my mind at any rate) clearly Steerpike's. Only the word 'tangent' sits uneasily with this: Peake is already slipping back into the perspective of the narrator, for whom Steerpike's mind is geometrically precise.

Readers tend to assume that a unit of text like a paragraph represents a single point of view until a unequivocal sign (such as a quotation mark) flags a change of centre of consciousness or perspective. Because free indirect style does not offer such unambiguous signs, it demands closer attention. These things are best demonstrated with an example. Here's a complete paragraph from the scene of the Earling in *Titus Groan*:

> Steerpike was watching Fuchsia through the branches. She would be difficult, but it was only a matter of careful planning. He must not hurry it. Step by step. He knew her temperament. Simple – painfully simple; inclined to be passionate over ridiculous things; headstrong – but a girl, nevertheless, and easy to frighten or to flatter; absurdly loyal to the few friends she had; but mistrust could always be sown quite easily. Oh, so painfully simple! That was the crux of it. There was Titus, of course – but what were problems for if not to be solved? He sucked at his hollow tooth.
>
> (TG492–93)

Only the first and last sentences represent the narrator's point of view (external perspective). They frame Steerpike's train of thought (internal perspective), which is identifiable not only by the opinions expressed but also by the characteristics of free indirect style: idiosyncrasies of lexis, short clauses, verbless sentences, interruptions, exclamations, rhetorical questions, and so on. Free indirect speech and thought enable Peake to shift rapidly from the point of view of the narrator to a character and back again. It is the verbal counterpart to his sudden changes in visual perspective that we have already observed. By this means Peake's 'roving ear' can tune in to the minds of his characters.

As with the eye, the unexpectedness of these aural shifts can catch us out. On that occasion when the Countess finally gets round to taking Titus for a walk, he says, 'Yes, mother,' whereupon 'a shadow settled for a moment on her broad brow. The word *mother* had perplexed her. But the boy was quite right, of course' (G315; Peake's emphases). The final sentence contains the Countess's unspoken thought, not the narrator's comment, as is clear from the opening 'but', the reference to Titus as 'the boy' and the familiar 'of course' at the end. It's all over in a flash, for the following sentence (a fresh paragraph) returns to Titus's perspective: 'Her massive bulk had always impressed Titus.'

Occasionally, Peake will throw in as little as a single word of free direct or indirect thought. Take the moment when Steerpike indulges in the sadistic pleasure of making Cora and Clarice crawl under the carpet (which in itself literalizes an idiom):

> The Twins, acting together, rose from their chairs and started moving across the room. They paused a moment and turned their eyes to Steerpike in order to make sure that they were doing what was expected of them. Yes. The stern finger of the young man was pointing to the heavy damp carpet that covered the floor of the room.                    (G48)

That 'Yes' in the middle quotes what the Twins are actually thinking – and it's part of the comedy of *Titus Groan* and *Gormenghast* that, since they are 'so limp of brain that for them to conceive an idea is to risk a haemorrhage' (G12), the only thoughts that Peake attributes to them are minimal tokens such as this. This instance is easy to decode, being framed by their point of view in both the preceding and the following sentences.

More often, however, the frame is absent (as we might expect from Peake), so that the narrator's voice merges seamlessly with the character's, as when Irma Prunesquallor is thinking of her ideal lover:

> She did not want him, this hypothetical admirer, necessarily to dedicate his whole life to her, for a man must have his work – (as long as it didn't take too long) – mustn't he? But if he was wealthy and wished to dedicate his life to her – well, she wouldn't make promises, but would give the proposal a fair hearing.                    (G28)

By slipping the words 'hypothetical admirer' into the opening sentence, Peake ensures that we enjoy the irony of the narrator's external perspective while listening to the idiosyncratic convolutions of Irma's thought and speech.

The frame is entirely absent (with the exception of one clearly marked paragraph) from the passages of 'stream of consciousness' (as they used to be called) or 'Reveries' (Peake's title) in *Titus Groan* (392–402). They should present no problem – Peake helpfully heads each section with the name of the character whose thoughts are represented – although the absence of punctuation does require a little effort from the reader. Yet in a recent British dissertation a student who claimed to be impressed by Peake's style dismissed the paragraph of Cora's thought as 'gibberish'!

The real difficulties are elsewhere. Rhetorical questions and exclamations are frequent indicators of free indirect style, yet Peake's narrator uses them too, raising doubt as to whose thought is being represented. During the romantic meeting between Bellgrove and Irma in the arbor,

> The night poured in upon them from every side – a million million cubic miles of it. O, the glory of standing with one's love, naked, as it were, on a spinning marble, while the spheres ran flaming through the universe!
>
> (G243)

The exclamation could be Bellgrove's or the narrator's. The tense of 'ran' points to it being Bellgrove's (for the narrator would have said 'run'), but is it in character for him to have quite such a thought at quite such a moment? Much depends on the reader's sense of irony. A few pages later, Irma is wondering,

> Had she said something so stupid, that no headmaster, worthy of his office, could ever consider accepting her? Had she unwittingly lifted some hatchway of her brain and revealed to this brilliant man how cold, black, humourless and sterile was the region that lay within?          (G252)

The first question is patently hers. The second opens in the same way, but then – would Irma spatialize her brain and refer to its contents as 'cold, black, humourless and sterile'? She is surely far too vain to denigrate her own mind in such terms; the question must belong to the narrator (who is liable to spatialize thought in this manner). But the *form* is that of free indirect thought, and therefore – supposedly – of the character. In this way, Peake blurs the usual narrator/character distinction to the point where their respective voices merge.

There may be reasons for this. In a radio talk, Peake tells how he realized that a good book illustrator needs 'the power to slide into another man's soul. The power to be identified with author, character and atmosphere' (BI14). It is now a commonplace among admirers of Peake's illustrations to affirm that he possessed this ability in abundance; it also applies to his prose writing. He can 'slide into the soul' of his characters and identify with them so closely that narrator and character seem to merge. *Mr Pye* offers an extended example of this, as we shall see in the next chapter.

'Boy in Darkness' is characterized by this mingling. On the third page of the story, the 14-year-old Boy

> longed (he knew it now) to turn his anger into action – to make his escape from the gaols of precedent; to make a bid if not for final freedom then at least for a day. For a day. For one tremendous *day* of insurrection.
>
> Insurrection! It was indeed nothing less. Was he truly contemplating so radical a step? Had he forgotten the pledges he had made as a child and on a thousand subsequent occasions? The solemn oaths that bound him with chords [sic] of allegiance to his home.                    (BiD159; Peake's emphasis)

The opening words are certainly the narrator's; then the three-word sentence, 'For a day', appears to flag the start of free indirect thought. The next paragraph seems to bear this out: the form suggests the Boy's thought – but the content (at least by the end) is narrator's report.

Frequent ambiguities like this can be found in the early pages of the story, with the narrator exclaiming and questioning in a manner that mimics free indirect thought with words and concepts that do not:

> For what is exploration without peril?
>
> But no. He would not start away in darkness. That would be madness. He would start a little before dawn with most of the Castle asleep, and he would run through the half-light, and race the sun – he on the ground and the sun in the air – the two of them, alone.
>
> But how to bear the cold, slow-footed night – the interminable night that lay ahead? Sleep seemed impossible, though sleep he needed.
>
>                                                                           (BiD161)

A phrase like 'the cold, slow-footed night' belongs to the narrator, but expresses the Boy's point of view. It is as though the narrator is thinking for the Boy, which brings us particularly close to him. By limiting the narrator's (and thereby the reader's) perception of events to the character's perspective, Peake makes the story more credible. Other people's dreams are inherently unexciting because we cannot share the intensity of the dreamer's perspective. Here, proximity of narrator to character lends veri-similitude to a nightmare. This technique goes a long way to explaining the particular effect of Peake's books on their readers.

Time and again his writing confirms the truism that, in fiction as in life, inside views evoke sympathy. Behaviour that we might reject as inexplicable, ill-mannered or plain unacceptable can become understandable, justifiable in the circumstances, and even acceptable once we have shared the other's view of the world and the inner processes that lead up to that behaviour. In a novel, the amount – and degree – of internal perspective has a powerful effect on the reader. This is amply borne out by the story of Steerpike in *Titus Groan* and *Gormenghast*. No objective summary of his career can evoke a shred of sympathy for him, yet to judge by the Internet forums (and letters I have received) he is the favourite character of many readers; they leap to his defence.

Combining direct and free indirect forms – external perspective indicated by inverted commas followed by a sudden shift into internal perspective – is a technique much favoured by Peake. It lends itself to comedy, offering us a sudden glimpse of a character's view. For instance, when Irma Prunesquallor is giving her brother a hard time, the narrator slips into his mind:

> 'I wonder if I'm getting old,' thought the doctor, and he put his hand to his forehead and shut his eyes. When he opened them she was there again – but O creeping hell! what had she done?  (G206–07)

The change of register and the typographical flags (the opening dash, the phatic 'O' and the exclamation mark) ease our descent into the bathos of the doctor's unspoken reaction.

A technique for rendering a character's world-view without these formal flags is to have the narrator adopt a character's vocabulary, but it is risky. As Stanzel pointed out, 'contamination of the narrator's language by the speech of the fictional characters … can frequently be observed in Victorian novelists such as Dickens, George Eliot and Meredith' and 'was already employed with virtuosity by Jane Austen' (Stanzel 192), yet it is easily misunderstood. In Joyce criticism it is known as the 'Uncle Charles Principle' following his contentious use of it in *A Portrait of the Artist*, and Peake similarly fell foul of the critics. Reviewing *Titus Groan* in the *Sunday Times* for 31 March 1946, Charles Morgan denounced as 'sloppy writing' a passage in which Peake allows his narrator to adopt the idiolect of Nannie Slagg. On the day of Titus's Christening,

> Nannie was practically insane with excitement and without Keda's silent help would have been incapable of coping with the situation.
>
> The christening dress had to be ironed, the christening rings and the little jewelled crown to be procured from the iron case in the armoury, and only Shrattle had the key and he was stone deaf.
>
> The bath and dressing of Titus had to be especially perfect, and with

everything to do the hours slipped away all too quickly for Mrs Slagg and
it was two o'clock in the afternoon before she knew where she was.

(TG101)

Peake brilliantly renders Nannie Slagg's preoccupations and perception
of events by allowing her cliché-ridden speech to flow into the narrative.
He has a sure ear for the language of a fussy old woman and the whole
passage echoes with her simple-minded sentimentality. Each paragraph
being a single sentence containing two or three clauses linked simply by
'and', the structure also reflects a mind that works only by accretion and
not by contrast or analysis. It deserves comparison with similar passages
in *Ulysses*.

However, Peake does not generally use the technique over several
paragraphs, as in this instance; he prefers to dip in and out again more
quickly, or simply to list the phrases that come to a character's mind.
Fantasizing about Irma, Bellgrove sees himself as 'an unquestioned patri-
arch, a symbol of success and married stability with something of the gay
dog about him too – of the light beneath the bushel, the dark horse, the
man with an ace up his sleeve' (G200). None of these clichés belongs to
the narrator. Over the years, Peake fine-tuned this ability to represent
the 'mind-style' of his characters. On the day of Mr Pye's arrival, Miss
Dredger dismisses her cook, although this means that 'she would have to
prepare another kind of lunch altogether and if it was late Mr Pye could
bally well wait for it' (MP27). The bathetic change of register builds up
our impression of Miss Dredger's independence of mind in order that her
fall under Mr Pye's power should be all the more spectacular. 'Oh, she
would show him!' she thinks a few lines later:

> But on reflection she was damned if she would be seen waiting for Mr Pye
> at her own gate as though she were interested in his miserable existence.
> No! Let the drive look like the Pennine Range! What did she care?

(MP27)

Numerous ironies – from 'damned' to her conversion to Mr Pye's religion
of the Great Pal a few pages later, and Mr Pye's spontaneous raking of
the gravel as soon as he alights from the carriage, not to mention his
preparing lunch and actually *waiting* on her – are made possible just by
this monologue. Representation of the individual voice is the cornerstone
of Peake's style.

Admirers of *Titus Groan* and *Gormenghast* tend to assume that
they represent 'Peake's style' and that any other work falls short of it.

Attributing the change in style of *Titus Alone*, for instance, to his terminal illness fails to recognize that it attempts something very different and fails to account for the variety within it. In the court scene, Peake quotes a letter from the Magistrate to his friend; its tone, structure and lexis are unlike any other passage in the book. Such appropriate variety could not be achieved by a writer whose pen was out of control. Like his characters, each of Peake's works has its own unique voice.

# Mr Pye

I am metaphorizing something and one day we'll
know what it is.                    (Mr Pye, MP229)

I have no flair for real evil.          (Mr Pye, MP175)

Him the Almighty Power
Hurled headlong flaming from th' ethereal sky,
With hideous ruin and combustion, down
To bottomless perdition.
            *(Paradise Lost*, I.44–47: NAEL 1: 1819)

IT IS HIGH TIME that we came to 'Peake's other novel'. Less than half the
length of either *Titus Groan* or *Gormenghast*, *Mr Pye* unites, develops
and deepens all the themes and motifs that I have been examining. Until
now, no one has considered it in the light of Peake's other works, with
the result that they have come away baffled. In his pioneering study John
Batchelor damned it with faint praise. 'Of its slight kind *Mr Pye* is an
attractive work,' he wrote, justifying his dismissal by quoting C.S. Lewis:
'One must not munch whipped cream as though it were venison' (Batchelor 114). I too enjoy the *crème chantilly* of Peake's humour in this novel
– but I also concur with its narrator, who observes of Mr Pye that 'the
little man had given Sark so much food for thought that it was no wonder
that it suffered from flatulence' (MP182).

At first sight, *Mr Pye* is simply a comic tale about a self-appointed
missionary who tries to convert the inhabitants of Sark to his own variety
of Christianity, and is prevented from doing so by supernatural events.
Angelic wings unaccountably sprout from his shoulderblades; to make
them go away he turns to evil, whereupon devilish horns grow on his

forehead. See-sawing between acts of good and evil to keep both wings and horns at bay, he exposes himself as a goat at a cattle show and then uses his wings to fly from the island. These bare bones became a Channel 4 telefilm that was shown around the world; it misses the point almost as widely as Batchelor did.

To start with, a story of good and evil featuring wings and horns had haunted Peake's imagination for at least ten years before he wrote *Mr Pye* in the early 1950s. In *Titus Groan* the 'fierce figures' on the stage of Fuchsia's attic 'brooded like monsters or flew through the air like seraphs' (80). The opening of *Gormenghast* links similarly contrasting pairs with a metaphorical island that is Sark in all but name:

> About the rough margins of the castle life – margins irregular as the coast-line of a squall-rent island, there were characters … wading out of the tides of limitless negation. … Yet what are these that set foot on the cold beach? Surely so portentous an expanse should unburden itself of gods at least; scaled kings, or creatures whose outstretched wings might darken two horizons. Or dappled Satan with his brow of brass.          (14–15)

Later, in the evocation of Steerpike's hell, we find 'the breasts of the plumaged seraphim; the scales of Satan' (G263). Mr Pye, whose round face 'might have been described as cherubic' (MP129), turns out to be 'half seraph and half devil' (220). Figures like these suggest a thoroughly serious intention behind the comic façade of this novel.

Foremost among Peake's preoccupations is solitude. Prior to the opening of the story, Mr Pye has been 'intensely lonely' (138), perhaps the loneliest of all Peake's characters. His condition may be gauged by the nonsense poem that he claims to have scribbled on the back of 'a proce-dure form' (230) at a business meeting. It's actually a parody of the hymn, 'From Greenland's icy mountains' that Mr Pye sings to himself more than once in the course of the novel.[1] He recites it when his wings make him feel 'more lonely than ever' (143), 'immeasurably lonely' even (208):

> O'er seas that have no beaches
> To end their waves upon,
> I floated with twelve peaches
> A sofa and a swan.

---

1. I have examined more of Peake's parodies in *Vast Alchemies*, p. 103 and in 'Parodies and Poetical Allusions'.

[...]
There was no one to love me,
Nor hope of being found –

When, on the blurred horizon,
(So endlessly a-drip)
I saw – all of a sudden
No sign ... of any ... ship.
(230)

From the foregoing chapters it will be evident that these lines express Peake's 'logical' sequence: no beaches, so no islands; no ships either; so no people, and therefore no love.

Unlike the Lost Uncle who resolves his physical solitude first, Mr Pye has invented a god whom he calls his Great Pal. They have a jolly time together, he and his Pal: 'never once have we found ourselves chattering at cross-purposes. Oh yes, and we have our jokes, too, my Pal and I' (60). It is a relationship that has taken him 'many years to perfect' (62), but of course, like all gods, the Great Pal observes a 'universal and ubiquitous silence' – he is not the sort to give his disciple 'something he can hear and touch and see and smell' (60) – so the friendly chats and shared jokes are in fact entirely one-sided. This Great Pal may satisfy some of the yearnings of Mr Pye's soul, but cannot cure his desire for flesh-and-blood companions. So he seeks to make converts to his faith.

In this process he employs metaphors that (predictably enough) are based on boats and water. He enrolls Miss Dredger – a dredger serves to to make harbours more accessible by deepening channels – by persuading her that the river of her life has hitherto been flowing the wrong way. Until now her virtue has been

> a thwarted, inoperative thing. It is dried up for lack of air and the waters of that broad clear river that flows through to God. Your trickle is running away downhill, my dear, and between the wrong rocks. (61)

So he invites her to 'double back' until her 'little stream' meets his big river. 'Join me in my skiff – and together, paddling happily to Zion, find with me, one glorious day, that we are particles, motes as it were, dancing in a haze of sunbeams' (61). The motifs and the ambition (like Keda's) of the part to fuse with the whole are familiar. Miss Dredger, nicknamed Sailor, becomes his first disciple, and he her Captain.

As we know, food for the soul and company for the body is not enough.

What Mr Pye wants is love, so he crosses the sea to the island he 'craves' for (10). Disembarking on Sark, he declares that he brings 'Just … Love' (20) and professes his ambition 'to turn this island into a living entity, a cosmos of healthy and far-reaching love' (58). In other words he hopes to make it love him and fill the emptiness in his life and heart. He has chosen the isthmus cure for solitude, attempting to turn something material into something spiritual, the reverse of simony. Of course, he fails. To start with, the isthmus cure is a pipe dream. Two islands 'joined together by the Coupée' like 'the unborn child to its mother' (249) are more solidly united than ever two people could be, in the womb or out of it. Not that Sark is two islands; it is one island in two halves 'with a wasp-like waist' (62) between them. Moreover its towering cliffs speak eloquently of its hostility towards uninvited guests. It does not want Mr Pye.

In this novel, then, Sark is no mere lump of rock in the sea; it is also a living creature, and its inhabitants stand for every man and woman. As Mr Pye puts it, not without humour: 'Here in this little island I have watched, in microcosm, the "world and his wife" go by – and sometimes I have seen, unless I am mistaken, the world go by with someone else's wife!' (103–04). His observation that our choice of partners is not always moral is highly ironical, for he is planning to enter into an intimate relationship with an island that is by no means his lawful spouse. In fact, he has chosen Sark in the manner that another man might select a prize animal for breeding:

> There she lay at full stretch upon the skyline, her attenuated and corus-
> cated body reaching from north to south, the morning sunbeam playing
> along her spine and flickering upon the crests and ridges of her precipitous
> flanks. … 'It is just the right size,' he murmured. 'It will do very nicely.'
>
>                                                                              (11)

The change of gender from the narrator's 'she' to Mr Pye's 'it' is unsettling (although characteristic of Peake's treatment of animal companions). It happens again in the passage describing how Mr Pye appropriates the island, and reveals the difficulty of making an island simultaneously a place and a partner. It is not an agreeable description, for Mr Pye physically possesses Sark, down to its most intimate nooks and crannies, without so much as a how-d'you-do:

> He was preparing his way: and at the same time he was preparing her
> – his island – for a revolution of the heart, for already he felt that she
> was his. A strange, proprietary instinct told him that … he should hold a

spiritual mandate over the wasp-waisted rock. That he had been treading its [sic] bony back for no longer than six weeks was of no significance. What mattered was that he had forced his way to the very core of what made the island into Sark, and Sark into the island. He had wormed his way into her dank, primordial caves; had stared his fill at her emblazoned flanks; had dived, a pear-drop in his mouth, into her cold April tide; had sat for an hour upon a fallen tree and drunk his fill of the sweet of Dixcart Valley where the primroses, the bluebells and the celandine, smothered the wooded slopes; and exposed himself like a sensitized plate to her every whim.                                                            (49)

It starts with the language of romantic love – 'already he felt that she was his' – framed within threats of political action, 'a revolution'. This is not 'love itself cry[ing] for insurrection' as at the end of *Titus Groan* (506), but 'proprietary instinct': Mr Pye wants to overthrow the current ruler and impose himself upon the island's heart, over which he thinks he holds 'a spiritual mandate'. Yet there is nothing elevated about it at all. Phrases like 'treading its bony back', 'forced' and 'wormed his way', 'stared' and 'drunk his fill', suggest something more like rape, male possession of the female object. Mr Pye rides roughshod over both the island and the islanders, regardless of their feelings. The closing phrase, 'her every whim', usually complements verbs like 'to give in to' and 'to indulge', but Mr Pye has merely 'exposed himself' to her whims, not satisfied them in any way. Later Peake has Mr Pye, rather appropriately, expose himself like a prize animal, with horns, at Sark's cattle show. At this point, though, the satisfaction is all his, not hers. Rarely does Peake show a man's love to be so selfish, or so thoroughly invested with lust for power.

In his insufferable self-assurance, his cocksure belief in the intrinsic rightness of his mission, Mr Pye aims to take political control of Sark, 'to inspire confidence on such a scale that it became the natural thing for island problems to come direct to him, shortcircuiting the famous Chief Pleas, the island Parliament' (78–79). He outclasses the Seigneur of Sark, knowing 'a hundred times more about those he passed on the stony lanes, than they knew about him' (54). In fact, acting as though he has 'private knowledge of something very droll denied not only to those who watched him but to mankind in general' (9), he seems god-like. In his bounty he intends to

offer back to the islanders that which was theirs, but not before they were ready to receive it, for they must learn that it was to their ultimate good that he should hold a spiritual mandate over their wasp-waisted rock. (49)

In other words, he takes it upon himself to judge when the islanders deserve to have their stolen property returned to them. This sounds like old-fashioned colonialism of the sort that still haunts those parts of the world where politicians play God. Men who go around telling people that 'they must learn that it was to their ultimate good' that they should rule over them are putative despots. No wonder Peake has a character ask 'What about Russia?' every now and then. (*Mr Pye* was published some six months after the death of Stalin.)

When it comes to wanting power over others, Mr Pye is close to Steerpike, who makes Cora and Clarice set fire to Sepulchrave's library while they are clay in his hands (TG288). Then they resist him: 'clay no more' they change into 'a sister medium', stone (G260) – another instance of the material change at crucial moments that we have already noticed. Like the Lamb of 'Boy in Darkness', Mr Pye wants to re-form the stone island of Sark and its inhabitants. He thinks that Miss Dredger will be 'like clay on the wheel of his love. As a potter with his medium, so he would throw her and fire her' (43). Thereafter, the metaphor of firing clay to make it harden in a new shape undergoes a strange transformation. Likening the island to a ship, Mr Pye argues with himself that 'it would surely be not only premature but dangerous to accost the crew aboard her with his love. He must fire them by degrees' (48). After 'accost', that 'fire' awakens disquieting echoes. Then we learn that as 'an experienced crusader', Mr Pye knows the value of having 'a trump card up his sleeve and playing it at that moment when the island was clay in his hand'. The next sentence confirms our misgivings by revealing that he plans to 'fire the first salvo on the night of the midnight picnic' (79). These mixed metaphors move from firing clay to firing guns, and they go on: when a delegation of islanders comes to reproach Mr Pye for his behaviour, he attacks their leader, saying, 'You have wasted your opening round – and you know what that means in battle' (193). So the crusading evangelist gradually comes over as a Christian soldier 'marching as to war' rather than the bringer of peace and love that we might wish to believe in. Remember, military images are what characterize Steerpike at the end of *Gormenghast*. As for the islanders who were supposed to be clay in Mr Pye's hands, they turn into stone on seeing his horns at the cattle show (254).

Mr Pye and Steerpike are also linked through the goat as the emblem of evil. Steerpike's walk is goat-like:

> There could be no mistaking that nimble, yet shuffling and edgeways-on
> – that horribly deliberate motivation that was neither walking nor running

– both close to the ground as though on the scent, and yet loosely and
nimbly above it.                                              (TG469)

This association of evil with the goat through its gait goes back to the
Bible (Daniel 8.5 to be precise – and one of Mr Pye's favourite hymn
lines is 'Dare to be a Daniel'); Peake repeats it in 'Boy in Darkness' (205),
so it is no coincidence. In *Mr Pye*, though, the association is generally
through the goat's horns, but also 'the mouth – a thoroughly unpleasant
line, where Satan had obviously been at work' (179). When Mr Pye starts
to worship this goat he realizes to his horror that 'it was no longer difficult for him to sin. It had become natural. And worse than this', for like
Steerpike again, he has 'developed a taste for it' (179). He also 'rejoice[s]
in his insurrection' (179), just as Steerpike does. Although he manages to
pull himself back from the brink of no return and 'banish the goat from
his mind' (rather as Steerpike banishes his conscience), he continues to
resemble Steerpike in being largely unaware of the changes that come
over him: 'he could not (being so close to himself) feel or see any difference in his nature … yet a change nevertheless had taken place' (205).
Ultimately the main difference between the two is that Mr Pye is goat-
like only when he does evil.

At this point, you may be thinking something like, 'Wait a moment! I
thought this Mr Pye was supposed to be a good guy with an angel face and
wings to match – and so far you've painted him all black.' True. In this
book Peake counts on the reader's automatic assumption that a missionary
and his work are by definition *good*, and he almost never allows us to
assess Mr Pye at anything but his own valuation. The narrator constantly
colludes with him, misleading the reader to the point where we condone
damage to property and even physical assault as Mr Pye struggles to solve
the problem of his wings.

It starts on the first page: introducing the scene in the harbour of St
Peter Port, Guernsey, the narrator informs us that the sky is 'stainless' (8),
the houses look down 'benevolently', and Mr Pye's paunch is 'benign' (9).
We accept the attribution of positive moral qualities to the sky as a cliché,
and to the houses as the conventional pathetic fallacy of fiction. Having
done so, we swallow the third without a second's thought – and pass over
the nasty little crane with 'murderous hooks' which 'soar again, out of the
shadow of the harbour wall, and into the upper sunlight' (8). This action
anticipates the final scene of the novel; few first-time readers are going to
suspect that Mr Pye might be like those hooks – yet by the end he has
caused two deaths, one internment in a mental hospital and numerous

broken legs. He even 'murders' gladioli by breaking off their heads (147). The truth is that the narrator shares Mr Pye's primly puritan view of himself and the world, which lulls us into sharing it too. So when a sailor slips and breaks his leg, we are inclined to attribute to Mr Pye, who in fact blithely ignores the accident, the narrator's unsympathetic complaint that the sailor mouths an 'extraordinarily offensive oath' (4). This narrative voice merges with Mr Pye's, vehicling his inner monologues. Only once does it stand back and warn us, in no uncertain terms, that Mr Pye is going to 'turn the island inside-out like a salted leech' (17). Otherwise his apparent goodness goes unchallenged by the narrator.

This blinkered narratorial perspective shapes the opening interaction of the novel, when Mr Pye buys his passage to Sark. He asks for a single ticket, but the vendor wants to give him a return, saving him two shillings. This kindness is rejected and the man made to appear a dimwit. Mr Pye is going to Sark to save its soul and there is no return – as Mr Pye himself points out later on – from such a course of action. The man in the little hut shrugs his shoulders. 'Some people, he reflected, were beyond hope' (8). To prevent us from thinking of Dante and sharing this profound assessment of Mr Pye, the narrator immediately 'dazzles' us with Mr Pye's smile as he calls the man his friend (8). From the ticket vendor's perspective, though, Mr Pye is indeed a hopeless customer, impatient and domineering, handling his money just as he plans to deal with the islanders: 'he placed some silver coins upon the table and ... jockeyed them into a straight line.' Since the vendor is no more used to 'having coins marshalled along his trestle table as though they were soldiers' (7) than he is to being compulsorily saved and turned into a Christian soldier, he is understandably irritated. At this Mr Pye takes out his watch and starts to count the seconds, awaiting delivery of his ticket! He is the most infuriating of customers, the sort that treats other people as inferior from the vantage point of their moral high ground. This is always provoking. What Mr Pye calls goodness 'can be as disrupting as evil' (18).

Believing oneself to be all goodness – 'the sweetest cherub to have ever twinkled on his very own little feet!' (102) – is so unbalanced that it affects other people, causing them to have accidents. From the moment Mr Pye arrives, Miss Dredger wonders, 'What had he done to put her off her balance?' (21). Soon she finds herself fighting down 'a desire to smash the window to let out her soul' (29). Given Peake's image of the daily need to break out of the glass room that we live in, she should probably have done so. Instead she breaks it by accident:

she started to her feet and, marching to the window, flung it open. …
    The violence of her action broke both its hinges and it fell with a crash
and a splintering of glass to the gravel below.                          (30)

Mr Pye's lack of balance causes the sensitive fulcrum of life to tip until,
in this case, the hinges themselves break under the strain. With stupen-
dous pride, he believes that 'the whole world is unbalanced' and claims
to be one of the 'very few, who fight to keep it upright' (100). He is like
a marching soldier who tells the rest of the squad that *they* are out of step
with *him*.

    There is a gradation in the accidents that Mr Pye causes, starting with
broken limbs and ending with broken necks. Legs come first because Peake
saw the leg as an expression of the dynamic nature of life, balanced but
not symmetrical. In a drawing of a leg, 'only in one sense is [it] standing
still on the ground. The lines are restless though the limb is balanced.
Search for this quality,' he tells the art student. 'With its discovery, you
enter a world apart' (CLP10). Thus Peake underlines our need to discover
this balance, in life as in art, that he calls *equipoise*. Throughout the novel
Mr Pye is 'forced to walk the tightrope of his brain'. Ultimately 'the strain
of so exquisite a balance' is 'overpowering' (216) and in the final scene his
black horse and carriage, 'losing balance', go over the edge, while he uses
his dazzling white wings to fly off into the sky. If Mr Pye is an angel, then
he is the angel of destruction through imbalance.

    Not unlike Steerpike, this self-appointed missionary does exactly what
he wants with other people. On the first evening of his stay, he doses
Miss Dredger's chicken soup 'with a strong sedative' because 'it was plain
that the good woman needed a full night's sleep' (43). (Did he steal the
potion from the local doctor's dispensary?) He introduces his own choice
of food (including 'exclusive China tea, dispatched regularly to Mr Pye
from Swanage') at the Clôs de Joi and repaints Miss Dredger's kitchen in
his own choice of colours: 'Mr Pye had decided on lemon yellow walls
and dove grey woodwork' (57). On his second day, he visits Miss George
and determines that she shall come and live with Miss Dredger too. 'I
will settle with your landlord. You have no more to fear,' he informs her.
'But this is my house: I bought it,' protests his unwilling victim. 'Then I
shall sell it for you, my dear, and you will be free,' he answers (81). Free
to enter Mr Pye's service, that is.

    Mr Pye is not just manipulative; he's a bully. He bludgeons Miss
George into joining his community: 'you are a great big lonely woman,'
he tells her.

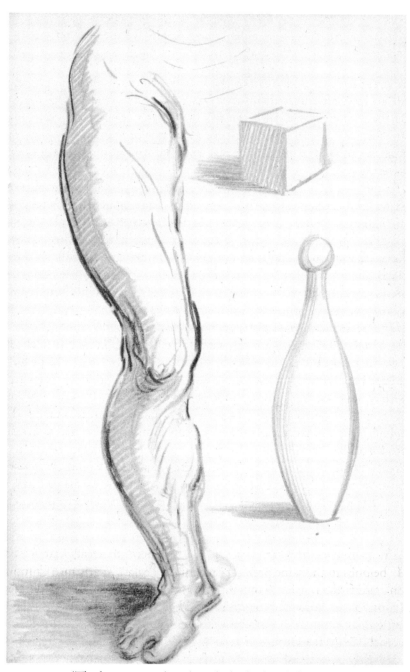

'The lines are restless though the limb is balanced':
Peake's drawing of a leg from *The Craft of the Lead Pencil*.

'Would you like to have something important to do? ... Something that made you proud to be alive? Would you like to feel a part of some great plan? Would you like to join me, and never be lonely again?' (80)

She capitulates. To 'convert' equally big, strong men, he turns Sark's cliffs into an implicit threat: he 'would take the man to the edge of a cliff, and there they would stand in absolute silence', after which 'the huge, sour-visaged, red-necked, sea-booted mariner would ... proceed with trembling legs upon his way' (77). The bigger his prey, the more Mr Pye savours his power.

As this last quotation suggests, Peake explicitly evokes Coleridge: Mr Pye holds the island, 'like the Ancient Mariner, with his glittering eye' (76). He mesmerizes his victims, the better to overpower them (as does Steerpike, by the way). 'Acting in unison, as though they were all part of one enormous machine, the scores of Sarkese rose to their feet, and drifted like somnambulists in Mr Pye's direction' (107). He robs them of individual will, an evil sign that points forward to the host of anonymous faces at the windows of the 'factory' in *Titus Alone*.

Mr Pye seduces people by appealing to their taste for good food. As Miss Dredger's paying guest, he turns the tables at lunch on his first day by serving her an omelette with 'the seductive bloom of an aromatic miracle' (34). Later he digs out 'a Château d'Yquem which he knew Miss Dredger was fond of' (226). This is the wining and dining technique that Captain Slaughterboard used on the Yellow Creature, and Mr Pye deploys it on a grand scale at his sumptuous midnight picnic, which the narrator calls 'a perfect affair'. However, 'any future banquet had little hope of being unequivocally appreciated – for there would always be a few to remember this classic spread' (103). Mr Pye is excessive in all he does, to the point of spoiling the future by setting too perfect a precedent. His lack of balance ruins everything.

To understand what's going on, we need to recall that *Mr Pye* belongs to the same period of writing as Peake's 'Christmas Commission' radio plays, which oppose art and creativity to technology and religion in the persons of the artist and the Little Man. Mr Pye is literally a little man – the only character in Peake's work to be so described – and also a Little Man. He has 'a certain inventiveness' (229) – after all, he invented his Great Pal – and he is mechanically minded, mending Miss Dredger's guttering and her lawnmower. In fact, he grips the island 'in the sharp, neat, shining vice of his brain' (48) which 'ticked away like a miracle of modern machinery' (120). (Notice the potential pun in 'vice', and the misuse of 'miracle' for the second time. Under Peake's pen, these are damning terms.) This again recalls Steerpike, whose mind works 'like an efficient machine' (TG225). Lacking heart in all he does, Mr Pye eventually realizes that he has 'flouted' his Great Pal 'with the intelligence rather than the heart' in his attempt to 'draw the island into the vortex of his love' (203).

Little Men are Philistines, unable to appreciate art; for them, 'Soutine is "ever so pretty" and Rembrandt "ever s-so sweet"', as Sark's resident painter, Thorpe, puts it bitterly (184). They fear originality because it threatens their superficial religious beliefs. So they either deny the artist his right and ability to create, or else reduce art to child's play, a mere matter of 'mixing your colours and all that' (W&D113). Peake uses Mr Pye to illustrate both attitudes (which correspond to Freud's superego and id); he even divides his psyche into 'his subconscious', which congratulates itself, and 'his conscious self' which has 'no time to dwell on anything that was not on the highest level of humility and leadership' (119). Speaking in what we might call his seraphic mode, Mr Pye exhorts Thorpe to 'leave the actual process of painting to the Deity. ... Fall back into the arms of Our Pal, and let your pastels do the work for you. After all, you are only the medium – the glass pipe as it were,' he tells him (88). Thorpe, who does not 'care much for religion' (215) protests that it 'would put [him] off f-frightfully' (88) to have God looking over his shoulder. In his demonic mode, Mr Pye suggests that it suffices to

> wield a full brush and slap the colours on, one! two! three! and away we go, plunging into the golden ochre, whisking the crimson from the palette, flicking on the viridian and hey presto! there you are, a thing of beauty, a radiance, an act, an utterance!               (183)

This stings Thorpe, who is generally shy and tongue-tied, into an eloquent denunciation of the 'organized racket' of galleries and critics that exploits both art and artists. He ends by tartly informing Mr Pye that he hasn't

> got a c-clue to what it's all about, as your ridiculous 'slap it on', 'whisk it off', and 'hey presto' attitude shows all t-too clearly. Your idea about colours is 'the m-more the b-better', and 'bright as p-possible', like a herbaceous b-border. Colour, Mr Pye, is a process of elimination. It is the d-distillation of an attitude. It is a credo.'               (185)

And with the word 'credo' we come to the crux of the matter. As beliefs and lifestyles, both art and religion spring from fear and create vision. Contrasting responses to the same stimuli, they 'sail on separate keels through separate waters' (W&D111).

Fear is something that Mr Pye does not know 'because it never occurred to him that there was anything to fear. His self-esteem and his self-confidence were almost palpable' and his pride 'quite unpuncturable' (76). His religious beliefs wipe out all sense of fear. Yet fear is essential – as he himself points out with reference to Miss George, whom he selects as an unwilling martyr to promote his cause (rather as Steerpike makes martyrs of the Groan family in the library fire). 'It is through fear that she is being purged,' he proclaims. 'Were she without fear she would be no better than a crocodile. Crocodiles are fearless through stupidity. We do not look to them for spiritual guidance' – which quite robs Mr Pye himself of any credibility as a spiritual guide. (He 'did not really believe in pain, but was full of compassion for those who imagined themselves to be suffering' (126) just as the crocodile lacks sympathy for the suffering of others, and is as impervious to art as 'the hippopotamus, the scorpion, the gadfly and the python' (W&D114).) He goes on: 'They cannot recognize fear any more than they can recognize evil' (118). Precisely: because Mr Pye has no fear he does not recognize the evil he causes. Blinded by belief in his own goodness he has no self-awareness, no sense – until the last – of his appalling pride and self-sufficiency. In fact, so great is his sense of self that he believes that God has found in him 'His perfect resting place' (124). This is the part offering accommodation to the whole.

Thorpe, the artist, is the opposite of this in every way; he experiences fear every time he thinks of painting and is acutely aware of his own shortcomings (which is no doubt why he stammers, in contrast to Mr Pye's skill with words). His confidence in himself and his ability to express beauty are sapped by doubts that can be summed up by 'everything's been DONE' already. (Tintagieu has a wonderfully earthy response to this: 'Don't let that upset you, dear ... it's still nice to do it' (on page 69, too, if you please). And they re-enact the original sin a few pages later.) He is unflinchingly honest with himself, having the intelligence to recognize, for instance, that the sudden anger he feels on seeing a photograph of 'smirking playboys' sitting in a nightclub, looking 'idiotically happy', is really jealousy. He can see that

> the glossy group had no need for art or the eternal verities. And suddenly
> he felt that he had no need for them either. He would like to sit in

nightclubs with a group of friends, and share with them their horror of
anything serious.                                                    (40)

So debilitating is his lack of self-confidence that the life of empty-headed
inanity enjoyed by the 'apes' in London can seem tempting. At such
moments, he finds beauty 'nothing but a bloody irritant' (92). A life
devoted to expressing 'the eternal verities' takes energy, courage, determination, honesty and willingness to accept one's own shortcomings
– virtues found in Thorpe, but not in sufficient quantities to make him
successful. In fact, he looks 'like something out of a book, something
pale, shadowy, a man in search of a personality' (69) – one of Peake's
most apt meta-comments.

The notion of *vision* is equally important. In a radio talk, Peake
contrasted the way the artist sees with what he calls functional vision.
The artist's vision is the product of his imagination, the fruit of having
the heart open to the world and letting beauty enter. For Peake,

> the marvels of the visible world are not things in themselves but revelations
> to stir the imagination – to conduct us to amazing climates of the mind,
> which climates it is for the artist to translate into paint or into words.
>
>                                                                    (AW4)

Conversely, 'there is no essential difference between the vision of a dog
and a practical man' (AW3) like the inventor and the Little Man. 'Total
blindness is reserved for those whose vision is functional' (AW3).

Peake contrasts the respective visions of Thorpe and Mr Pye in two
stages at the midnight picnic. Wondering if there's a painting to be made
of the scene, the artist strolls away across the beach. When he looks back
towards the bonfire where duck and pigeon are roasting on the spit, he sees
his footprints in the sand and is 'appalled. He had never known until this
moment that he was pigeon-toed'. In the end though, he considers that
it does not matter if one walks 'like a duck or an ant-eater'. 'Rembrandt
was no beauty,' he says to himself, 'and nor was Toulouse-Lautrec. I'm
an artist, not a *matinée* idol' (92). 'A *matinée* idol': that's what Mr Pye
amounts to. His picnic is his show – yet vision, Peake punning reminds
us, 'needs no spectacles' (112) – and ugly ducklings like Thorpe who do
not adulate him can go roast on the spit.

In contrast to Mr Pye's irrepressible buoyancy, Thorpe lives with a
sense of 'melancholy', of 'heroic deeds', 'golden pilgrimages' and 'splendid
dreams that had passed him by. … Yet there was always that flicker of

hope … that … a centrifugal moment' (16) of vision would come like a gift from heaven, enabling him to express 'the eternal verities' in a great painting. (Notice how that 'centrifugal moment' physically contrasts with 'the vortex' of Mr Pye's love. For Peake, creation involves flinging out, and therefore separate identity, whereas Mr Pye's centripetal love threatens separateness.) Until that moment comes, Thorpe can but wait.

Mr Pye, on the other hand, has constructed a spectacular vision, a 'splendid dream' of his own kind of 'golden pilgrimages':

> the vision of a Sark, purified by its own recognition of the supernatural, purified by the ceaseless battle for self-improvement, purified and made happy by this common aim, so that it became the Mecca, the panacea, the envy, not only of other little islands, thwarted and eternally bruised with internecine warfare – but the envy of the whole world, who would come to know of this little paradise, not more than three miles long, and would set sail for its rugged coast, that they might learn the Faith.                    (115)

It has nothing to do with the vision that an artist wants to 'translate into paint or into words'. This is functional vision, social engineering, a dream of community in the mind of a lonely man. Peake peppers it with terms like 'supernatural', 'self-improvement', 'Mecca', 'panacea' and 'envy' that from his pen are ambiguous, suspicious or even downright reprehensible. Its realization is prevented by a 'technicality' (48) – the favourite stumbling block of the Little Man. It does not occur to Mr Pye

> that he was taking upon himself a crusade of a kind well calculated to try the strength and patience of an archangel or a god with a soul as clear as the highest quality glass and the physical strength of the abominable snowman.                                              (48)

Since Mr Pye has none of these qualities, his self-imposed mission is a lost cause, 'beyond hope' (8). Indeed, he loses everything, not only Sark, but the whole world – for where on earth could he possibly land, or live, with wings such as he comes to possess? His natural habitat is the mythical realm of archangels and abominable snowmen.

Thorpe's vision comes moments after realizing that he is pigeon-toed. Looking at the beach scene, he attempts to turn it into a painting, telling himself that he 'must make marks, coloured marks, any marks, that might convey at least a fragment of the scene; the gloating light; the rhythm of the rocks'. But inspiration is not to be commanded. 'The whole thing stank of false romanticism. It reeked of a million postcards.' 'Oh, God,' whispers Thorpe to himself, 'why didn't I stick to life insurance!' (92). It is often at such moments when we give up *trying* that what we seek comes to us. Suddenly, he is filled with 'a kind of exultation'; he has seen

> in his mind's eye, a picture, dynamic, vital, savage, frozen into geometry ... a painting unlike any other painting – yet in the tremendous tradition of the masters. Who cared if his toes turned in?                    (93)

This work would have 'that most magisterial of qualities, "equipoise"' (D9) that Mr Pye is so lacking in; he is 'half seraph and half devil' (220), flung between superego and id. Thorpe is ego, balanced 'on a razor's edge between the passion and the intellect' (D9). But instead of quickly sketching his vision, he starts to run 'with his arms stretched out stiffly behind him like wings or like a child pretending to be an aeroplane'. Abruptly, he finds himself 'soaring through the air ... with a suddenness that gave him no time for fear'. Have his imaginary wings worked? Has he achieved the fearless state of the evangelist? No. 'As he galloped around the base of a high solitary rock he had tripped' and he finds himself 'lying on his face in a rock pool' (93). He never recovers the vision of that great painting.

This scene bathetically anticipates Mr Pye's ultimate fall and flight (and in this paragraph I have italicized the links). Filled with 'the breadth of his vision and the intensity of his drive' (45), Mr Pye flees from the enraged islanders, standing with his *wings outstretched* in a carriage pulled by a *galloping* black horse. However, he is not going 'around the base' of the island but approaching the knife-edge of the Coupée on Sark, that 'high solitary rock' in the sea. Then comes the *moment of renunciation*: 'he drew forth his soul and tossed it skywards to his God. "Oh, catch it, if you care to,"' he cries, beating his wings 'in an earthless *exultation*'. (This 'earthless exultation' recalls Keda's experience. Mr Pye is last glimpsed doing just what she no doubt imagined, 'beginning to soar in slow wide arcs, and ... dwindling until ... only visible to those of keenest vision' (MP254).) At once, the horse *stumbles* and, still pulling the carriage, *plunges* (in Peake's best Miltonic prose) 'a hideous conglomeration, down, down, down, vaulting horribly as they descended in giant arcs to the shingle far below.' Mr Pye himself is hurled '*high into the air*', *soaring* 300 feet above 'the wide and sweeping bay ... where he had once despoiled the castles of the *children*.' He starts to fall 'like a stone', but at the end of his 'long hurtling flight' (253–54), he spreads his miraculous wings and, clumsily at first but with increasing skill, flies away on them. The wings save his life at the expense of his vision.

The motif that serves to contrast the world-views of the Little Man and the artist is the moon. The three key scenes of the novel, Mr Pye's discovery of the Coupée, the picnic and his final flight from the Coupée, all take place by the light of the moon. We know that for Peake the moon is negatively connoted; this story confirms it on every page. The effect of Mr Pye's preaching, for instance, is invariably associated with lunar inanity: of 'the scores of moonstruck faces' (106) in his 'moonlit congregation' (116) that shine 'vacantly in the moonlight' (117), 'there were [but] three who had their mouths shut' (106). Mr Pye's wings are best viewed by the mendacious light of the moon: 'the moonbeams, streaming through the window, lit up with dazzling whiteness a wing the size of a swan's' (247). As he flies out of the story, their chief characteristic is this 'dazzling whiteness' (254). On seeing Mr Pye as 'a moonlit seraph', Thorpe is dumbstruck, unable to 'close his mouth, into which the moonbeams poured' (250–51). He won't listen to the sermon but he still gets the moonlight.

Every word of Mr Pye's discovery of the Coupée (which repeats Steerpike's experience on the rooftop of Gormenghast), is pregnant with meaning, especially the opposition between light and darkness.

> And then suddenly the moon broke free and fled across the night, only to be lost immediately in the black surges of the sky.[2] But in that moment of silver radiance Mr Pye had seen the Coupée. ... Within a few feet of where he stood, and upon his right hand, a moonlit wall of rock fell in precipitous rhythm to a wilderness of dazzling foam. ... Equally close to him, upon his left, the cliff plunged down into the moonless shadows where the foam roared and tumbled in the darkness. Ahead of him the high, dangerously narrow track of La Coupée ... seemed to be suspended in the air. The iron railings on its either side shone balefully. And then the wild moon fused and Mr Pye was left in darkness.                    (45–46)

All the way from 'broke free and fled, only to be lost' down to 'fused' we have evidence that Peake associates the moon with sin, Satan's revolt against God. Decisions made by the moon's light are fallacious and fundamentally flawed, for it misleads the senses and dazzles the mind; even the

---

2. 'Surges' is an odd word in this context; is it a misspelling for 'serges', the metaphorical thick cloth in Steerpike's experience (TG133)?

iron railings that protect the strait and narrow path seem baleful rather than reassuring. At the end, Mr Pye's 'hideous conglomeration' of horse and carriage crash through them, just as Miss George mows down the banisters 'like ninepins' (163) in her fall. So while Mr Pye is quite correct in observing that 'this is where the wisdom begins' (46), the immense irony is that the light of the moon leads to self-deception and self-aggrandisement, the belief that the part can accommodate the whole. Witness Mr Pye's words to his god: '"Have faith in me," he whispered to the Great Pal, who glimmered in every drop of the moonlit rain. "Have faith in me, and forgive me, and nothing can go wrong"' (204). At this point, humility is a feeling quite unknown to Mr Pye. Hubris awaits him.

True wisdom lies in recognizing that light makes the darkness, and vice versa; you can't have one without the other, any more than you can have birth without death, love without hate, or good without evil. Mr Pye believes that he can have one without the other, a stance that Peake had anticipated (in the comic mode) in *Gormenghast*:

> Who could imagine, while Cutflower was around, that there were such vulgar monsters as death, birth, love, art and pain around the corner? It was too embarrassing to contemplate. If Cutflower knew of them he kept it secret. Over their gaping and sepulchral deeps he skimmed now here, now there, in his private canoe, changing his course with a flick of his paddle when death's black whale, or the red squid of passion, lifted for a moment its body from the brine.                    (G217)

Dazzled by the moon, blithely paddling his skiff (61), Mr Pye obstinately reads meanings into the natural world about him. The raindrops on his window send him out to explore the island, when a wise man would have stayed at home. But 'no midwife is more at the mercy of being shaken from her bed than the man who follows the flights of his own soul: the man of private faith: the perfectionist: the sleuth of glory' (42). Moments later, a falling branch almost kills him. The stink of a dead whale might disrupt his grand rally but deters him not a jot. 'The whale had been sent. There had been a change of plan. That was all. He would have a chat with the Great Pal and proceed upon the next stage of his evangelical mission' (122). Tintagieu intuits that Mr Pye, that 'enigma of noon' (48), belongs to the night world: 'Perhaps you were made for the moonlight, chief. ... Perhaps you ...' (248), and her voice fades away. She is lost for words, like everyone else when it comes to drawing conclusions about Mr Pye. What he truly is is beyond words.

The artist, Thorpe, knows better than to believe the light of the moon. Kneeling down 'on the wet sand' to sketch the midnight shore, he finds that 'it was the moon itself that baulked him. The moon, that fatuous circle. That overrated face that spawned the light; and it wasn't even her own light' (92). Rejecting it he envisions a painting with 'a kind of leper whiteness – the paint all thick and crusty – I'll mix the stuff with sand. *And no moon*' (93; my emphasis). Mixing sand with the paint may be an original idea for a nocturnal seascape; it also takes us back to the glassblowers that so impressed Peake, 'wheedling alchemy / From the warlock sand' (Gb19). Furthermore it contrasts ironically with the fall of Mr Pye, for whom

> all things were penultimate. He was always on the threshold, dealing with that minor technicality that had, of necessity, to be cleared up before the trumpets rang, and the heavens opened and the moon at last showed him her other side.                                              (48)

When those trumpets finally ring out, so to speak, and he crosses the 'threshold' of the Coupée, he gets to see that 'other side': 'from the reflecting shore the wet face of the moon shone up at him' (253). With his imagination, Peake's artist aims to spiritualize matter by transforming it, whereas his evangelist succeeds only in reducing the spiritual into matter.[3]

The counterpoint between Thorpe and Mr Pye illustrates the separate courses taken by art and religion from the same point of departure. Mr Pye is 'proud to belong to the tiny company of zealots who were prepared to stake their faith in the spiritual values and to have the courage to voice their belief to the world' (132). Recalling Peake's notion that great artists are 'rebels' (D8) whose works depict 'eternal values', we find that, with the smallest of changes, this same statement applies to artists. They belong to the tiny company of *rebels* who are prepared to stake their faith in *eternal values* and to have the courage to voice their belief to the world. The religious and the artistic conceptions of the world function in exactly the same way, yet have fundamentally different aims and – as we saw in the previous chapter – very different consequences. Through his satyrical depiction of Mr Pye (if I may be permitted the pun), Peake shows his understanding of the zealot's outlook and deplores its effects, in particular its rejection of the artist's world-view and lifestyle.

---

3. This parallels the notion of simony in Joyce's *Dubliners*, just as Peake's wholes and parts parallel Joyce's Euclidian gnomon.

So far, this discussion of the conflict between art and religion in *Mr Pye* has concentrated on mind and spirit, at the expense of the body, as represented by Tintagieu. (Her name, by the way, derives from an immense rock off the coast of Sark; she's a mini-island in herself.) By no means should the body be neglected, for unless we satisfy its appetites, neither mind nor spirit last long in this world.

Tintagieu leads a life of pleasure, indulging her body's natural lust with the unselfconsciousness of a monkey (MP69). 'To talk with Tintagieu was to experience childhood all over again. She loved to make love as a child loves to play' (110). Recognizing what she represents, Mr Pye sends Miss Dredger to recruit her as one of his missionaries. 'It is not that your morals are bad,' she observes,

> 'it is because you simply haven't any. That is what appeals to the chief. ...
> In his opinion you are absolutely innocent like a piece of clay, or like a bird
> of prey that has no choice. It can only be itself.'                    (152)

Responding to the call, Tintagieu comes dressed in what she thinks is missionary attire, the tightest of black skirts and a black blouse with 'a small white collar like the frills which butchers put round mutton chops' (154), turning herself into 'five-foot-three inches of sex, lagged like a boiler-pipe in mourning' (156)! When it comes to Peake's animal companions, eating and sex are never far apart. In front of Mr Pye, she too loses her balance and falls 'in a voluptuous heap' at his feet. Just for once, no bones are broken, but the scene enables Peake to surround Mr Pye with two emblems, the virgin Miss Dredger and Tintagieu the whore, a literal fallen woman.[4]

Seeing her there, Mr Pye tries yet again to do evil and thwacks her on the rump. He is rewarded with 20 minutes of laughter,

> as uninhibited as the howling of a wolf pack, but there was nothing hungry
> or vicious in the noise. It was simply uncontrolled to such a degree that it
> seemed to belong more to the animal than the human kingdom. It was
> Tintagieu laughing: laughing helplessly, her diaphragm shuddering like a
> plucked wire, her body sprawled out like something that she had no longer
> any control over or any wish to control, as it rolled this way and that in an
> agony of mirth.                                                        (158)

---

4. This constellation was first noticed by François 41.

As suggested previously, if animals could, they would laugh at man's pretensions. With her laughter that is 'more animal than human' Tintagieu does just this – and Mr Pye learns from it. He accepts his animal side, exposes himself like a prize goat at the cattle show and then uses his wings to escape. To do this, he shuts off 'that part of his mind which made decisions', clears his conscience and feels full life in his body, 'a kind of radiance of the heart' (252). Ultimately, his bird-like pinions save him, not his pious preaching.

Until that moment, Tintagieu has been the only person on the island to remain unmoved by Mr Pye's campaign:

> To those whose contact with Mr Pye had already resulted in a marked moral improvement, and who made solicitous enquiries as to the state of her soul, Tintagieu merely raised her thick eyebrows and blew a long and ruminative raspberry.                                                    (78)

Since animals do not have souls, Peake maintains the ambiguity of her status with this thoughtful 'raspberry'. But as Mr Pye takes leave of her, he thanks her, and she suffers 'so sweet a pang in her breast – a pang of such pure affection – that no one who only knew her as Sark's least virginal of daughters, could ever have believed' (250). He awakens in her the love that raises humans above animals, and she proves to be capable of greater altruism than any other character in the novel, Mr Pye not excepted.

Appropriately Tintagieu also provides much of the humour in what is, after all, a moral comedy. She participates in Peake's playful depiction of the Sarkese view of tourists, which happens to reflect his ultimate belief that it is impossible to share an island – any island – with another human being:

> These day-trippers, in the unanimous opinion of *all* islanders, were the lowest type of animal life. Tintagieu and Thorpe, sitting on the sea wall, watched them as though they were witnessing the disembarkation of thrice murrained cattle.
>   Certainly there was an awful lot of meat coming ashore.
>                                                    (180; my emphasis)

Part of the irony is that the male tourists, with 'their shorts rolled up to their crutches' (53 – Peake delicately writes 'crutch' for 'crotch') are Tintagieu's source of livelihood, her stock-in-trade. Thus she makes a perfect 'goatherd' for Mr Pye at the cattle show, reversing their respective

roles. In hoping for venison, Batchelor had got the wrong meat: the characters of this book eat only seafood, birds and eggs. No pork, or lamb.
And thanks to Tintagieu, the beef is consumed in other ways.

While some have found *Mr Pye* indigestible, I find it a feast. It is the
most consciously constructed of Peake's prose works, with fine control
of language and layered meanings. Its irony makes it funny as well as
profound, and the philosophical or metaphysical considerations are
anchored in concrete events. On one level it is about vision and belief in
art and religion; on another it dramatizes Peake's impression that love is
not 'rock-like' but 'a bird of the air' (Gb6). On yet another, it may be just
a multiple pun: if you prey on a granite island and make it your quarry,
all you get is stone. And the reader can enjoy all three at the same time.

# Theatre

What else is there but volcanic search? The pain; the dark propulsion; the bonfire in the heart: the sounds of footsteps leaving the comfortable house for the fields of thorn and those cold shores in mountain shadow where the dead sea fruit lolls in the ashes of apples. (*Cave*, Act III)

Each on his rock transfixed, the sport and prey
Of racking whirlwinds, or for ever sunk
Under yon boiling ocean, wrapped in chains,
There to converse with everlasting groans.
(*Paradise Lost*, II.181–84; NAEL 1: 1839)

Trust nothing that can ever be explained. (PP335)

So far this study has concentrated almost entirely on Peake's fiction and poetry, yet throughout the 1950s, he channelled most of his creative energy into writing plays. If the themes and motifs presented in the foregoing chapters truly represent his main preoccupations, Peake's theatre should corroborate my findings, rounding them out with additional evidence and filling in areas I may have neglected. So let us consider the most successful of his plays, *The Wit to Woo*, which had a brief run at the Arts Theatre in London in the spring of 1957. Since then, no one has offered a critical analysis of it.

There were good reasons why Peake should consider the theatre to be a natural venue for his talents. We have seen how his characters would come to him primarily as voices and then take shape as he allowed them 'to strut, to mime upon, to creep or float across' the stage of his imagination (D7). In his fiction he described and animated numerous scenes as though in a theatre, complete with backdrop and proscenium arch. So I feel that John Watney underestimated Peake when he suggested that money was his primary motivation for becoming a playwright. Given the state of his finances, the hope of making 'an instant fortune' (Watney 175) in the theatre was no doubt great, but Peake only entertained it because his creative process inclined him in that direction.

His growing interest in writing for the theatre can be observed in his fiction. On three occasions, for example, he has Titus hear a disembodied voice. In *Gormenghast*, the mountain challenges him with a repeated question: "*Do you dare?*" it seemed to cry. "*Do you dare?*"' (G97). The quoted speech, the italics for emphasis, and the inquit (or subjective discourse tag) all belong to the traditional techniques of fiction-writing. 'Boy in Darkness' is equally bookish:

> The whisper that breathed between his shoulder-blades as though urging him to fly ... was growing in volume and intensity. 'Just for a little while,' it said. 'After all you are only a boy. What kind of fun are you having?'
>
> (159)

In *Titus Alone*, on the other hand, the presentation is that of a play script:

| | |
|---|---|
| A voice. | 'O Titus, can't you remember?' |
| Titus. | 'I can remember everything except ...' |
| Voice. | 'Except ...?' |
| Titus. | 'Except the way.' |
| Voice. | 'The way where?' |
| Titus. | 'The way home.' (TA33) |

Peake does this more than once in *Titus Alone*, making some pages look as though they have been lifted from a play. Abandoned passages in the manuscript also adopt this form of presentation.

The novel reader's experience of dialogue presented in the manner of a play script differs fundamentally from that of the theatre audience. In print, the identification of the speaker (be it only 'a voice') functions as an implicit narrator. Herein lies the first problem that Peake had to contend with in turning to playwriting, for he was heavily dependent on the narratorial voice. So we should not be surprised that his first plays were for the radio. The very difficulty of conveying everything to the audience by sound alone makes it an apposite medium for Peake to exercise his talents in. Moreover, it was common in radio drama of the 1950s to have a storyteller set the scene. (*Under Milk Wood*, by Peake's friend Dylan Thomas, which was broadcast twice in January 1954, has multiple narrators, a 'first voice' and a 'second voice' in addition to a character-commentator, Captain Cat.) Thus his first works for radio, two Christmas plays, are introduced by a storyteller – but this device could barely cope with the moment when the artist hears in his head the painters Giotto and El Greco advising and encouraging him. The BBC dropped these lines in performance (in October 1954), and Peake omitted them from the expanded version of the play that he prepared for broadcasting in December 1956 (see PS 9 (April 2005), ii: 12). His second radio play (aired on the Third Programme in February 1956) was a 60-minute compression of *Titus Groan*, narrated by the animated 'spirit of Gormenghast'. Finally, in his adaptation of *Mr Pye* (BBC, July 1957) he dispensed with a narrator altogether, as he did in his stage plays, of course. However, the temptation to include unidentified voices remained. In *Mr Pye* this works well enough, given the large cast of islanders, but in *The Wit to Woo* an unknown person, who plays no part in the plot, twice looks in through the window, asking, 'Would this be Crouchingfold?' (PP289 and 330), which is quite at variance with the rest of the play. As in Peake's fiction, some of the main characters are heard off-stage several minutes before they make their first appearance, which makes of them, if only momentarily, a form of disembodied narratorial voice.

The other problem that Peake had to contend with in writing plays was his inclination to backtrack from the opening situation instead of developing it. The idiosyncratic structure of the Titus books, which omit the 'point of departure' with Titus aged 40, can be found in *Noah's Ark* and *The Cave*. In their different ways, both plays return to the distant past to account for man's present condition, but neither makes this intention very clear. On the other hand, there is little evidence in Peake's stage plays of his temporal backshifting on the purely verbal level. Only the summary of *The Cave*, 'Act I being several thousand years before Act II, and Act II being several hundred years before Act III', emphasizes precedence rather than sequence. Reversed order of action, using the phrase 'but not before', can be found in the stage directions of *The Wit to Woo*. Percy, wearing a suit of armour, is interrupted by a funeral attendant as he attempts to pick up his drink:

> Watkins returns up the cellar steps but not before Percy has stooped down in order to fish up the elusive glass at his feet. When at an angle of ninety

degrees, he is frozen stiff by the reappearance of Watkins, who straightens him out, and leans him against the bannisters, but not before Percy has scooped up the glass.                                                                    (PP357)

It takes a second reading to establish the actual sequence of events, yet actors need to have their moves prescribed in strict chronological order. Apart from the occasional lapse, then, Peake overcame his tendency to backtrack.

Nevertheless, his most successful play, *The Wit to Woo*, develops the consequences of an action that has taken place before the curtain rises: having been unable to verbalize his love for Sally Devius, Percy Trellis has faked his suicide. The play opens with his return in the guise of his own imaginary cousin, the grandiloquent artist October Trellis, on the morning of his own funeral. Thus it repeats Peake's technique of omission of the 'real reason' at the same time as differing completely from it by progressing (with flashbacks to explain the situation to the audience) to resolution: Percy finally wins Sally's heart. The curtain comes down on a perfect love match.

It took much work and rewriting over a period of five or six years to achieve this. For instance, the back of one typescript was used as 'the scribbling ground for a new version' (Watney 175). Unfortunately *Peake's Progress* reproduces not the script as ultimately performed (which itself shows signs of revision, with additions pasted in on the backs of the duplicated pages) but one of Peake's many drafts, full of minor incoherences. Its main lines correspond to the staged version, but many speeches are slightly longer or shorter, the byplay is different, and the naming of the secondary characters is inconsistent. As the version that was performed is regrettably still unpublished, I shall quote from *Peake's Progress*, borrowing from the staged version on just one occasion and signalling divergences between the two.

In addition to the hard work and rewriting, Peake found a major source of inspiration in a classic play, *Volpone, or The Fox* (1606). Ben Jonson's plot, itself developed from Horace's satire on legacy hunters (Book II.7), revolves around the character of a devious miser, Volpone, whose god is gold. To make himself even richer, he pretends to be dying and has his business friends informed that, if they give him suitable presents, he will make them his heirs, thereby multiplying their 'investment' on his demise. His friends respond in kind, demonstrating how low a man will stoop for financial gain: one disinherits his son, another breaks the law, and a third is willing to prostitute his wife. This would be simple enough were it not that Volpone's manservant, Mosca, who has been aiding and abetting his master, turns out to be feathering his own nest at the same time. All this is mirrored in a sub-plot involving a couple of English tourists, as well as a dwarf, a eunuch, a hermaphrodite, sheriffs (Commendatori) and lawyers. When finally everyone is arrested and tried, each attempts to deceive the court, but in the end, they are all punished according to their merits. Jonson was a determined moralist.

As in *Volpone*, the plot of *The Wit to Woo* proves to be more complex than it first appears. Old Man Devius (whose very name harks back to Jonson's play) pretends to be dying in the hope of precipitating the marriage of his daughter Sally to Percy Trellis. Only halfway through the play does Peake reveal that Devius is bankrupt and hoping that Percy, whom he fancies to be rich, will pay off the debts once he is married to Sally. (It is never made clear just how much money – or how little – Percy actually has.) At the same time, the manservant Kite, who is Percy's prime accomplice in his deception, turns out to have been aiming to make away with what he imagines to be the fortune of Old Man Devius. So while the latter is feigning illness and Percy faking suicide, Kite is deceiving them both. Yet another parasite, Dr Willy, colludes with Old Man Devius in exchange for liberal quantities of his patient's best brandy; while completely befuddled, he has been made to sign Percy's death certificate. So he too is a deceiver deceived. Peake does not bring them to trial, but he introduces the law in the shape of a Bailiff – a 'nasty little man' (338) – and his men who come in blind obedience to orders from head office and seize Devius's possessions. It's also there in Percy's inextricable problem: he cannot regain his old identity because he is legally dead.

Peake acknowledges his debt to *Volpone* in various ways. He puts the word 'fox' into the mouth of no less than three characters: realizing that October is in fact Percy, Sally exclaims, 'The vixens of the world inhabit me / And bark for vengeance on this wily fox!' (342). Old Man Devius swears by 'the love of foxes' (299) and Percy qualifies Kite as 'foxy' (314). Peake also creates similar scenes. One of Volpone's prospective 'heirs' proposes his young and pretty wife, Celia, as a cure for the old miser's supposed illness. Once alone with her, Volpone throws off his fox furs and bounds out of bed, declaring – to her horror and amazement – how lucky she is to have acquired such a generous lover as he. Sally Devius is equally unaware of her father's true condition, both financial and physical, so she too is astounded when he suddenly leaps from his bed. Furthermore, rather as Volpone is expected to be revived by having Celia in his bed, so the decrepit Dr Willy is rejuvenated by the sight of Sally in her under-wear: 'she can titillate and twitch my senses / Into a second youth' (324), as he puts it.

Jonson signalled his satirical intent by giving many of his male charac-ters the names of parasites and scavengers, especially birds. The malcon-tent Mosca is a fly – a name that Peake used in *Gormenghast* – and Devius calls his daughter a 'disobedient fly' (297); the advocate, Voltore, is a vulture; one merchant, Corvino, is a raven; and another, Corbaccio, is a crow. In the sub-plot, the English couple are deceived by Peregrine, a young gentleman on his Continental tour. Peake repeats this device by calling his malcontent Kite, another bird of prey. The word also has the most appropriate obsolete meaning of 'a person who exploits or preys on others' (NODE). Moreover, Peake had already used the kite most ambigu-ously when he wrote of love that it proves to be 'A heart-shaped kite / On the winds of the world' (Gb67). As for the other raptors, Peake has Kite call the four mutes both 'crows' (282) and 'vultures' (283), and makes the chief undertaker allude to the raven (272). By way of comparison, the eagle gets two mentions, the peregrine, the hawk and the falcon none. But Kite calls the house 'a rookery of robbers' (361); Devius calls Dr Willy a magpie and the Bailiff's men, who are carrying off his furniture, both jackdaws and magpies: three more scavengers. So Peake includes all of Jonson's birds except for the peregrine – replaced by the eagle? – and adds others in the same vein.

Nor is this all, for Peake punctuates *The Wit to Woo* with numerous owl and cuckoo calls which both echo its punning title and comment on the plot. In fact the play opens with the sound of birds. As the curtain rises on the hall of an English country house, complete with portraits of grotesque ancestors and stuffed animal heads on the walls,

> there is music interwoven with the hooting of an owl. There is then a complete silence on the empty stage, except for a fluttering sound like that of a bird caught in a greenhouse.                                    (271)

Could anyone in Peake's 1957 audience identify that sound, never mind intuit its significance for him? It's a complex symbol, recalling both the fluttering of a heart desirous of love and the need for the artist to break out of the glass cage of habit and convention.

The one character whose name seems to be quite out of place is Percy Trellis, who becomes the artist October Trellis. How did Peake arrive at 'Percy'? Are we to think of Percy Shelley, the poet who fell in love with

Bird-like undertakers in Peake's sketches for *The Wit to Woo*.

'a green schoolgirl' (361) like Sally, 'the kind of flower that only blooms / Once in a hundred years' (314)? As an artist, Percy became 'Giuseppe' in one of the drafts (depicted in PP320), which was probably another nod towards *Volpone*. He ended up being called 'October' which has an appropriate absurdity to it, at the same time as being situated in the season of natural maturity, contrasting with Sally's green of inexperience. This gave Peake an opportunity to toy with different meanings of *season*: as an amateur actor, Percy has played heroes and villains 'In and out of season' (313) but now he has 'had [his] fill of seasons' (362). In any case, Percy's first name seems to have been less important than his family name, which departs radically from Peake's habitual characternymy and remained unchanged through several drafts. Here I have another suggestion as to the source.

In the late 1970s, Lee Speth came across some verses beginning 'Let me linger by the trellis' by an obscure American poet, Mabel Ingalls Wescott, in a volume published in New England in 1937. They use the same trochaic rhythm and 'old fifteener' line as Tennyson's 'Locksley Hall', from which Ms Wescott 'appropriates whole phrases'. Speth also noticed that the verses spoken by the Poet in *Titus Groan* use the same meter and repeat the key verb, 'to linger' (which is not prominent in Tennyson, nor is there any hint in Peake that he was aware of 'Locksley Hall'). 'The only differences are that Peake uses two lines where Ms Wescott uses one and therefore doubles his rhymes, and that Peake varies his chant with a four-line refrain.' So Speth wondered, 'Is Peake's effusion a parody of Ms Wescott's poem?' It seems highly improbable that, writing *Titus Groan* in wartime England, he should know of 'Let me linger' and, what is more, *bother* to parody it, yet the similarities are undeniable. Speth concludes: 'if Peake did not know Ms Wescott's poem, how sure can anyone be about *any* derivation? We may even have to face the possibility that the author of Genesis had never heard of Gilgamesh' (Speth 47).

Had he known of Percy Trellis in *The Wit to Woo*, I doubt whether Lee Speth would have had a moment's hesitation. Mrs Wescott's poem is all about the trellis that she has often gazed upon 'from window casement' – remember that the Poet declaims his lines through the open window of his garret. At the foot of this trellis her 'thoughts will ever linger' when 'at last the *dusky twilight*, that is near and nearer drawn / Mingles with the light of heaven, in the merging of a dawn' (Wescott 17, my emphasis). Everything points to Peake borrowing this 'trellis' for his hero loved by a girl who pours out 'her girlish soul / Into the *dusky night* like golden syrup' (PP302; my emphasis) in the manner of Mabel Ingalls Wescott.

The uneven course of true love between Percy/October and Sally Devius is the main theme of *The Wit to Woo*. It opens with them as isolated as any characters in Peake; in particular, their respective families are minimal: neither seems to have a sibling and no mention is ever made of Sally's mother, or Percy's father. As for his mother, Sally confesses that she 'never quite believed he was the child / Of anyone' yet 'he must have *had* a mother' (306; Peake's emphasis). Seeing Percy disguised as an artist, Kite exclaims, 'Why, your mother wouldn't know you', and Percy responds laconically with 'She never did' (314). So Percy is another literary orphan. Moreover, Peake's mothers (like Gertrude in Gormenghast) may forget their sons but sons (like Titus in the world outside Gormenghast) do not forget their mothers. As Dr Willy puts it, the bailiffs overlooking the liquor in the cellar is 'like a man / Forgetting his own mother' (352). (The remark is most apposite in the mouth of Dr Willy, for he imbibes brandy from the bottle like a baby.)

Percy and Sally are typical Peake characters in desiring love as the cure for loneliness, ever aspiring to end their solitude by fusing with one another. Percy hopes that he and Sally will

> melt into a realm
> Of dew and sunbeams intermingled
> With lawns of light that scoop the startled heart
> Out of the breast,
> There to ache together, and dissolve in love!
> (301; staged version)

Only readers aware of the cosmic perspective of Peake's fiction, of the desire of the part to merge with the whole and yet remain separate, can appreciate the weight of these words, which recall the Edenic perspectives of the golden oak wood, shortly before Titus glimpses the Thing in *Gormenghast*.

In this play, loneliness and solitude are figured right from the start by the empty hall on which the curtain rises to the sound of a fluttering bird. The bailiffs empty the house of all its furniture; when finally the last object – the suit of armour with Percy inside it – has been carried out, the hall seems 'twice as big and twice as empty' (359). Rather appropriately, Sally feels that the dead Percy 'haunts the aching / Halls in [her] heart'

(358). Emptiness links with the misleading light of the moon: Percy observes bitterly that

> The very moon that has seduced so many
> And drawn them down through dooms of disillusion
> Is only rock and stone – its glamour light
> A mere reflection, cold ... cold ... cold and empty
> As a woman's heart.
>
>                                        (351)

and Sally makes an identical speech, ending with 'a man's heart' (358) (which shows that Peake can be a moralist too). The heart and the bird combine in another image that we have already identified, the nest. Sally complains

> I only wish
> My heart was not as empty as a nest
> Abandoned in a tree.
>
>                    (294)

Preparatory to ending their respective solitude by joining her in that nest, so to speak (rather as Lord Sepulchrave joins the owls and their love-lined nests in the Tower of Flints), Percy clears the hall of other characters with a switch of foliage, declaring as he does so that he is 'tearing off, one by one ... all the little / Civilized twigs that get in the way' (367). Thus Peake combines emptiness, birds and nests in a characteristic complex of motifs.

He even connects his nests and birds with Jonson's theme of legacy hunters. Percy's fear 'that at any moment [Sally] might turn / Into a cuckoo' (300) is invidiously encouraged by Kite, who suggests:

> with a legacy alive
> And twitching in your wallet you will find
> That everybody starts to love you deeply –
> (Including your beloved?).
>
>                                        (312)

Percy finds this thought 'contemptible': 'To follow up your reasoning / Is to be led into world of worms', he snarls, cleverly linking the food of birds with the body as food for the worms in the grave which he has just evaded. For him of course, Sally 'must accept me for myself alone. / Not for a legacy, but for *myself*', which is highly ironic: at this point he has just buried Percy and hardly begun to know himself as October. '*Which self?*' comments Kite in a sarcastic aside (312; Peake's emphases).

In the end, Percy becomes 'a deathless bird' in Sally's eyes, stepping 'like a phoenix out of all / The accumulated ash'. This is a bit much for him. 'Oh steady on!' he protests. 'Deathless bird?' To which she responds with Peake's characteristic bathos: 'What would you rather be? A budgerigar?' (372). She even tells him that she is his 'love-bird, top to toe', whereupon Percy asks 'Or beak to claw?' (371). So alongside all those Jonsonian birds of prey, Peake manages to fit in his birds of love as well.

Peake's favourite of image of man's solitude, the island, is there too, or rather, the terms that Peake employs depend on it or derive from it. For instance, when Percy deplores the perfidy of women, he exclaims: 'There is no haven. / But what of those who tread the slippery springboard?' (351). We need to know of Peake's basic metaphor to understand such a brief allusion to attempts to cross the water and reach another person. Sally's phrases are less obscure: after Percy's 'death', she feels 'as though a great tide had gone out' (with a superfluous past perfect) leaving her 'all sand' (308).

The solitude of Old Man Devius is figured by the bed to which he has retreated in his supposedly fatal illness. It is lowered to the stage by winch (like a lifeboat from the davits of a ship), whereupon he 'weighs anchor' (299) and orders Dr Willy to steer him around in it:

> Starb'd a little! Starb'd, my old rudder. Nor'west
> By west and mind that coral reef! that's it, and
> Very nicely navigated. Fetch up alongside, Willy,
> There's a bantam. Drop anchor, dear.
>
> (318)

Peake transforms Volpone's bed into his own favourite metaphor of the ship.

Beneath the slapstick of this play lies Peake's basic preoccupation with the difficulty of communicating love and its close link with identity. After all, saying 'I love you' in all sincerity posits the identities of both speaker and addressee. It may even be thought of as defining the speaker: 'I am the person who loves you.' It also requires a voice to say it with, and (for the communication to be successful) ears to hear it. Peake ironically highlights the theme by having four *mutes* open the play. This term for professional mourners or funeral attendants derives from the French for *dumb*; as an adjective it still means 'temporarily speechless' (NODE). He has them garrulously fill us in on the situation and in particular on Percy's problem: he cannot tell Sally that he loves her. Whenever they are alone together, his voice 'Fills up [his] throat and [he] can make no sound' (285). Walking with him in the village, Sally

> waited for 'is voice –
> But though 'e tossed 'is head 'n jerked 'is jaw
> As though to shake the words out, nothing happened.
>                                                    (277)

She knows that he loves her, but because he does not express it in *words*, his behaviour awakens no response in her. So she is like a blank page waiting for the words of the poet to breathe life into her. 'What was the use of being loved', she wonders, if she feels within her 'no echo to the muffled chimes / Of his heart?' (293; not in staged version). This metaphor combines the motifs that we have seen from the start, the vast space beneath the ribs, like the hollow halls of Gormenghast, a cavern or a belfry, where beats the heart as the voice of the imagination. They all belong to the moment preceding the act of creating a work of art.

Moreover, Percy is just too *nice* for her, 'too much the gentleman' (275 and 311): he can't 'let 'imself go' (275) and hold her tight. So Sally, considering her own attractiveness, wonders

> When all is said and done, what is the point
> Of looking lovely if you can't arouse
> The beast in men – however nice a beast,
> Still, it must be, a beast.
> Dear Percy's beast was always half asleep.
>                                                    (294–95)

Her partner must not be so civilized that the animal in him has been completely tamed. Now that Peake voices the woman's point of view on this matter, he makes the purpose of animal companions quite plain. One of the functions of the Thing is to arouse the beast in Titus – which is just what the frigid Cheeta rejects. Adding to Peake's metaphors of fire for physical love, Sally declares that she wants 'a man of fire to tame [her]' (309).

She seems not to notice that Percy has already demonstrated his predatory animal nature by hunting wild beasts in Africa; their heads decorate the walls of the set. Moreover, he is presented from the first as one of those gentlemen who are 'queer as bloody centaurs, / 'Alf one thing, half another' (276); he is as 'tongue-tied as that bloomin' antelope' (277) on the wall. Thus to *Volpone*'s theme of man's rapacious desire for money, Peake adds man's equally urgent search for love, linking predation and exploitation with the same pun as in *Mr Pye*: treating another person as a *quarry*. (John Donne, an immediate contemporary of Jonson's, uses a similar pun in Elegy 19 when he calls his mistress his 'mine of precious stones' (NAEL 1: 1256).)

Man's dual appetite for money and sex is underlined by questioning Percy's motive for pursing that 'golden creature', Sally: was it love, 'like a great rash across the globe, / Itching like no one's business, / Or was it greed?' (277). The answer is both, for Devius observes that Percy has 'returned like a lamb to the daughter, / A sheep to the gold' (361). The play ends with Sally pouring out Percy's tea (echoing celebrated literary tea parties from *Alice in Wonderland* to *The Importance of Being Ernest*). Unlike the Yellow Creature serving Captain Slaughterboard and Jackson waiting on the Lost Uncle, this 'golden creature' can speak and asks 'how many lumps' he wants. '*Four?* I must remember that' (373; Peake's emphasis). In this way Peake keeps before us the animal and purely material sides of man's desires at the same time as assuring us that when the soul gets the nourishment it needs, the sugar lumps of love are not rationed.

But this is to anticipate Percy's transformation. His 'death' makes Sally 'think of life. / It is the Universe! It is creation –' (294). After his 'tongue-tied love' (309) she wants a creative man, able to 'express himself' (302) in paint and words,

> someone with his head
> Among the Pleiades – for some fanatic
> Remorseless in his brimstone lust for beauty.
> (309)

She believes that she would make 'so wonderful a wife / For a difficult man' like this, the kind of artist who would never 'put women first'. In Kite's words,

> She sees herself
> As someone sent to succour some foul beast
> Who bites the hand that feeds it.
> (309)

In short, she wants 'A beast of genius to bully her' (303) and an artist dedicated to his art. 'Creation!' she exclaims, 'Creation / Is everything' (303).

With discouraging directness, Kite informs Percy that she wants 'a man as different from you / As he can be' (302). Having excelled in amateur theatricals in the village hall, Percy is confident that he can rise to the challenge and pass for the 'selfish and inordinate parasite' she desires. The term *parasite*, uttered in the presence of Kite, the most parasitic character of Peake's play and the closest to all the parasites in Jonson's, suggests that although the artist's 'Remorseless ... lust for beauty' may seem like an animal appetite, only 'something fiercer, not to be denied' (367), it in fact raises him above the animal. Love and money serve his creative urge. In this way then, Percy becomes Peake's exemplum not just of an artist but what it means to be an artist. Behind the flippant humour and the dreadful puns, there lies a serious purpose. (In fact, the puns seem to be at their worst when Peake is at his most serious.)

First of all, Percy has to realize that

> There comes a time
> When to be tongue-tied is to be a fool.
> I know the music but have lost my voice,
> And so I had to die: to kill myself: to start again.
>                                         (286)

Committing suicide in order to gain a voice is just what Lord Sepulchrave and Keda do, but Percy's is not a literal death. It is the metaphorical death of the artist that seemed so melodramatic in the context of Peake's manifesto; as we saw at the start of this book, the need to 'go over the edge' in order to bring a work of art to life renews the identity of the artist himself. Thus Percy becomes the proverbial 'man who slew himself for love' (363) who 'like a phoenix' (372) or 'a man of fire' (309) is reborn from the 'ashes' of his past, as an artist.

Committing oneself like this is the act that distinguishes the artist from the technologically minded man. Percy dismisses the mechanism for raising and lowering the bed that Devius has installed at great expense as 'a crude contraption' (327). When it jams, leaving the bed suspended in mid-air, Devius hesitates to jump. 'This is madness!' he exclaims. 'I'll break my bloody neck' (329). He lacks the 'madness' (the *furor poeticus*) that gives the artist his courage and is saved from having to 'ease [him]self over the edge' (330) by the restarting of the winch. The mindset that produces technology prevents a person from being an artist.

The verbal part of his new role is easy for Percy to play. He knows that disguised as another person he can find his voice and be fluent, for after a certain Lady Twigbrain introduced him on a social occasion as 'the Duke of Clapham' (286) he 'proceeded / To rule the roost' (316). (Both her name and this phrase participate in the complex of images around birds and their nests.) Freed from his stutter, he became 'a loquacious peer' who 'charmed the maiden' (287). So we find him declaiming melodramatically

> O I have words I've hardly ever used,
> New minted, shining, ready at the lips,
> For I have barely dipped into the well
> Of language with a tea-spoon!
>
> (286)

He uses words as Peake does, liberating the phrases 'Imprisoned in the brain' (286) through new words and new metaphors. As the artist October, the first thing he does is to roar 'No!!!!' (330), exactly like Peake's ideal artist who is not 'afraid to shout across the lethal stillness of good taste and moderation' (D8). Naturally, Sally finds it 'splendid to cry out / So unequivocal a "no" as that, / In someone else's house' (330).[1]

On the other hand, being an artist is less easy. Percy claims never to have met an artist and 'wouldn't be seen dead' (316) with one anyway. (Peake is both mocking the English social snobbery that disdains the artist and punningly anticipating the moment when, as the artist October, Percy is finally 'seen' for who he is.) He doesn't know 'how they walk or how they talk', but he can imagine, or rather *conceive* (Peake's emphasis) of being one – 'and I can act him. / Isn't that creative enough?' (316). His ability to *create* (as opposed to *invent*) his new character makes him a suitable artist for Sally. It also turns him into a work of self-creation, a living work of art.

That Percy cannot draw for the life of him matters little. If anyone notices how he has despoiled 'this innocent, this virgin whiteness' of the sketchpad page, Kite suggests that he

> Call it 'Vitalitism',
> 'Impressionism' or whatever comes to mind.
> And when in doubt, sharpen your pencil.
>
> (317)

---

1. This resembles Herman Melville's claim, in a letter (dated April 1851) to Nathaniel Hawthorne, that the writer should say 'No! in thunder' to all the most common and cherished beliefs of his society.

In satirizing all artists, Peake produces self-parody, down to the Pleiades beneath the ribs. The terms with which Kite schools Percy in his role are typical:

> Follow your nose and as the need arises
> Prattle of palette knives and canvases,
> Or studios with their windows facing north.
>
> (317)

Even the way of walking – '*trample* the floor; / Restless, relentless: struggling with your vision' (317) – is important, as it was with Pentecost, the gardener of Gormenghast, who is an artist in his relationship with flowers and plants and apple trees. It contrasts with the walk of Steerpike, who 'was not the artist' but 'the exact imitation of one' (TG164). Percy may not be able to draw, but he creates. He is no mimic artist.

As we saw in *Mr Pye*, vision starts with 'the marvels of the visible world' which 'stir the imagination' and awaken in the artist's heart an inspiration that he wishes 'to translate into paint or into words' (AW4). At the beginning of the play Percy's problems of self-expression parallel Thorpe's stammering, but he outgrows this handicap. He starts to look at things as an artist does – in Peake's term, to 'stare long and hard' (CLP2). A very pretty girl like Sally, a 'marvel of the visible world', inspires him. 'You will forgive me if I stare at you,' he says. She is unused to such direct admiration: 'What are you doing? Have a heart,' she protests. To which he retorts: 'I've little else at this amazing moment! / Who let you out alone on this raw planet?' (334). Her beauty makes him fearless, and he moves closer, saying, 'The creative half of me is thirsty stuff.' Sally backs away as though he were a vampire. 'And what about your other half, Mr Trellis?' she asks. 'That is my hungry side,' and a stage direction specifies that he is 'about to touch her hand' (334). This is where we came in: food and drink for the soul plus animal desire are the terms with which we began our exploration of the artist's loneliness in Peake's world.

Once Sally has accepted this new Percy, she warns him that 'life with me will be a kind of vision'. He responds gravely, 'It will certainly *need* vision' (372; Peake's emphasis). A successful love relationship is like a work of art: neither can be realized without vision, which inspires the voice of the heart to express itself. This is why Percy feels obliged to check with her that she does indeed 'hold a brief for the imagination' (333). By the end of the play, there is little to distinguish Percy's and Sally's love for each other from a work of art, and in the printed version they fuse to the extent of speaking the closing words in unison.

This consciously novelettish romance forms part of Peake's process of creating works of art within his works of art. Just as Sally establishes a parallel between life and fiction when she declares,

> Life's what I want – the endless panoramas
> Unfolding, like a book, page beyond page,
> Of painted marvels
>
> (294)

so Percy makes of his life a modern work. Heavyweights of nineteenth-century literature like 'Scott and Trollope' (285) get placed in the coffin and buried instead of Percy: as a work of art, he supplants the calf-bound creations of previous generations. Childhood reading, on the other hand, survives: Devius rediscovers with delight a boys' adventure storybook, *Under the Serpent's Fang* (340), that he (and Peake too, incidentally) loved in his youth.

On the subject of how an artist should behave, Kite tells Percy to be 'simple as a little child … and self-absorbed and merciless / As a little child. … Vain as a little child, your manners horrible / As those of a delightful little child' (316–17). The grotesque – to which Peake draws attention by having one of the mutes pronounce it 'gro-tes-cue' (353) – paradox of being 'Horrible and delightful at the same time' (317) brings us to the heart of Peake's work. All the antithetical terms associated with the artist, the 'brimstone lust for beauty' and the foul 'beast of genius' (309), express demonic energy in unbridled search of expression, rather as the child's behaviour (and view of the world) is unmediated by adult concepts and rationalization. Observed with unsympathetic or functional eyes, such behaviour has all the appearance of evil (hence the 'brimstone'), which leads, as we have seen, to the fundamental misapprehension of art by the Little Man.

Percy's remarks about darkness shed similar light on Peake's other works. In the guise of October, he initially proclaims with brash confidence,

> I never have believed in darkness.
> It is a trick and Rembrandt cornered it,
> Three hundred years ago.
>
> (319)

As illustrated in *Mr Pye* and the Christmas plays, the false belief that 'it has all been done before' is liable to paralyse the artist. Looking at Sally makes Percy realize his mistake: 'I see it now! I have neglected darkness' (332). As we saw with *Mr Pye*, it is not possible to set darkness aside. Rather appropriately, it is Percy's love for Sally that makes him see this; love turns darkness into light, so to speak. And this is the function that it performs throughout Peake's fiction. (By my count, *dark/darkness* and *light* – along with *voice* – are the most common nouns in Peake's work after parts of the body: head, eyes, face and hands, in that order.) In the world of Gormenghast, where '*darkness winds between the characters*' (G7; Peake's emphasis), love brings light, as announced by the 'flame-green daybreak' in the closing lines of *Titus Groan*, when 'love itself will cry for insurrection' (506). No wonder Percy believes in 'another world / Where love can make the very darkness shine!' (302).

The transformation of the voiceless Percy into the artist October rehearses everything we have seen about identity in Peake: the same person under a different name, he unites sameness and difference. The outrageous clothes that Kite has prepared for him not only parody Peake's own sartorial excesses as a young man, but also initiate the process of change. Clothing does not constitute identity any more than a name does, but dressing like an artist helps Percy to believe in his role. We find this theme in one of Peake's early cartoons (as 'Nemo'), captioned, 'He must be an artist … / Look at his shirt!' (*Satire*, December 1934, p. 17). In *The Wit to Woo* it's 'A man can be himself, I hope, and wear / What the hell he wants to, can't he?' (326). Percy hesitates to wear the clothes and at various moments is tempted to tear them off, which externalizes the inner transformation he is undergoing. Sally's first appearance in her underclothes, followed by the visit of her couturier, suggests a similar process in her.

In presenting himself as his own cousin October (a variation on the doubling we noticed earlier), Percy has to avoid being too similar to his old self, lest he be recognized, and too different, lest he lose Sally. At one point he pursues her so hotly round the stage, asking 'Can you not hear my heartbeats hammering / The morse of love?' (335), that she regrets Percy, who would never have stooped so low. Ironically, she asks him to 'be the gentleman your cousin was' (335). Thus Percy's progress towards integration has to walk 'the razor's edge between the passion and the intellect'. Ultimately he has to achieve 'that most magisterial of qualities, "equipoise"', just like 'the finest examples of any master's work' (D9). He has to become an artist and a work of art, in one.

He must be an artist...
  Look at his shirt!
He must be a genius...
  Look at the dirt!
My deah! How too thrilling!
  My deah! What a shriek!!
His work must be *brilliant*...
  Just *look* at his beard...
So to speak.

'He must be an artist ... / Look at his shirt!'

Behaviour being the expression of identity, Percy achieves this union through action. After Sally has seen through his subterfuge, he tries to revert to the old Percy, for he wants to be loved for himself, but – as we have seen – he cannot 'return to what [he] was before' (365). Confusing himself with his name, he complains that 'Pale documents [i.e. a death certificate] have trapped me / And now I am unable to exist' (365). The paperwork of bureaucrats excludes him from the land of the living:

> These men, the vicar and the coroner,
> Have every kind of crested document
> Relating to my death and burial. And I,
> Against all this have only my poor limbs
> To brandish for my proof – my voice
> To shout 'Look! Look!' My hands to clap,
> My flesh for pinching, but all this is nothing
> In the sour eyes of the official tape-worms.
> For *them* the centre of reality
> Is made of ink and paper; and a seal
> Is more to them than breath,
> And so I find, I'm dead against my will.
>
> (365)

This poetic statement of his predicament – closed by an atrocious, yet most appropriate pun – neatly contrasts with Peake's assertion that a great work of art transforms the paper it was executed on 'into a cosmos of such vibrancy as made the room we stood in [seem] like a land of the dead' (D7). Percy has to learn to identify with the artist and distinguish between his self and what he creates. In doing this he confirms Peake's other statement at the end of his introduction to *Drawings*: the 'native forms and denizens' that people his work 'have their roots in [his own] experience', and yet when he looks at his works, he can truly say, 'This isn't me!' (D11). The artist puts himself into his work, where it takes on independent life.

The climax comes when Sally scorns this 'feeble' and 'emasculate' Percy (366) who allows a mere piece of paper to deny his existence. 'To the devil with the law,' she exclaims (366). Thanks to his feeling that 'a jungle' is closing in on him 'with every breath', he makes contact with his core self. 'In a brimstone mood for justice' and declaring that 'the niceties are over' (367), he behaves like 'a child inspired' (368), demands 'more space' and clears the stage with a branch, 'tearing off [his] graces' (367) as he does so. The terms not only qualify the apparently uncivilized behaviour

Official red tape was associated with this image for Peake
after he had depicted Joad's Young Soldier in Search of
the Better World confronting 'the Red Tape Worm'.

of the artist for Peake, but also recall Titus's integration of the childlike Thing, 'the original branch / Naked and unadorned' (367) at the end of *Gormenghast*. In this way Percy fuses his old self with his artist self into a new identity, the same and yet different – and thereby wins Sally's heart.

Discovering – and being true to – one's core self helps others to be genuine too. In language that exploits the autumnal maturity of October, Sally tells this new, congruent Percy that 'Just as you've shed your ghost, I'm shedding now / A part of me that was a counterfeit' (373). It also liberates, as we saw in the chapter on identity. Delightedly Sally declares,

> I am free at last.
> Free of the battle. Free of subterfuge.
> Free to give in. Free to give out.
> Free to adore you.
>
> (372)

This is the freedom enjoyed by Titus, once he has affirmed his identity separate from Gormenghast.

AT FIRST SIGHT, THE wild comedy of *The Wit to Woo* might seem quite unlike the Titus books, but in the end it reflects the same preoccupations, expressed in a different mode. To appreciate (and begin to understand) any single work of Peake's we must set it in the context of his other works, for they are mutually enlightening. It's a matter of parts and wholes. Whereas disparate works seem enigmatic, putting them together enables us to grasp the overall shape that they belong to. This book has not assembled all the different parts of Peake's oeuvre, but they suffice to point to the meaning of the whole. And this metaphor is part of that meaning. All Peake's work is about the relationship of the part to the whole.

The pattern is present, on both the cosmic and the personal levels, in Peake's sense of man's solitude in the absence of God, and in the sense of separateness that starts at birth. Every person is an island, detached from the continent that bore them. The inefficacy of human love to bridge the gap between islands heightens that isolation and leads to a search without end (which was to be the main theme – and possibly the title – of the fourth Titus book). Changing metaphor (but not the basic pattern), we could say that, like Lord Sepulchrave, Peake's characters aspire to build a love nest, only to find themselves with separate twigs. (Being a comedy,

*The Wit to Woo* ends without putting the new relationship between the lovebirds to the test of time.)

Peake explores his homomorphic pattern through the youth who leaves home and discovers that he cannot return. Identifying the whole from which he has issued, he learns to accept his separateness, thereby becoming whole in himself. In the alternative story the youth is so terrified by the wild beasts in the jungle 'out there' that he scuttles back to fuse with home, abandoning separateness – and therefore identity. Another variation is self-aggrandizement, considering oneself so great (the universal pie, rather than a mere slice, so to speak) as to absorb other parts, even the whole, but this leads to emptiness, not plenitude. Inner space cannot surpass outer space. Peake's ideal is the balance between separation and integration, sameness and difference, being a part and a whole at the same time.

Just so long as Peake viewed the world from the perspective of one of God's creatures – the worm's eye view – he could feel only separation from the whole. Worse, it left him face to face with man's animal nature and our ill treatment of our fellow creatures, whether human or animal. Creating works of art (drawings, paintings, carvings, poems, stories, novels, plays and even an opera) gave him a completely different perspective: the vertical god-like view. It made him feel whole – a whole that flung out works, parts of that whole. As each fresh act of creation rehearses the separation of the part from the whole and at the same time makes the creator whole, it reconciled Peake with his human condition and healed his sense of isolation.[2] He replaced the pain of feeling separate with the joyful pain of separating from parts.

As 'Authorjehovah', Peake created works out of the vast inner space within him and breathed life into them. This act of creation affirmed and established his identity. It said 'I am.' And of course, those works are unique, just as their creator was. Creation also gave him a 'fantastic' sense of power; he greatly enjoyed 'the sheer excitement of having a piece of white paper and a pen in one's hand', for at that moment 'no dictator on earth can say what word I put down' (RTO8). However he was fully aware of the corrupting potential of such power, and would consequently have wished to withhold the vertical perspective from those who do not,

2. Was Peake familiar with T.H. Huxley's oft-quoted phrase, from his lecture 'On the Physical Basis of Life' (1868), about 'the iron law under which men groan' – and did it provide Titus with his family name?

like him, create from the heart – particularly those who invent with the brain and reject the civilizing power of art. For he loved the worlds that he imagined and peopled with characters, good and bad. Just as God created the universe and lovingly allowed it to evolve freely, so Peake made his creatures independent and separate from himself, allowing them to develop as they would.

Naturally, Peake's works reflect their creator and his process of creation. It was with this thought that he concluded the Introduction to the book of *Drawings*:

> For it is one's ambition to create one's own world in a style germane to its substance, and to people it with its native forms and denizens that never were before, yet have their roots in one's experience. As the earth was thrown from the sun, so from the earth the artist must fling out into space, complete from pole to pole, his own world which, whatsoever form it takes, is the colour of the globe it flew from, as the world itself is coloured by the sun.                                                                (D11)

As has become apparent in the course of this book, the Titus books tell not only of the birth, growth and education of a boy called Titus; they are also about the genesis and reception of a work of art. The meanings are stacked one within the other, as in the autobiography that Peake thought of writing; he titled it 'Chinese Puzzle' and conceived it as a series of boxes within boxes, starting with China and moving in through the house to the child, and then the same 'in reverse until the child steps out of China' (PP471). His works – parts that he flung off – are wholes that contain further parts that are in themselves wholes, and so on. Like Crab-calf's great work (with poems 'interlarded') in *Titus Alone*, they constitute a summation of 'everything I know of life and death' (TA186).

All Peake's characters are potentially artists; a few are truly creative artists, struggling with poverty and self-doubt yet fired with the belief that they are doing the right thing, dealing in truth and beauty. Moreover, it is possible to be an artist without creating works of art. As an attitude towards oneself and a perspective on the world, it is a way of life, what one is and not what one does. Sally – ironically glimpsed 'at her dressing-table / Creating eyebrows' (283) – sums it up when she says, 'Creation is everything' (303). Percy becomes both an artist of life and, like Titus, a work of art in himself.

The imagination that dwells in the heart and is inspired by love is the means by which this may be accomplished. The fusion of living,

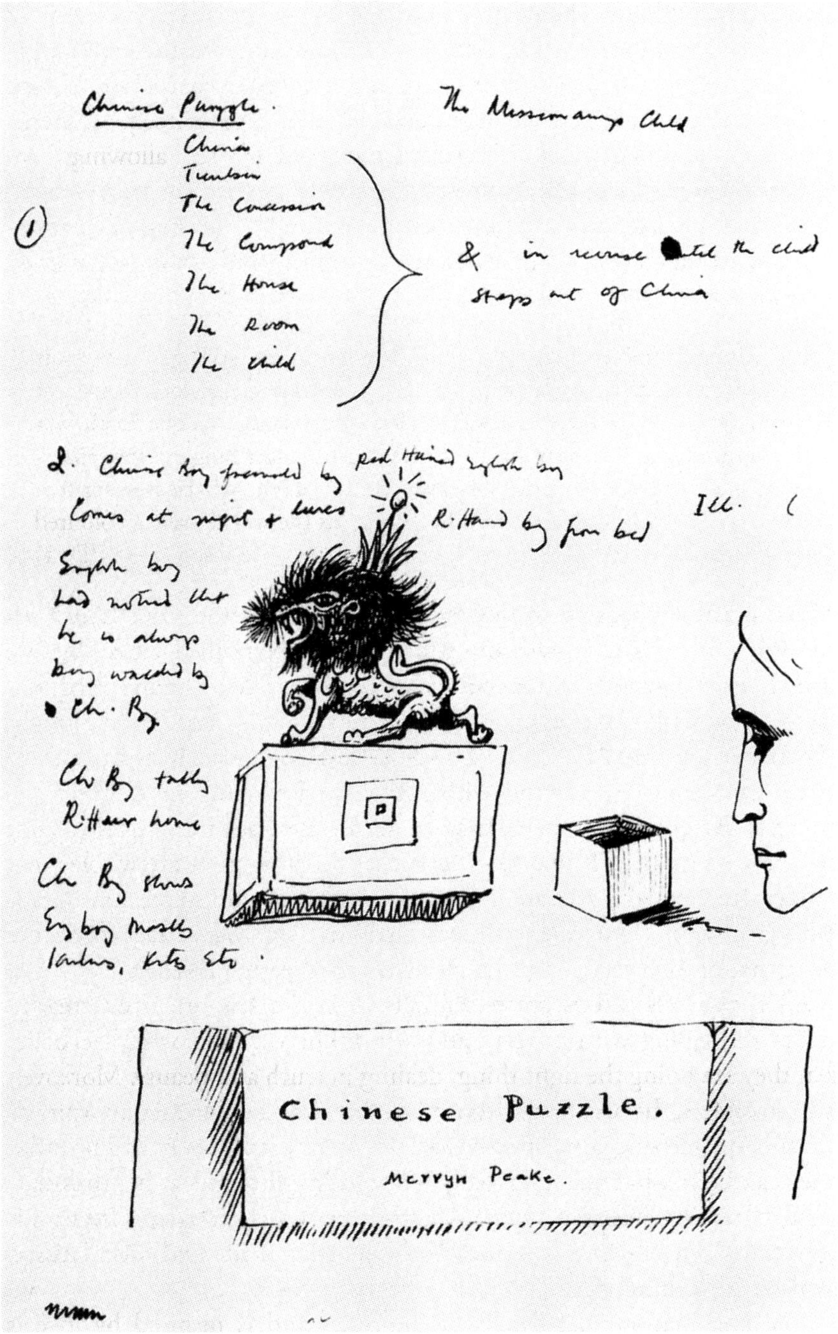


‘Chinese puzzle’ from Peake’s ‘Notes for an Autobiography’.

loving, imagining and creating produced what Peake called miracles, and he rejoiced in the work of his hand. Thus, while his works (like the Bright Carvings themselves) 'exude a kind of darkness for all their colour' (TG16), they shine with the joy of creation, and pass on to the reader or viewer something of what it is to be a creator rather than just a creature.

By exploring the relationship between the whole and the part on every level from the cosmic to the microscopic, and by attending to the voice that fed his imagination – the most ancient of creative processes – Peake placed himself among visionaries like Milton and Blake. The voice of the heart is where it all begins.

# Index